THEATRE CRI

THEATRE CRITICISM

CHANGING LANDSCAPES

Duška Radosavljević

Bloomsbury Methuen Drama
An imprint of Bloomsbury Publishing Plc

B L O O M S B U R Y
LONDON · OXFORD · NEW YORK · NEW DELHI · SYDNEY

Bloomsbury Methuen Drama

An imprint of Bloomsbury Publishing Plc

Imprint previously known as Methuen Drama

50 Bedford Square	1385 Broadway
London	New York
WC1B 3DP	NY 10018
UK	USA

www.bloomsbury.com

BLOOMSBURY, METHUEN DRAMA and the Diana logo are trademarks of Bloomsbury Publishing Plc

First published 2016

British Library Cataloguing-in-Publication Data
A catalogue record for this book is available from the British Library

ISBN:	HB:	978-1-4725-7864-8
	PB:	978-1-4725-7709-2
	ePDF:	978-1-4725-7710-8
	ePub:	978-1-4725-7711-5

Library of Congress Cataloging-in-Publication Data
A catalog record for this book is available from the Library of Congress

Illustration by Alice Marwick
Cover design by Eleanor Rose

Typeset by RefineCatch Ltd, Bungay, Suffolk
Printed and bound in India

CONTENTS

Contents

Part IV   Samples of Critical Practice

ACKNOWLEDGEMENTS

Over the years at the University of Kent, I have encountered growing enthusiasm among students for the subject of Theatre Criticism. Partly as a result of theirs and partly as a result of my own interest, in March 2011, I organized a research symposium entitled 'What is Theatre Criticism For?', which featured the Kent alumni Lyn Gardner and Mark Fisher, my colleague and co-teacher of the subject Patrick Marmion, scholar Paul Prescott, and Irving Wardle, former critic and the author of what appeared to be the latest and most influential book on the subject, published in 1992. Sponsored by the Kent Institute for Advanced Studies in the Humanities (KIASH), European Theatre Research Network (ETRN) and the School of Arts, the event was surprisingly well attended with many audience members – students, scholars, theatre and media professionals – travelling in from London and even further afield. I take this opportunity to say thank you for pointing out to me the need for a book like this one to everyone involved on that occasion – students, panellists, audience members, colleagues and sponsors, as well as Talia Rodgers of Routledge who was also present and supportive of the project from the start.

The necessity for this book became even more apparent to me during the Unpack the Arts European Residency Programme for Cultural Journalists at the New Circus Festival in Zagreb in 2012. Even though, sadly, none of the participants of that residency (except Nataša Govedić who we met as part of the programme) have contributed to this book, the cultural and discursive diversity I experienced at the meeting was deeply inspiring and influential for the development of this idea, so I thank everyone who has made this possible.

Special thanks are due for the enthusiastic and warm support of Bloomsbury Methuen Drama, particularly editor Anna Brewer and her colleagues, as well as the anonymous readers who provided valuable feedback. One of them, Karen Fricker, has gracefully stepped outside of the cloak of anonymity to become a valuable collaborator, adviser, editorial consultant and draft reader on this project – for which I remain indebted and hopeful that our conversations continue for many years to come.

In addition to Karen, I am grateful to Andrew Haydon, David Roesner and Tatiana Oskolkova for recommending and brokering relationships with particular contributors and interviewees on my behalf. My admission into the International Association of Theatre Critics has also been hugely helpful in sourcing some of the contributions, so thank you Ian Herbert and Mark Brown for endorsing my membership.

It is with great regret that I acknowledge the input of contributors whose work, for one reason or another, did not make it into the final version of the manuscript: Ian Herbert, Polly Carl, Nicholas de Jongh, Paul Prescott, Yohann Floch, Maka Vasadze, Holger Syme, Dan Rebellato, Catherine Love and Stewart Pringle. Let's hope there will be a second volume, or at least some other opportunities for collaboration on this subject.

Lyn Gardner, Andrew Dickson, Alistair Smith, Andrzej Lukowski and Anne Peter have all generously contributed their valuable time in agreeing to be interviewed as part of my research – I am grateful to them and to Elly Hopkins who has painstakingly transcribed their words. In the area of field research, special thanks are also due to Catherine Comerford, former Executive Director of *The Stage* and Scott Matthewman, former online editor at *The Stage*, Natasha Tripney, founding editor of *Exeunt*, and Jake Orr, co-founder of *A Younger Theatre* for providing historical information about their respective publications.

All contributors to the volume have my eternal gratitude for their stimulating ideas, insights, patience, responsiveness and spirit of generosity, even when my requests might have been ill-timed and overly fastidious.

I'd like to thank Paul Allain, Cecilia Sayad and Karen Fricker for their close reading and extremely valuable comments on my introductory essay.

In addition, I owe my thanks to George Rodosthenous for over fifteen years of tireless support, patient advice and helpful feedback on everything I do.

Last but not least, love and thanks to Tobi, Joakim, Katarina and my parents for making it all possible.

LIST OF CONTRIBUTORS

Vasco Boenisch has worked as a freelance theatre critic for the *Frankfurter Rundschau, Theater heute, Theater der Zeit* and the *Süddeutsche Zeitung*, and as a cultural correspondent and television presenter for WDR television. Currently he works as a Dramaturg at the Ruhrtriennale, the international festival of the arts in the Ruhr area of Germany. He is the author of several volumes of non-fiction.

Mark Brown is theatre critic of the *Sunday Herald* and Scottish critic of the *Daily Telegraph*. He is a member of the executive of the International Association of Theatre Critics (IATC) and of the editorial board of *Critical Stages*. Currently a doctoral researcher at the University of Dundee, he teaches at the Royal Conservatoire of Scotland. He is also the editor of *Howard Barker Interviews 1980–2010: Conversations in Catastrophe* (2011).

Valda Čakare is a theatre critic and Professor of Theatre Studies at the Academy of Culture in Riga, Latvia. Her areas of specialism are the theatre of the twentieth century, performance theory and theatre semiotics. She is currently working on theatrical gesture and acting in recent history of the Latvian theatre. Parallel to her academic career, Čakare writes reviews on theatre and performance.

Maddy Costa writes about theatre and music and works with theatre-makers, producers and venues to engage audiences in critical discussion. She is critic-in-residence with Chris Goode & Company, co-founder of Dialogue, and associate artist with Something Other. She contributes reviews to *Exeunt* and *The Guardian*, and blogs at Deliq. (http://statesofdeliquescence.blogspot.co.uk/)

Alison Croggon is a Melbourne poet, novelist, librettist and theatre critic. She ran the respected blog Theatre Notes (theatrenotes.blogspot. com) from 2004 to 2012 and was the 2009 Geraldine Pascall Critic of the Year. Her other work includes eight collections of poetry, nine novels and nine opera libretti. (alisoncroggon.com)

Diana Damian Martin is a writer and critic. She is Performance Editor for *Exeunt Magazine* and has published extensively for both print and online in UK, France, Belgium, Germany, Czech Republic and Australia. She is founder of the Institute of Critical Practice and Lecturer in Performance Arts at Royal Central School of Speech and Drama. (http://dianadamian.com/)

Jill Dolan is Dean of the College and the Annan Professor of English and Theatre at Princeton University. She is the author of *The Feminist Spectator as Critic* (2012) and *Utopia in Performance: Finding Hope at the Theatre* (2006). Her blog, *The Feminist Spectator*, won the George Jean Nathan Award for Dramatic Criticism. (http://feministspectator.princeton.edu)

Mark Fisher is the Scottish theatre critic for *The Guardian*, a former editor of *The List* and a freelance contributor to *Variety*, *The Scotsman* and *Scotland on Sunday*. He is the author of *The Edinburgh Fringe Survival Guide* (2013) and *How to Write About Theatre* (2015).

Nataša Govedić is employed at the Academy of Dramatic Arts, Dramaturgy Department in Zagreb. She has been a theatre critic since 1995 and is the editor and co-founding member of several magazines. Author of eleven books on theatre and performance studies and several novels for children, she also works as a dramaturg and performer.

Andrew Haydon is a freelance theatre critic (*The Guardian*, *Nachtkritik.de*, *Frakcija*) based in Manchester. His account of British theatre in the 2000s is published in *Decades – Modern British Playwriting: 2000-2009* (2013), edited by Dan Rebellato. He blogs at Postcards from the Gods. (http://postcardsgods.blogspot.co.uk)

George Hunka, author of *Word Made Flesh: Philosophy, Eros and Contemporary Tragic Drama* (2011), has written several plays and essays, as well as reviews, theory, and feature stories for *American*

Theatre, The Guardian (UK), *Theater, Contemporary Theatre Review* and the *New York Times*. From 2003 through 2013 he wrote the popular web journal about theatre, drama, and performance *Superfluities Redux*. (http://www.georgehunka.com/)

Margherita Laera is Lecturer in Drama and Theatre at the University of Kent. She is the author of *Reaching Athens: Community, Democracy and Other Mythologies in Adaptations of Greek Tragedy* (2013) and editor of *Theatre and Adaptation: Return, Rewrite, Repeat* (2014). She writes about London theatre for Italian publications.

Michelle MacArthur teaches at the University of Toronto. Her work has appeared in *Theatre Research in Canada*, *Canadian Theatre Review*, *alt.theatre*, as well as several edited collections. Michelle is also the lead researcher for the Equity in Theatre initiative (http://www.eit.playwrightsguild.ca), a campaign focused on redressing gender inequities in the Canadian theatre industry.

Kristina Matvienko is a theatre critic and researcher based in Moscow. A former Artistic Director of the New Drama Festival, she currently works for The Golden Mask Festival and is a curator for The School of Contemporary Spectator in Electroteatr 'Stanislavsky'. She reviews for Russian newspapers and magazines and teaches theatre history at the Russian State Institute for Cinema Arts (VGIK).

William McEvoy is Lecturer in Drama and English at the University of Sussex. His main research areas are contemporary playwriting, the language of theatre criticism and theory, theatre and ethics and the writer–director relationship. He is the author of a recent essay on the Irish playwright Enda Walsh and a chapter on site-specific theatre and visibility in *Theatre as Voyeurism* (2015), edited by George Rodosthenous.

Open Dialogues (Rachel Lois Clapham and Mary Paterson) is a writing collaboration that produces critical writing on and as performance. Open Dialogues work with festivals, artists, curators and audiences around the world, including PERFORMA, SPILL and SHOWTiME. In 2010 they launched NOTA – a long-term research framework that presses on the time, place and quality of notes in relation to performance. (www.opendialogues.com)

Savas Patsalidis is Professor of Theatre History and Theory at Aristotle University (Thessaloniki) and the Drama School of the State Theatre of Northern Greece. He is the author of eleven books on drama criticism/theory and co-editor of another thirteen. He reviews for the daily newspapers *Aggelioforos* and *Eleftherotypia* and is the editor-in-chief of *Critical Stages* (the ejournal of the International Association of Theatre Critics).

Duška Radosavljević is a writer, dramaturg and Senior Lecturer in Drama and Theatre Studies at the University of Kent. She is the editor of *The Contemporary Ensemble* (2013), and author of *Theatre-Making* (2013). Since winning the Harold Hobson Student Drama Critic Award in 1998 she has written hundreds of reviews for the *Stage* as well as numerous articles in academic journals and edited collections. In 2002 she was shortlisted for the Allen Wright Award. She also writes for *Exeunt*.

Matthew Reason is Professor of Theatre and Performance at York St John University (UK). Publications include *Documentation, Disappearance and the Representation of Live Performance* (2006), *The Young Audience* (2010) and co-edited with Dee Reynolds *Kinesthetic Empathy in Creative and Cultural Contexts* (2012).

Alice Saville is a London-based freelance theatre critic and arts journalist who writes for *Fest* magazine, *Auditorium* and *Exeunt*, where she is also features editor. She was shortlisted for the Allen Wright Award in 2013 and has worked as embedded critic at the Camden People's Theatre.

Megan Vaughan is a writer, arts blogger and occasional fanzine-maker based in London. Her blog, Synonyms for Churlish, is largely flippant and cynical, but her most popular reviews have experimented with form, using concrete prose, emoji and the interactive storytelling software Twine, amongst other things. (synonymsforchurlish.tumblr.com)

CHAPTER 1
THEATRE CRITICISM: CHANGING LANDSCAPES
Duška Radosavljević

Define a landscape.

For a start, where does it begin and where does it end?

It depends on where you are standing, your point of view and the breadth of your field of vision. Inevitably, the notion of a landscape presupposes the existence of a viewer, and of a relationship between the human subject and an aspect of their environment. In geographical terms, a landscape is simply an aspect of landmass – mountains, rivers, seas – under consideration. In artistic terms, it is a genre of painting. According to Microsoft Word, it is one of two possibilities for your page orientation: specifically, the horizontal one.

(Horizontality is important – it will discretely become one of the keywords in this book.)

There is an irresistible paradox at the core of the term 'landscape'. As noted by Elinor Fuchs and Una Chaudhuri, on the one hand, it contains an implied 'systematicity and coherence', on the other, an elusiveness which also gives rise to a wide metaphorical use. But far from suggesting cultural insignificance, 'the instability and ubiquity of the term reflect the cultural need for this concept, making it powerfully generative for many fields, including ours' (Fuchs and Chaudhuri, 2002: 12). At the risk of stating the obvious, the notion of a 'field' itself embraces the metaphor too.

My initial choice of the term 'landscape' as part of the title for this collection was largely intuitive, prompted by its metaphorical potential and associative resonance. A 'changing landscape' is a phrase often casually invoked in relation to the ecologies of both theatre-making and theatre criticism at the beginning of the twenty-first century. But what does this really mean? Perhaps one of the first imperatives that the notion of a 'landscape' dictates is the focus on a wider and more geologically layered context: in this case the layers include cultural, geographic, economic, philosophical, technological, historical and authorial considerations. However, the possibility that what we are looking at is a 'changing' landscape (or indeed a series of 'changing landscapes') suggests a really exciting – potentially dramatic, potentially historic – prospect. Volcanoes, storms, hurricanes, tectonic shifts come to mind.

Sketch No.1: A turbulent landscape

In 2007, the Artistic Director of London's Royal National Theatre, Nicholas Hytner labels newspaper critics 'dead white men'.[1] In the same year, a number of theatre bloggers burst onto the London scene with such strength of conviction that theatres are forced to take notice.[2] In 2012, the reception of Simon Stephens' *Three Kingdoms* shows a very clear dividing line between two camps: the newspaper critics who almost uniformly dismiss the German director Sebastian Nübling's production as 'self-indulgent' and obscure, and theatre bloggers who provide a painstakingly detailed, sophisticated and impressively well argued defence of the director and playwright's work.[3]

In September 2013 The Critics' Circle in the UK commemorates its 100th anniversary, although in the same month both Kate Bassett of *The Independent on Sunday* and Libby Purves of *The Times* lose their positions as theatre critics for their respective papers.[4] The trend of ongoing job losses for newspaper critics both in the UK and the US and the simultaneous rise of deprofessionalized critical voices on the internet is frequently commented upon with some disdain by writers such as Mark Shenton, former critic of the *Sunday Express* (who also loses his position at his paper in December 2013 amid some controversy).[5]

This prompts often heated debate[6] as to what the future holds for theatre coverage itself, as well as for arts writers and journalists, specifically regarding sources of their remuneration and their ultimate survival. Meanwhile, following expansion to the US in 2011, *The Guardian* newspaper establishes its Australian section in 2013. In her inaugural public lecture 'The Rise of the Reader', Katherine Viner, the incoming editor-in-chief of *Guardian Australia*, celebrates the changes to both journalism and the public domain that the post-Gutenberg age has made possible.[7] Pessimistic and optimistic pronouncements regarding the status and future of arts journalism continue to succeed each other on a daily basis.

These patterns of upheaval are strikingly similar – and not at all unrelated – to the way in which the higher education sector is deeply embroiled in the changing notions of economic and epistemic values. Scholars and critics can be seen to have writing and intellectual labour in common, and the higher education sectors in the English-speaking world are producing increasing numbers of graduates in Drama/Theatre/Performance Studies, trained to think critically about live theatre and performance. In the twenty-first century, under the pressure of neoliberal capitalism, universities increasingly encounter the paradox of being expected to deliver not only high levels of knowledge and skills of reasoning but also a guarantee of employability. As a result we are witnessing an influx of graduates with high levels of critical skills, writing ability and specialized knowledge of theatre and performance who also happen to be digital natives. They may not have clear career paths ahead of them, but they do have the means to keep their love of theatre and writing going, by at least trading their skills for free tickets.

Theatre criticism in the twenty-first century

This volume is a series of snapshots documenting some of the changes suggested by the book's title. The collected articles capture aspects of the spirit of the time which have the potential to remain relevant to long-term study and understanding of the histories, theories and practices of theatre criticism in the early twenty-first century. The book is fuelled by an ambition for an international perspective, although its own most immediate context is that of the UK theatre and arts journalism scene and its focus can be seen to be predominantly Euro-centric.[8] By at least covering aspects of theatre criticism in both Eastern and Western Europe as well as the US and Canada, the book contributes more of an international perspective on the subject of theatre criticism than might otherwise be available.[9] I will return to the specific advantages afforded by this particular juxtaposition of insights later.

While contextually framing the range of works presented here (academic articles, surveys, personal reflections and examples of creative practice), this introductory essay also aims to tackle a research question of its own, chiefly: how can we best comprehend, absorb and harness the different levels of change affecting the practice of arts criticism in our age? How do we – to follow through with the ecological metaphor – make sure that we do not stand in the way of natural developments while at the same time averting natural disasters? And how do we conceive of the notion of a landscape in the digital age? Taking into consideration the predominantly urban rather than rural nature of our key subject matter – as well as the factor of human intervention in the digital age – should we not apply the metaphor of a cityscape in fact? Or more precisely: cyberscape, whereby we are no longer detached but increasingly immersed.

Methodologically, this introduction first of all situates online criticism contextually in relation to academic and print criticism before attempting to see it in evolutionary terms as part of a larger paradigm shift in order to frame the essays that follow. As befits the notion of a 'landscape' – and the purpose of an introduction – this chapter has elements of a survey, though hopefully one that ultimately achieves depth as well as breadth. It synthesizes various insights from aesthetics, journalism, technology and economic philosophy in order to provide a clearer and more nuanced picture of our subject. Necessarily, the initial part of the discussion that follows is a review of relevant literature and current thinking in relation to different forms of criticism. The second part of the essay proposes a radical change of perspective by arguing that the current landscape of theatre criticism must be viewed not as part of a historical continuum and in relation to the previous forms of criticism, but in the context of the changing nature of the public goods and more specifically of the intellectual commons in the digital age. While acknowledging the existence of as yet unresolved economic and ontological problems in relation to the current state of theatre criticism, the essay's conclusions also uncover certain advantages gained in the realm of innovation and emancipation.

Academic criticism – evaluation vs interpretation

Academic literature has in recent years more often approached the category of arts criticism rather than theatre criticism per se. A need for metacriticism seems to have arisen at the turn of the twenty-first century as a result of a specific kind of multi-faceted 'crisis' – to use the term that is at the etymological core of the word 'criticism' itself.[10] In 1998, cultural historian and art critic, Maurice Berger, was prompted to reflect on the state of American criticism by a controversial essay in the *New Yorker* in which the dance critic Arlene Croce refused to review a piece about AIDS made by terminally ill artists and non-artists. Berger appeared to condemn Croce's choice, not so much on moral grounds, but on the grounds of its professional sectarianism. Croce's refusal to engage was seen as a potential capitulation to the increasingly predominating erosion of the critic's significance at the time. Key factors contributing to these changes that Berger identified in the introduction to his collection were: de-professionalization, decentralization of both the arts and criticism (through increasing diversity), the profit-driven mentality of American culture, academization of criticism (specifically the use of jargon leading to a decline in the quality of writing), and perhaps the 'gravest' problem: the tendency towards insularity and provincialism (i.e. critics not responding to political changes that lower the status of the arts in the public domain). Some of these issues are still considered legitimate problems (commercialization of culture and apoliticization of the critic) while others are simply outdated – no one in Berger's position would dream to raise an issue against diversity at the beginning of the twenty-first century. As for the relationship between criticism and academia, a notable shift has occurred in this respect too.

Art historian Gavin Butt (2005), literary critic Rónán McDonald (2007) and aesthetic philosopher Noël Carroll (2009) have all identified a new point of crisis – namely the crisis of critical theory – which they all seem to see as an opportunity rather than a challenge. There seems to be a consensus, prompted perhaps by Terry Eagleton (1984), that the age of Enlightenment originally gave birth to the figure of the critic. Ever since then the critic occupied a position of authority as an arbiter of public taste and an 'expert' on a particular artform. In the introduction to his volume, McDonald notes that, until relatively recently, newspaper criticism and academic criticism still co-existed within interchangeable planes – '[h]igh profile critics of the mid-twentieth century were frequently university professors who wrote books and reviews for a non-academic audience' (2007: viii). A significant rift occurred in the year 1968. The atmosphere of anti-authoritarianism, which spilled across the globe and led to demonstrations in various countries, coincided with the publication of Roland Barthes' essay 'The Death of the Author'. Barthes' reader-oriented argument, which insisted on a separation between the author and the work and the ousting of authorial intention as a legitimate interpretative perspective, consequently exerted considerable influence on future theoreticians of literary criticism. Further development of left-leaning cultural theory deployed Marxist, feminist and poststructuralist perspectives in interpreting works of art in relation to their political context – uncovering their latent ideological content and the self-perpetuating workings of the dominant power structures – arguably taking academic criticism further away from the general public.[11]

According to Butt, McDonald and Carroll, this trend for interpretation reached a crisis in the early 2000s and a new way forward was needed. Gavin Butt noted an 'unease' and skepticism towards the 'heritage of criticism left to us by postmodernism itself', rooted in the fact that the very hermeneutic tools used to question power and authority came to be 'credited with a kind of authority of their own' (2005: 4). As a philosopher – and in the spirit of a 'new aestheticism' coming in the wake of this skepticism – Noël Carroll opted to rehabilitate the notion of 'evaluation'. Seen to be presupposing certain elevated standards against which the act of criticism occurred as well as a hierarchical relationship between the art, the critic and the reader, the method of 'evaluation' had previously been rejected by the cultural theorists as a politically questionable mode of criticism. However, Carroll's method of evaluation – which, it must be said, will be no news to newspaper critics – proposes instead that the work of art is evaluated in relation to how it is an achievement or a failure in relation to what the artist is deemed to have set out to achieve. Importantly, the focus is on the artist's agency rather than inferred intention:

> That which we value or disvalue in the work is the artist's exhibition of agency in the process of having created the artwork. The critic focuses upon the artistic acts performed in the work; the object of criticism is what the artist performs, his or her artistic acts, in terms of their achievement (or failure).
>
> 2009: 51–2

Performativity is a key theme for Gavin Butt as well. However, he is more interested in performativity as a means of legitimating the status of a critic and his/her 'right to speak' rather than that of the artist. By positioning itself as a paradoxical mode always already outside of conventional wisdom, criticism, according to Butt, must discover its agency 'within the very mode of critical address itself' (2005: 5–6). Butt invokes Aristotle via Derrida – and the ancient philosopher's rhetorical address 'Oh my friends, there is no friend!' – in order to demonstrate how criticism's paradoxicality (desiring consensus and dissensus at the same time, for example), eventness and performativity might work.

McDonald, on his part, takes as one of his departure points John Carey's anti-elitist assertion in his book *What Good Are the Arts?* that our sense of artistic value in a non-theistic world is necessarily individualist and subjective. This 'radical relativism' of artistic value and reduction of arts criticism to personal taste are condemned by McDonald as potentially responsible for a 'plunge in the public reputation of academic criticism' (2007: 25). Unlike Carroll who simply declares his return to evaluation, possibly on the strength of his standing in his discipline, McDonald seeks to problematize and achieve a consensus around the notion of 'value' before a pragmatic method can be proposed. He therefore calls for a middle ground whereby our sense of aesthetic values needs to be understood as culturally contingent, in the same way as our ethical values are. Ultimately, McDonald is optimistic about the return to evaluation and the trend of 'new aestheticism', seeing it as an opportunity for academic and non-academic criticism to meet again after a period of separation. Interestingly, the increasing success of creative writing courses in the early 2000s in the UK is also hereby linked with the return of evaluation as a methodology into English departments, as these courses have been more willing to embrace the method and capitalize on it. By extension, criticism, which is in itself a craft and a literary form according to McDonald, should follow in the footsteps of biography and memoir to become one of the genres taught as part of the creative writing courses alongside fiction (2007: 147).

Rónán McDonald is certainly not alone in advocating for a more creative and artistic status of criticism – Butt departs from the viewpoint that even the theorist is 'enmeshed in the very, perhaps even "creative", production of the cultural fabric itself' (2005: 3), while Berger sees the essays in his collection as representing 'the kind of aesthetic and intellectual self-awareness usually associated with artistic practice' (1998: 12).

What is standing in the way of criticism being more widely perceived as an artistic practice? The mantle of the expert traditionally associated with it? The binary evoked between the artist and the critic whose work is seen to exist only parasitically in relation to the artist's and whose efforts are perhaps defined by opposition to those of the artist as being more coldly analytical? Perhaps it is worth turning here to the form of criticism which is – or has been until recently – the most dominant form in the public domain: newspaper criticism.

Newspaper criticism – the past vs the future

In his 1992 book, British theatre critic Irving Wardle drew a significant distinction between an essay and a review – 'reviewing is for those whose minds are already made up and essays for those who write to discover what they think' (1992: 54). But a major factor in choosing between the two was whether a critic wrote for a daily or a weekly newspaper. There is no space here for a detailed historical analysis,[12] but suffice it to say that some of the most enduring aspects of British criticism stemming from its beginnings in the eighteenth century and identified by Wardle include 'bias in favour of actors and dramatic character, its suspicion of rules, its pragmatic reportage and its need (not felt by the writers of the other arts) to persuade the reader that the theatre will do him good' (1992: 32). The seventeenth century legacy of Puritanism followed by the Court-sanctioned decadence of the Restoration era had left a legacy in England of a dialectical relationship to morality and this continued to influence aesthetic judgement throughout the eighteenth century and beyond. Wardle is aware of cultural differences too and somewhat self-effacingly notes that '[e]very attempt to erect a critical scaffolding from neo-classicism to Brecht and structuralism, has met with the resistance of British reviewers – whom their Continental colleagues are apt to dismiss as a crowd of know-nothings' (1992: 25). By the mid-twentieth century, Wardle notes, the form and tone of criticism diversified and reviews were appearing in a variety of genres including even 'fairy tale, parody, pantomime couplets, one-act plays, "Dear Diary" entries and open letters to the artists concerned' (1992: 50). But the key components remain that the reviewer should define his/her relationship to the reader, define his/her relationship to the piece being reviewed, express his/her considered opinion by giving appropriate evidence for it, and do it all with style – i.e. the reviews should be well written although the quality of writing should only serve the discussion of the work being reviewed rather than the display of the writer him/herself.

Newspaper criticism can therefore be seen as a hybrid genre between literature and journalism – that is: between creative and factual writing, the latter function being determined by the nature of the medium itself. In the English-speaking world, theatre critics have often been graduates of English – and in the UK, they have tended to be Oxbridge educated.[13] As a result of their training, twentieth-century newspaper theatre critics, like many of their predecessors, could be seen to have displayed a literary bias in their appreciation of theatre.[14] A shift away from the primacy of the text gradually took place in Theatre and Performance Studies in the second part of the twentieth century, but its effect on newspaper theatre criticism would not be detected for a few decades to come.[15]

At the Critics' Circle Centenary Conference in September 2013, former *Evening Standard* critic Nicholas de Jongh delivered a speech, largely based on his 2001 book *Politics, Prudery and Perversions: The Censoring of the English Stage 1901-1968*, in which he noted the remarkable compliance of British theatre critics in relation to the establishment. For decades between the 'campaigning fervour of the Shaw brigade' in the 1900s and the arrival on the scene of Kenneth Tynan in the 1950s, there were no notable attempts, for example, at challenging the institution of censorship in the UK. Even Tynan was a lone voice among his generation. De Jongh (2013) attributes the British critics' habitual lack of defiance against the establishment to 'the nature and composition' of the newspaper industry in the twentieth and twenty-first century. Noting that the industry is 'controlled by practicing Conservatives who use their papers as propaganda sheets for the Conservative Party', de Jongh identifies the same allegiance in many of the most significant twentieth century theatre critics: Harold Hobson (1904–1992) and his predecessor on the *Sunday Times* – James Agate (1877–1947), the *Observer*'s Ivor Brown (1891–1974), the *Evening Standard*'s Sir Beverley Baxter (1891–1964), and even Michael Billington's predecessor at *The Guardian*, Philip Hope-Wallace (1911–1979). The fact that overt conservatism is not only a matter of the distant past was shown by the also recently departed *Sunday Telegraph* critic Tim Walker, complaining in *The Salisbury Review* that in 2015 theatre critics became 'a sorry sight': 'seldom if ever in suits, all too often laden with carrier bags, and, sometimes, so Quentin Letts of the *Daily Mail* used to complain, smelling very bad'.[16]

It is important to note that these critics are all men. Not until the 1990s did women begin to occupy the more prominent positions in the UK: Lyn Gardner at *The Guardian*, Kate Bassett at *The Times*, Susannah Clapp at the *Observer*. Meanwhile, in the United States, journalist and blogger Monica Reida pointed out in 2009 that of the 20 members of the

New York Drama Critics' Circle, five were women.[17] A *Howlround* article by Daniel Jones from 2013 notes that TCG's list of 'Top 12 Theater Critics' in America released in November 2011 featured only two female critics. The article further praised the situation in Britain as being different in that '[a]lmost every other review listed on *The Guardian* website is written by a woman' and nine of the 17 faces of the Guardian Stage Staff on Twitter were women. However, the latter observation must be understood in the context of online criticism – which represents a distinct and often diametrically-opposed domain to that of newspaper criticism – and the specific example of *The Guardian* newspaper itself.

Sketch No. 2: 'Public value, not private gain'

The Guardian newspaper, originally founded by the Manchester businessman John Edward Taylor in 1821, was bought by its editor CP Scott in 1907, but as of 1936 it passed on from private ownership into a trust. This act was beneficial for its former proprietor thus saved from a financial ruin, but also for the future of the newspaper itself which was therefore guaranteed political and financial independence and protection of its liberal values. The Scott Trust has represented a unique form of media ownership in the UK and beyond, which could be seen as a significant factor in the paper's own political identity. According to a statement on the Guardian Media Group website from 2007:

> Guardian Media Group does not seek profit for the financial benefit of an owner or shareholders – it seeks profit to sustain journalism that is free from commercial or political interference, and to uphold a set of values laid down by CP Scott, the great Manchester Guardian editor [. . .]. Simply, it exists to create public value, not private gain.[18]

In an interview he gave me in January 2015, former theatre section editor, Andrew Dickson, explained that this particular organizational model was also partly responsible for the success of the Guardian website – which is, as of 2012, the third most read news website in the world.[19] Dickson explained that one of the Trust's greatest and most influential decisions was 'to do digital, do it early and do it well' (Dickson in Radosavljević 2015b). According to *The Guardian* website itself, institutional plans for its launch were being laid out through the establishment of the New Media Lab in 1995, and following individual online ventures around the 1996 UEFA European Football Championship and the general election in 1997, the Guardian Unlimited network of websites was launched in 1999, achieving up to a million users by September the same year.[20] By 2006, as noted by critic/blogger Andrew Haydon, *The Guardian* realized that 'the future of journalism lay in online expansion, and set up a number of more informal, comment-friendly blogs – including one for theatre'.[21] Despite a gradual but steady fall in sales affecting all of the newspaper industry – this newspaper's sales fell by 48 per cent between 2008 and 2014[22] – *The Guardian* did, as noted above, embark on significant international expansion. 'By brilliant foresight, from having been this middle ranking newspaper in Britain, the *Guardian* was suddenly really big, globally,' concludes Dickson.

In her talk 'The Rise of the Reader', Katherine Viner reinforced that *The Guardian*'s ownership is the secret to its digital success and that its ownership model, free of proprietors or shareholders, was the source of editorial freedom – 'all money must be reinvested back into journalism, and being open to readers and the web fits the ethos' (2013).

Magazines – a relevant digression

Perhaps one final point to add about printed criticism, before moving on to the discussion of its nemesis – online criticism – is the notion of editorial agenda. Matt Trueman[23] rightly observes that art criticism –

and specifically selection of the work to be reviewed in the limited space of a newspaper – has traditionally been governed by the news agenda. The problem with this, he warns, is that such thinking reinforces existing hegemonies – London, big theatres, West End, Shakespeare, middle class, men, white, heterosexual.

In the context of arts criticism, it is important to also distinguish the category of listings and trade magazines. The news agenda and the organizational hierarchies do not necessarily apply in relation to these smaller circulation weekly publications in the same way as their main purpose is to cater for the specific interests of their readers. In recent years the editorial agenda in these cases has been more about survival as these publications are under greater pressure to respond to a changing nature of the consumption of arts criticism in the twenty-first century. For illustration, I will provide two UK examples,[24] including some basic relevant statistics and an outline of contrasting ways in which they are changing in the present climate.

The trade newspaper *The Stage* (founded in 1880) is focused on members of the theatre profession in the UK as their key readership.[25] *Time Out* magazine – originally set up in 1968 as a co-operative dedicated to covering the alternative scene in London – has increasingly developed as a consumer magazine and was by 2012 replicated as a publication model in 37 cities around the world (Sweney 2012). Up until 2012, both of these publications were paid-for and mostly sold by subscription.

The year 2012 was a turning point for *Time Out* as, following the example of London's *Evening Standard*, it became a free publication with a much higher circulation (increasing from 55,000 to 300,000) and therefore acquiring a greater appeal for advertisers. At the same time the original co-founder and owner Tony Elliot sold 50 per cent of the business to a private equity firm. The switch to free circulation seems to have re-invigorated the profile of the magazine on the ground, but this was also linked to the expansion of the magazine's significance online. Andrzej Lukowski, Theatre Editor of *Time Out London*, noted in an interview he gave me that the existence of a print version in London is 'an anomaly' linked to its historical significance for the local community whereas most other cities run only an online version

(Lukowski in Radosavljević 2014b). As of 2012 all theatre reviews are published overnight rather than once a week as was the case with the print-only model. The operative word-count for all reviews is now 300 words as opposed to a sliding scale that existed for the print version where shows with lower scores received shorter write-ups. Whereas all reviews are published in full online, they still are occasionally edited for the print version. As a result, the assumption behind the coverage published online is that it is aimed more at people who are 'habitually into theatre' (Lukowski in Radosavljević 2014b), whereas the coverage in the print edition should be accessible to all. Between 9 and 10 theatre reviews are published weekly and there are about 10–12 freelancers covering theatre for *Time Out London*. In 2015 the magazine paid its freelance contributors £60 for a review of 300 words.

The Stage newspaper has also introduced major changes in its organization and circulation model. In 2014, former Deputy Editor Alistair Smith took over as the Newspaper Editor and a new Online Editor Paddy Smith was appointed on an equal level for the first time. According to Alistair Smith, the paper's circulation was 10,000 but the number of online users was 300,000 at the end of 2014. Contrary to the move from paid-for to free, *The Stage* has opted for a move towards the paywall model for its website. The content between the two platforms (print and online) is the same, but there are different forms of access available to readers depending on the level of engagement they wish to have with the website – the highest level being equivalent to the subscription charges for the paper (£65 per year in 2015) and giving subscribers full access to both. *The Stage* conducts surveys of its readers to get an idea of their profile (30 per cent actors and 70 per cent other theatre professionals) and their needs (job adverts, information, data about the industry, career advice, regional reviews, social networking). The paper works with about 100 freelancers nationally and it publishes about 25 reviews per week (going up to 100 during Christmas time and the Edinburgh Fringe).[26] The average length is 250 words (and the payment for a 250-word review is £25). After a long-term resistance from the critics, but in response to the readers' demands, a star system was introduced to accompany *Stage* reviews in 2014, although as a means of a 'compromise' a 'conscious decision [was made] to place the star rating at the end of the review rather than at the beginning' (Smith in Radosavljević 2014a). Since 2015, *The Stage* has had two lead reviewers who cover higher profile events nationally – these are not staff positions but roles occupied by current freelancers. Interestingly, appointed to these roles in their inaugural year were two existing *Stage* critics who have a considerable digital influence of their own – Mark Shenton (blogging for *The Stage* since 2005) and Natasha Tripney (co-founder and editor of the online theatre magazine *Exeunt*). As of 2016, Tripney holds the newly created position of Reviews Editor at *The Stage*.

Although *Time Out London*'s online content has only taken on a life of its own since 2012, its first basic online presence was established in 1994 and the website became more active in the late 1990s. *The Stage*'s website was first switched on in January 1998, but it was only updated weekly with selected content until 2004, when it became more dynamic.[27] Confronted with the question of competition with the online media, Alistair Smith insists on the distinctiveness of *The Stage*'s theatre coverage (taking the industry professionals' perspective) as opposed to *The Guardian*'s (educated consumer) or *Exeunt*'s ('more of an academic' perspective). Meanwhile Lukowski notes that he looks to *Exeunt* as a potential source of writers for his publication. Lukowski is positive about the effect of the digital domain on theatre criticism in that it provides scope for a diversifying creativity of the form, which he ultimately considers to be an 'art'.

Online criticism

The rise of blogging and online arts criticism has met with skepticism coming both from newspapers and academia. In 2007, *The Guardian*'s chief critic Michael Billington contributed a piece of his own to the Guardian Blog in which he questioned the legitimacy of blogging as criticism. While recognizing the democratizing power of the internet, Billington's 'caveats' about blogs included their lack of rigour and what he seemed to perceive as the blogger's disrespect for the form and style of a newspaper review.[28] Meanwhile, scholar Rónán

McDonald identified the more philosophical problems of quality control, 'atomisation of cultural discussion' (in other words, '[w]hile everybody's interests are catered for, nobody's are challenged or expanded'), and what he perceived as the internet's inability to represent a public sphere (2007: 16). While I cannot argue against the evident atomization and the apparent pliability of the internet in being deployed in the interest of consumer capitalism, I intend to return to the notion of the 'public sphere' and of journalism as a 'public good' in the conclusive discussion to this chapter. I can only attribute Billington's criticisms to a conservatism characteristic of the position of seniority, which will therefore need to be addressed paradigmatically.

It is important to recognize that online criticism operates within a distinct technological and socio-economic sphere which inevitably necessitates a distinct sort of categorical consideration. Rhetorician Carolyn Miller deploys the rather useful notion of kairos in studying the development of genres from a Darwinist perspective. Kairos and chronos are both ancient Greek conceptions of time, but while the latter is linear, the former is more indicative of an opportune moment – closer to the notion of perfect timing. In one of the early and definitive articles about the genre of the weblog, 'Blogging as Social Action', Miller and Dawn Shepherd situate the emergence of the form in the late 1990s – a '*kairos* that has shifted the boundary between the public and the private and the relationship between mediated and unmediated experience' – a kairos of 'mediated voyeurism' (2004). They observe this trend as affecting the public sphere on all levels, including the behaviour of politicians (such as Bill Clinton at the time) and they see it as rooted in the increasing desire for information and readiness to share or disclose information in order to ensure continued access to it. Further, Miller and Shepherd identify two key features of blogging: 'self-expression' and 'community development', which are also analogous to the intrinsic and extrinsic functions of self-disclosure. This self-disclosure is not necessarily an unveiling of a pre-existing self, however, but a process which we might even see as performative:

The self that is 'disclosed' is a construction, possibly an experimental one, which takes shape as a particular rhetorical subject-position. In a blog, that construction is an ongoing event, the self being disclosed a continual achievement.

Miller and Shepherd 2004

In addition, 'relationship development' (building connections) and 'social control' (opinion manipulation) are aspects of this self-disclosure, used to build a community around the blogger. But self-disclosure and community-building are seen as osmotic, leading the authors to ask whether the newly normalized subject positions of the exhibitionist and the voyeur 'catalyze this new form of rhetorical action'. Ultimately, Miller and Shepherd see the blog as a positive outcome of technological evolution: it is a manifestation of the writers 'seizing the means of production', it is the progeny of a whole set of historical genres (diary, anthology, shipping log) and, in terms of identity-formation, it is a 'counter-movement to postmodern destabilization' and a 'particular reaction to the constant flux of subjectivity' (2004). Viewed genealogically in this context, online criticism can therefore be seen as distinctly emancipatory, community-oriented, performative and potentially non-literary in its nature.

I'll elaborate.

I am interested in the notion of the genre of weblog as a new 'rhetorical action', especially as it contains the inscribed etymological link to the performative act of persuasion through public speaking. In this respect it is important to separate the genre of the blog from a purely literary heritage and understand it within a different evolutionary context. A number of thinkers have seen the digital age as an age of 'secondary orality' (Ong 1982/2002), or, conversely – the age of the print media as the age of the 'Gutenberg parenthesis' (Pettitt 2007). More recently, bloggers An Xiao Mina (2015) and Zeynep Tufekci (2011), have both drawn on the analogy between digital and oral cultures in an attempt to raise awareness of the paradigmatic differences between verbal expression in print and digital media. Even though Walter Ong proposed his notion of 'secondary orality' well before the advance of the internet (he was referring more to the inherent orality required by the media of the telephone and the broadcasting technologies), he credits the electronic age for actually drawing our attention to the categorical distinction between orality and literacy. By orality he is interested in the human condition – and the associated model of cognition and communication – that existed not only pre-Gutenberg, but pre-literacy. He considers writing to be a 'particularly pre-emptive and imperialist activity that tends to assimilate other things to itself even without the aid of etymologies' (2002: 11). The 'mentality' of primary orality is not fully conceivable to a literate person, Ong claims, and it facilitated completely different cognitive faculties from those which developed in the literate age.

It is possible to question the relevance of this argument to digital expression on the grounds that digital writing is after all writing in its full literate form; however, it is Ong's method rather than his specific insights that are relevant to us here. In other words, we must categorically distinguish between digital communication as a paradigm and the forms of communication which preceded it. When it comes to writing, the hierarchies of the publishing world have demanded that we abide by certain orthographic standards. Even the pedagogies of literacy have been governed by the same rules. However, with the removal of those editorial hierarchies in the digital world we have been freed to revert to more personal, more creative and more conversational means of expression. Twitter in particular – with its limit of 140 characters per personal statement – has lent itself well to comparisons with oral conversation, and perhaps even the more specific rhetorical form of repartee. And this has ushered in innovations in orthography and in general coding in communication too.

In the late 1990s the American author and neuro-surgeon Leonard Shlain advanced the hypothesis that the advent of literacy also led to the predominance of patriarchy over matriarchy – being linear and goal-oriented the use of the alphabet ousted the more holistic condition of imagistic and synchronic thinking of the pre-literate age characterized by a veneration of female deities, and moreover it affected further cognitive development of humankind because of the different use of the hand and eye in the process of writing in particular. A similar idea about the relationship between technological and cultural development is present in the writing of the French philosopher of science Michel Serres. Serres goes further in detaching the conception of digital communication from the pre-existing modes by defining the new generation of digital natives primarily through their use of thumbs (in the act of texting). This new 'millennial' human – whom he affectionately calls Thumbelina (and Tom Thumb) – has a completely different relationship with knowledge and is therefore invested with the hope of being a harbinger of the 'civilization of access' (2014).

Online criticism must be understood as belonging to the realm of digital communication as a paradigm. As will be seen in the section below, this realm operates according to its own ethical, economic and epistemological forces. For this reason it cannot be subjected to the value system which had governed the print media.

The public sphere

Hungarian scholar Mihály Szilágyi-Gál has pointed out that the freedom of access available in the digital age can be seen as both an advantage and a disadvantage. On the one hand, similarly to Rónán McDonald, he thinks that the lack of rigour can diminish the power of criticism as a public good and the very integrity of the public sphere itself; on the other hand, due to technological developments, the participation of authors and readers is less dependent on material goods, which affords new opportunities. Comparing the hierarchies inherent to the different media, Szilágyi-Gál notes that 'the internet offers a horizontal landscape where it is virtually more possible for anybody to "appear on the scene"' as opposed to the vertical structure of the print media 'both in terms of material accessibility and hierarchies of content' (2014).[29] The paradox is that, despite this apparent openness of access, the actual hierarchies of opinions in the digital realm might become even stricter. The way I see this is through the shift of power from an editor (deciding on the publishability value of a text) towards the reader (deciding on the readability value of the text), and the latter being more difficult to discern or standardize. A solution that Szilágyi-Gál proposes is 'co-operation' – a combination of the vertical and horizontal models and a possibility of an internet ethic emerging, a set of new normative practices devised jointly between the users, the community and the government.

The research surveyed in Szilágyi-Gál's article falls broadly into two categories – pessimistic and optimistic. As I suggested above, the optimistic perspectives tend to operate from the standpoint that the digital domain is a new paradigm, which offers new opportunities. The advent of the internet has brought about the philosophical shift towards the 'Open Source' development model in technology, for example, where, following the principle of user initiative, networks of software writers add to the development of a particular product, thus replacing the model of corporate hermeticism, changing the notion of copyright and making intellectual and creative goods more widely available. One of the most remarkable attempts at paradigmatically redefining the digital domain came from four business analysts in 1999 in the form of an internet publication which *The Guardian* called 'a primer on internet marketing'[30] – *The Cluetrain Manifesto*. The manifesto consisted of 95 theses which attempted to put across the idea that the business companies needed to come out of their 'Ivory Towers' and connect with people, that we (businesses and customers) were all members of a more horizontal networked community and that in the new digital age the market was in fact conversation itself.[31] In 2015, two of the original authors, David Weinberger and Doc Searls, published a follow-on piece. *New Clues* forms an admission in some way that the original project was over-idealistic in that it had failed to see that the sociology of the internet, being composed of ourselves as individuals, would inevitably mirror the sociology of our non-digital lives. The new document takes as its departure point the fact that the internet community now consists of three hordes: The Fools ('the businesses that have merely adopted the trappings of the internet'), The Marauders (trolls, plunderers etc), and Us ('the most dangerous horde'). While still reinforcing the importance of conversation and community, the document urges us – in a gospel-like way – to 'live the values [we] want the internet to promote' (2015).

The frequent invocation of co-operation and community in relation to the digital age might raise some of the twentieth century concerns around those notions, which is why the final word in this section must be given to political philosophers. As I have argued before (2013), Jean-Luc Nancy's idea of community as 'being together', without any ideological essentialism imposed from above, is useful both as a means of rehabilitating the notion of community after the Cold War and capturing the spirit of participation of our time. The absence of ideological essentialism and the need for 'exposition' and 'sharing' of the self advocated by Nancy (1991) is easily analogous to our behaviour on the internet (provided the internet is genuinely free of any controls from above). Similarly optimistic ideas for the possibility of emancipation through the power of the 'network' are offered by Michael Hardt and Antonio Negri in their work *Multitude* (2004). Moreover, according to Hardt and Negri, at the end of the twentieth century 'immaterial' labour (service work, intellectual and affective labour) had replaced industrial labour in the hegemonic position (2004: 108), thus ousting the Habermasian conception of the 'public sphere' as defined within the category of a bourgeois society. The products of immaterial labour are not objects but relationships and they therefore form the 'biopolitical' commons. It is in the production of intellectual commons, in amongst other factors, that Hardt and Negri find the grounds for their optimism, although Slavoj Žižek has also cautioned that 'what Hardt and Negri celebrate as the unique chance to overcome capitalism is celebrated by the ideologists of the information revolution as the rise of a new, "frictionless" capitalism' (2012).

An additional, somewhat worrying perspective on the notion of intellectual commons and the state of the public good and the public sphere arises out of an increasing marketization of universities in the English-speaking world. It has been stated already how critical theory is deemed to have caused a rift between the academic and the public intellectual domain. Since the late 1990s British universities have seen an increase in student numbers, and since 2012 the introduction of the £9,000 annual tuition fee to be met by the students rather than the state has arguably changed the status of knowledge from a public good as defined by the age of Enlightenment to a marketable commodity.[32]

American scholar and publicist Mark Greif notes an additional layer of a crippling rift between the academic and commercial spheres. On the one hand, writers and critics – public intellectuals – need universities as a means of their own initiation and also, in some cases, as a source of extra income; on the other hand, any association with universities is necessarily played down: 'One must simultaneously differentiate oneself from the university spiritually and embed oneself within it financially' (2015). Establishing that 'something has gone wrong with our collective idea of the "public"', Greif revisits the mid-twentieth century to chart the ways in which the relationship between the state and the public has changed. The post-1945 state funding of higher education in the US was related to the idea that the public – improved through instruction and cultivation – was needed for the security of the nation. But as the threat from the outside diminished, labour was increasingly outsourced and the intellectual empowerment showed itself as potentially dangerous in the 1960s, the way in which the public was perceived by the cultural elites in America changed – now they were needed as 'continuing consumers'. The only solution Greif can see to this is for intellectuals to change their relationship to the public and start holding it in higher esteem: 'to participate in making "the public" more brilliant, more skeptical, more disobedient, more capable of self-defense, and more dangerous again – dangerous to elites, and dangerous to stability' (2015). Perhaps a response to this invitation is only possible in the digital version of the public sphere where the hegemonic relationships of the non-digital world do not actually apply (as yet).

Sketch No. 3: Public goods

The United Nations Development Programme publication *Global Public Goods*, defines public goods as belonging to a world 'outside the market places' (1999: 2). In economic literature, public goods are usually defined through two criteria – non-excludability (that they are available to all) and non-rivalry in consumption (that they can be consumed by many without being depleted). The authors of the above UN publication, Kaul, Grunberg and Stern, further define public goods as the goods that the market itself cannot provide even though the market might rely on them, such as laws, protocols, street names, peace and security, clean environment, education and traffic lights. Wikipedia also lists fresh air as a public good, while Tyler Cowen considers the World Wide Web as a source of public goods 'provided through fame incentives or through personal motives to do a good job' (2007). Kaul et al. note that the distinction between the private and public goods is not easy to draw as this is often a continuum. Public goods have many diffuse benefits and the difference between the private and public benefit of a public good – otherwise called externality – is hard to calculate. More precisely, the private benefit of education to an individual is not easily separated from the cumulative benefit of education to the public. Externalities are therefore 'by-products of certain activities – spillovers into the public sphere' (1999: 5). The abstract value of externalities can perhaps be seen as a reason why it is difficult to make a case for state subsidy of public goods such as education or journalism.

Nevertheless, in 2012, the Tow Center for Digital Journalism at Columbia University conducted an investigation into the state of post-industrial journalism and published a report concluding that 'journalism – real reporting, about whatever someone somewhere doesn't want published – is an essential public good' (Anderson, Bell and Shirky 2012).

In an age when the newspaper industry is diminished by an economic crisis and the advance of the open web-based journalism, in a post-Edward Snowden age of a growing distrust between the public and the state, the question remains: what will sustain the public good of free information?

Conversation

In a 2015 article on arts criticism in the digital age, Natasha Tripney quotes from personal correspondence with blogger Megan Vaughan to illustrate the nature of the genre:

> it does kinda feel like those of us working on the internet have a responsibility to exercise all the freedoms it gives us to play with words and structure and form, because criticism should be a LANDSCAPE. Digital criticism, for me, is the freedom to be different, but implicit in that is an obligation to be different, for the sake of a healthy culture of discourse, now and in the future.
>
> Vaughan in Tripney 2015

Vaughan's conception of a 'landscape' (or 'LANDSCAPE', as she puts it) implies an intrinsic plurality, and this plurality is realized to its full potential in the unregulated and freeing domain of the internet. Moreover, the 'freedom to be different', in Vaughan's view, ensures a 'healthy culture of discourse'. By extension, one might argue that this also enables the health of the public sphere itself.

In the 2000s there was an increased interest in the idea of 'space' occurring in many subject areas including Performance and Theatre Studies. (Fuchs and Chaudhuri's book quoted at the beginning of this article was part of this 'spatial turn'.) Prompted by an interest in ecology and site-specific theatre for example, performance scholars began turning to geography for theoretical frameworks of their analyses. In 2005, in her editorial for the journal *Transactions of the Institute of British Geographers,* Susan Smith noted that geography had become 'too important to leave to geographers'. As a result, she observed the increased importance of 'conversation' as a means of ensuring the vitality of 'geography as an enterprise of relatedness' (2005: 389). Clearly the same process has been necessitated and facilitated by the digital domain whose health or 'vitality' also appears contingent on 'conversation' itself.

Katherine Viner refers to digital journalism as 'the truth made better by conversation' (2013). Conversation is the key term for the advocates of the orality view of digital communication. And in an interview she gave me as part of this research, Lyn Gardner noted that her work was always dependent on conversations with people in real life and that 'Twitter has only made this continue in a different way' (Gardner in Radosavljević 2015a). Meanwhile, in the first significant academic article on blogging in theatre, Fricker has also isolated 'dialogism' or 'networked conversation' as one of the key features of the form (2015: 42).

This is not without problems. One of the contributors to this volume, Matthew Reason, argues that the notion of 'conversation' made possible by the internet is often overrated as it remains a 'metaphorical' or at best an 'aspirational' rather than a 'literal designator'. Another contributor, Michelle MacArthur, in highlighting the unique values of 'crowdsourced criticism', notes the unresolved issue of a lack of remuneration methods for the labour that goes into it. Many online magazines contend with the same problem, although there are regional differences in this respect. The increasingly influential UK-based *Exeunt*[33] does not as yet remunerate its writers on a regular basis, although its German counterpart *nachtkritik.de* does – mostly thanks to the heavily-subsidised theatre sector in Germany whose funds spill through to the online publication via advertising and commissioned festival projects.[34] Meanwhile Anderson et al. (2012) are skeptical about advertising as a source of subsidy for journalism in the digital age as its own form and function are changing too. In the United States a business model has been trialled whereby individual theatre productions commission reviews directly from a database of writers, and although this was introduced as part of a wider mission to 'raise the standard' of theatre criticism, it has met with a strong disapproval from The American Theatre Critics' Association and the print sector.[35] In the second decade of the twenty-first century, therefore, the question of economic sustainability for digital arts journalism remains. However, it is interesting to note that the compulsion to offer a response to a work of art and thus produce criticism has thus far appeared stronger than a desire to be remunerated for that labour. It is perhaps this immanent nature of criticism that will guarantee its survival from potential crises, as well as the survival of the public sphere itself and the public intellectual within it.

Although my argument so far has emphasized the categorical difference between online and print criticism, it must be observed that online criticism allows for a useful synthesis of some of the print heritage too. The form of online criticism facilitates a much easier cross-pollination between academic writing and the more indigenous digital forms. This may be an outcome of a more direct influx of university students and scholars, accustomed to academic writing, into the blogosphere. Additionally as Karen Fricker has noted, 'academic settings are an opportune place to bring concerns about the changing face of our field to light' (2014) and can provide a forum for discussion. And the blogosphere – as shown by many academic-bloggers, including Fricker – also has the potential to demystify and popularize the intellectual commons of academia. As pointed out by Miller and Shepherd, the origins of weblog are to be found in archival activity and even today blogs share with academic writing the practice of meticulous referencing of other works dealing with the same subject matter. Hyperlinking allows for a much more efficient referencing than is currently possible in print. In print the referencing convention can be seen as tedious, in the blogosphere it is able to immediately manifest its original function – conversation.[36]

As far as geographical metaphors go, this volume too represents a meeting ground for scholars, critics and bloggers with the shared interest in the subject of theatre criticism;[37] and their works exist in a multifaceted conversation with each other. Although the contributors were not aware of each other's papers at the time of writing, discernable running themes – as well as some points of contention – resonate throughout the volume. More specifically, the majority of the contributions are concerned with evaluating the extent of change to the practice of criticism caused by circumstantial factors. Neo-liberalism, technology, craft, power, horizontality, democracy, performativity emerge as key terms even when they are merely implicit in the discussion. The material is organized into four sections, namely Contexts and Histories of Theatre Criticism, Critics' Voices, Changing Forms and Functions of Criticism, and Samples of Critical Practice. The volume does not presuppose a binary between a critic and an artist as is evident in some of the contributions which claim the status of an art or craft for the practice of criticism. Additionally, the samples presented in the final section were selected mostly on the basis of the levels of innovation and creativity they epitomize.

The reader is invited to make their own connections and tease out new issues too, rather than follow any potential narratives preordained by the volume's own structure. Insights gained through seemingly inadvertent juxtapositions of articles can sometimes be revelatory too. For example, George Hunka finds that the *New York Times*' readers have historically required consumer guidance from their theatre reviews while Valda Čakare notes that post-Soviet Latvian critics increasingly seek to escape commercial pressures by defecting into academia. Given the separate political genealogies and functions of theatre criticism within those two distinct contexts, emerging resonances really highlight the question of the possibility of criticality in capitalism. For this reason the volume opens with the pairing between George Hunka's overview of post-war American theatre criticism and Valda Čakare's re-examination of the reliability of theatre reviews as historical documents in communist and post-communist Latvia. Savas Patsalidis' history of theatre criticism in Greece ends up highlighting the inadvertently positive influence of an extreme economic situation on the status of theatre and criticism, thus offering a unique perspective on the notion of 'crisis'. Similarly to these three contributors, Kristina Matvienko traces a genealogy of Russian theatre criticism from its origins in the Enlightenment era to the present day, focusing on the repressed practices and the potential for their survival. Two of the contributors take a more empirical approach to analyzing their cultural contexts – Margherita Laera's study of the ethical issues within Italian criticism and Vasco Boenisch's study of the critics' own and the readers' perceptions of the function of newspaper criticism in Germany are both based on detailed statistical analyses of completed questionnaires. Some of the authors above, such as Hunka and Laera also touch on the practice of blogging in the US and Italy respectively and its sometimes precarious status in both of those contexts. Andrew Haydon's account of the development of online criticism in England concludes the first section of the volume by combining archival research, interviews and personal insight, resulting in the first comprehensive document of its kind.

The second section is more directly concerned with the voices of theatre critics – although they are not restricted to this section exclusively. At one end of the spectrum of personal reflections, critic Mark Fisher offers an entertaining and impressively rich survey of fictional representations of theatre critics; at the other, in contrast to many other contributors to the volume, Mark Brown takes on a decidedly skeptical stance towards the proliferation of digital criticism to argue for the protection and cultivation of theatre criticism as a craft. Meanwhile academic/blogger Jill Dolan and former *Guardian* staff journalist Maddy Costa offer unique contributions to the field of criticism by retracing their career steps and reflecting on their evolving practices in the context of feminist and 'embedded' criticism, respectively. These elegantly written insights also form a generous resource and an important reference point for future study.

Opening the section which deals with the changing forms and functions of criticism, Diana Damian Martin takes the cue from Jacques Rancière to offer a rigorous theorization of criticism as a political event with a specific emphasis on the 'possibility of dissensus'. This resonates well with the notions of 'conversation' explored with exemplary originality and rigour by British scholar Matthew Reason focusing on post-show discussions and by Canadian scholar Michelle MacArthur investigating comment threads in digital criticism. In an anticipation of the book's conclusion, Croatian critic Nataša Govedić advances the notion of 'articism' in an erudite essay which delivers a performance of its proposed principles, while William McEvoy's essay recapitulates many of the themes raised in the volume through an analysis of selected samples of contemporary British criticism (predominantly by female writers) through the lens of performativity. Methodologically, some of these essays, and most explicitly McEvoy's, aim to emphasize the possibility of criticism transcending the subjective/objective binary and of different forms of critical writing being perceivable as part of a 'continuum'.

Thus the final section is appropriately framed by the preceding one(s). As noted before, the drive towards criticism as an art is by no means a new development, but the decision to end the collection on this note is indicative of a desire to draw attention to the possibilities created in this respect by the digital paradigm shift. In this vein, the final section anthologizes four samples of critical practice published previously online: Alison Croggon's prose poem *How to Think Like a Theatre Critic*, Mary Paterson and Rachel Lois Clapham's performance script *NOTA*, Alice Saville's *Exeunt* review of children's show *Huff* written in the form of a picturebook, and Megan Vaughan's blog review of *Teh Internet is a Serious Business* written in emojis.

The fact that these examples are all authored by women is incidental but certainly not insignificant. At the core of the paradigmatic changes occurring to the various landscapes of theatre criticism is certainly a key issue thus far circumnavigated in this discussion, but by all means crucial and very familiar to the field of gender studies – power. At the end of the discussion new questions for future research are made apparent in this – landscaped – field: What is the relationship between creativity and emancipation? Is changing the world rather a matter of perspective? Could it be that the digital paradigm shift has also inadvertently redressed the power imbalances of the previous centuries, resulting in a long-awaited triumph of the previously repressed?

A final word about change. We are used to the notion of a geographical landscape as a relatively static concept. It takes years, or at least months for any changes to a landscape to become noticeable. This is in direct contrast to the word 'criticism' – and 'crisis' contained therein – which implies the idea of change in a most acute sense.[38] Semantically, change is therefore implicit in the process and in the very idea of criticism. This may not mean that any single act of criticism will move mountains or part seas, but the cumulative effect of criticism as a collective endeavour is certainly linked to the idea of progress (also characteristic of the era of Enlightenment). Thus criticism cannot exist in a vacuum as a freeze-frame of a place or a moment in time, it is always already a moving image, a time-lapse sequence. By finally freeing it from the constraints of the pre-Enlightenment structures of authority and power hierarchies, the democratizing and creatively empowering technological developments of the twenty-first century are potentially making it possible for the idea of criticism to redeem itself of its association with power and authority, and to actualize its full creative and intellectual potential. And that is why the changes happening to our particular landscape are in fact dramatic.

Notes

1. The original reference: Hoyle, Ben, 'Dead white men in the critic's chair scorning work of women directors', *The Times*, 14 May 2007. Because *The*

Times' digital archive is situated behind a paywall, the reader can more easily access the follow-up piece – Hytner (2007) 'What I really think about theatre critics', *The Guardian*, 3 June, http://www.theguardian.com/ stage/theatreblog/2007/jun/03/whatireallythinkaboutthea (accessed 24 February 2015). In the spring of 2015, Hytner was succeeded to the role of the Artistic Director of the Royal National Theatre by Rufus Norris.

2. This is recounted in detail in Andrew Haydon's article in this volume.

3. For more detail see Radosavljević (2013).

4. The changes at *The Independent on Sunday* were described as downsizing following a change of ownership. Libby Purves denied that the termination of her contract was part of the same phenomenon. Merrifield, N. (2013) 'Times axes theatre critic Libby Purves', *The Stage*, 16 September, https://www.thestage.co.uk/news/2013/times-axes-theatre-critic-libby-purves/ (accessed 24 February 2015).

5. Shaikh, T. (2013) 'Sunday Express theatre critic Mark Shenton "fired over nude gay website pictures"', *The Independent*, 06 December, http://www. independent.co.uk/news/media/press/sunday-express-theatre-critic-mark-shenton-fired-over-nude-gay-website-pictures-8988525.html (accessed 24 February 2015).

6. An interesting instance of this can be inferred from Karen Fricker's blogpost from September 2014 'The crisis in theatre criticism is critics saying there is a crisis' http://karenfricker.wordpress.com/2014/09/11/ the-crisis-in-theatre-criticism-is-critics-saying-theres-a-crisis/ as well as Dan Rebellato's response to the same prompt in 'Critical Thinking', http:// www.danrebellato.co.uk/spilledink/2014/9/17/critical-thinking (accessed 24 February 2015).

7. Viner, K. (2013) 'The Rise of the Reader', *The Guardian*, http://www. theguardian.com/commentisfree/2013/oct/09/the-rise-of-the-reader-katharine-viner-an-smith-lecture/print (accessed 25 February 2015). On 1 June 2015, Katherine Viner succeeded Alan Rusbridger as the first female Editor-in-Chief of *The Guardian*.

8. Ten out of 22 contributors are British-born, only four are from non-European (although still English-speaking) contexts; however eight contributors including the editor are originally from non-English speaking European contexts.

9. The International Association of Theatre Critics' biannual journal *Critical Stages* (http://www.criticalstages.org/) must be commended for offering a more global perspective. The Special Topics section of Issue 9, February 2014, focused on 'Alternative Criticism', featuring articles from international contributors.

10. According to the Online Etymology Dictionary, the original Greek 'krisis' as used by Hippocrates and Galen meant 'turning point in a disease' and was related to the verb 'krinein' – 'to separate, decide, judge'. http://www. etymonline.com/index.php?term=crisis (accessed 26 February 2015).

11. I say 'arguably' because, paradoxically, one of the most formidable contemporary cultural critics who is very much present in the popular media nowadays is the Marxist Lacanian philosopher from Slovenia Slavoj Žižek.

12. Wardle traced its origins back to schismatic pamphlet ('a form with no literary grace, expressly designed to wound the object and bludgeon the reader into agreement' 1992:17), as well as theatrical listings and insider's gossip (the latter particularly popular at the time). As indicated above, the early critics of the Enlightenment era had high standards.

13. Wardle himself studied at Oxford, as did Michael Billington, Michael Coveney, Libby Purves and Charles Spencer. Benedict Nightingale, Mark Shenton, Ian Shuttleworth and Kate Bassett are Cambridge alumni. (Thanks to Ian Shuttleworth for also offering, 'as an example of hermeticism', that he overlapped at Cambridge with Bassett and Shenton as well as Dominic Cavendish and Simon Edge.)

14. For more detail see W.B. Worthen (1997).

15. An interest in non-literary aspects of theatre can certainly be discerned in the work of the Guardian critic Lyn Gardner who is a Drama and English graduate from the University of Kent.

16. Tim Walker (2015) 'Theatre of Blood', 3 March, http://www.salisbury review.com/Editorial_Blog/critic.html (accessed 3 March 2015).

17. This remained the case in 2013–14, although, notably, Elisabeth Vincentelli (*New York Post*) is listed as a Vice-President of the organization. In March 2015, these records on the organization's website were not yet updated.

18. 'Scott Trust', http://web.archive.org/web/20070922153023/http://www. gmgplc.co.uk/ScottTrust/tabid/127/Default.aspx (accessed 2 March 2015).

19. 'The Guardian is now the world's third most read newspaper website', http://www.theguardian.com/gnm-press-office/8 (accessed 2 March 2015).

20. 'History of the Guardian website', http://www.theguardian.com/ gnm-archive/guardian-website-timeline (accessed 2 March 2015).

21. Andrew Haydon (2013), 'Crisis, what crisis?' http://nachtkritik.de/index. php?view=article&id=8662%3Aa-debate-on-theatre-criticism-and-its-crisis-in-the-uk&option=com_content&Itemid=84 (accessed 2 March 2015).

22. 'ABC figures show papers' efforts to stem circulation decline', http://www.theguardian.com/media/greenslade/2014/oct/10/abc-figures-show-papers-efforts-to-stem-circulation-decline (accessed 2 March 2015).

23. Matt Trueman (2015) 'Choosing what to review is a critical decision', *What's On Stage*, 2 March, http://www.whatsonstage.com/london-theatre/news/matt-trueman-critical-choices-blog_37274.html (accessed 2 March 2015).

24. In the US, New York's *The Village Voice* is perhaps comparable to this genre of magazine, although it was originally conceived as an 'alternative weekly' and has traditionally featured news coverage, investigative journalism and opinion pieces as well as criticism and listings.

25. Its closest US equivalent would be *Variety*.

26. The reviews have historically been co-ordinated by a dedicated administrator but as of 2016 a Reviews Editor will be appointed.

27. Thanks to Catherine Comerford, former Executive Director, and Scott Matthewman, former Online Editor/Digital Project manager at *The Stage* for providing this information.

28. Michael Billington (2007) 'Who needs reviews?', The Guardian Blog, 17 September, http://www.theguardian.com/stage/theatreblog/2007/sep/17/whoneedsreviews (accessed 3 March).

29. Horizontalism is an important concept for Andy Horwitz too, who has proposed a critical framework he calls 'critical horizontalism', discussed in more detail in Maddy Costa's contribution to this volume. Horwitz, A. (2012), 'Culturebot and the New Criticism', 31 March, http://www.culturebot.org/2012/03/12883/culturebot-and-the-new-criticism/ (accessed 4 March 2015).

30. Jack Scofield (1999) 'Netwatch', *The Guardian*, http://www.theguardian.com/technology/1999/apr/15/onlinesupplement7 (accessed 5 March 2015).

31. Thanks to Matthew Reason for initially bringing this text to my attention.

32. British academic Stefan Collini (2012) has provided interesting commentaries on this topic.

33. *Exeunt* was founded in 2011 by two writers; in 2015 it has a team of ten editors, headed by Tripney. There are about 25 regular contributors and a larger pool of occasional ones. The site's main revenue is through advertising, though this is limited. Additional sponsorship has been obtained on a project by project basis (in 2015 Nick Hern Books provided sponsorship for a podcast series). Tripney notes that the 'social/community aspect of Exeunt is one of its strengths' and this is nurtured

through regular get-togethers of writers for which refreshments are provided by the publication (Tripney by email, 2015).

34. *Nachkritik* was founded in 2007 by four theatre critics and one web designer; in 2015 it has ten editors. It is currently one of the most significant online theatre publications in the German-speaking countries. Its core content comprises of theatre reviews which often function as prompts for reader discussion. According to one of its current editors Anne Peter, in 2015 *Nachtkritik* reviewers are remunerated €80 per review. The site is funded mostly by theatre advertising (80 per cent), but they also receive donations, patron contributions and payments for projects they do for particular festivals (Peter in Radosavljević 2015c).

35. See Carey Purcell (2015) 'Is Paying for Reviews the New Journalism? Time Out's David Cote Weighs In', *Playbill*, 17 June, http://www.playbill. com/news/article/is-paying-for-reviews-the-new-journalism-time-outs- david-cote-weighs-in-351494 (accessed 17 June 2015).

36. This is also the key mechanism behind Matt Trueman's notion of criticism as a 'team sport'. Matt Trueman (2013) 'Vlog: Criticism as a Team Sport' http://matttrueman.co.uk/2013/10/vlog-criticism-as-a- team-sport.html (accessed 6 March 2015).

37. The contributors were approached both personally and via a call for papers to the International Association of Theatre Critics (which yielded three contributions). As already noted, approximately half of the contributors are British-based although not all of them are British by birth. Approximately half of the contributors have the English language as their native language (the US, Canada and Australia are represented in addition to the UK). Contributors from non-English-speaking backgrounds are all from European countries, namely Greece, Russia, Latvia, Croatia and Germany.

38. See footnote 10.

Works cited

Anderson, Chris, Bell, Emily and Shirky, Clay (2012) *Post-Industrial Journalism: Adapting to the Present,* Columbia Journalism School | Tow Center for Digital Journalism, http://towcenter.org/research/post- industrial-journalism-adapting-to-the-present-2/ (accessed 6 March 2015).
Berger, Maurice (ed.) (1998) *The Crisis of Criticism*, New York: New Press New York.

Butt, Gavin (ed.) (2005) *After Criticism: New Responses to Art and Performance*, Oxford: Blackwell Publishing.

Carroll, Noël (2009), *On Criticism*, New York and London: Routledge.

Collini, Stefan (2012) *What Are Universities For?* London: Penguin.

Cowen, Tyler (2007), 'Public Goods' in The Concise Encyclopedia of Economics, http://www.econlib.org/library/Enc/PublicGoods.html (accessed 10 March 2015).

De Jongh, Nicholas (2013) 'On Criticism and Censorship' talk at The Critics' Circle Centenary Conference, Royal Central School of Speech and Drama, 27 September, available on http://www.theatrevoice.com/audio/the-critics-circle-centenary-conference-how-did-it-start/ (accessed 6 March 2015).

Eagleton, Terry (1984/2005) *The Function of Criticism*, London and New York: Verso.

Fricker, Karen (2014) 'The crisis in theatre criticism is critics saying there's a crisis', *Karen Fricker blog*, September 11, http://karenfricker.wordpress.com/2014/09/11/the-crisis-in-theatre-criticism-is-critics-saying-theres-a-crisis/ (accessed 6 March 2015).

Fricker, Karen (2015) Blogging, *Contemporary Theatre Review*, 25:1, 39–45.

Fuchs, Elinor and Chaudhuri, Una (eds) (2002) *Land/Scape/Theater*, Ann Arbor: University of Michigan Press.

Greif, Mark (2015) 'What's Wrong With Public Intellectuals?', The Chronicle Review, February 13, http://m.chronicle.com/article/Whats-Wrong-With-Public/189921/ (accessed 6 March 2015).

Hardt, Michael and Negri, Antonio (2004) *Multitude: War and Democracy in the Age of the Empire*, New York: Penguin.

Jones, Daniel (2013) 'Blistered and Burned: The Absence of Female Critics', Howlround, 13 July, http://howlround.com/blistered-and-burned-the-absence-of-female-critics (accessed 6 March 2015).

Kaul, Inge, Grunberg, Isabelle and Stern, Marc A. (1999) *Global Public Goods – International Cooperation in the 21st Century*, New York, Oxford: Oxford University Press (United Nations Development Programme).

Levine, Rick, Lock, Christopher, Searls, Doc and Weinberger, David (1999) *The Cluetrain Manifesto*, http://www.cluetrain.com/ (accessed 6 March 2015).

McDonald, Rónán (2007), *The Death of the Critic*, London and New York: Continuum.

Miller, Carolyn R. and Shepherd, Dawn 'Blogging as social action: a genre analysis of the weblog' in L.J. Gurak, S. Antonijevic, L. Johnson, C. Ratliff, & J. Reyman (eds) (2004), *Into the Blogosphere: Rhetoric, Community, and Culture of Weblogs*, http://blog.lib.umn.edu/blogosphere/blogging_as_social_action.html (accessed 6 March 2015).

Mina, An Xiao (2015) 'Digital culture is like oral culture written down'
https://medium.com/the-civic-beat/digital-culture-is-like-oral-culture-
written-down-df896b287782 (accessed 3 March 2015).

Nancy, Jean-Luc (1991) *The Inoperative Community*, Minneapolis and
Oxford: University of Minnesota Press.

Ong, Walter (1982/2002) *Orality and Literacy: The Technologizing of the World*,
London and New York: Routledge.

Pettitt, Thomas (2007) 'Opening the Gutenberg Parenthesis: Media in
Transition in Shakespeare's England', paper written for media in transition
5: *creativity, ownership and collaboration in the digital age* Conference
at MIT, April 27–29, 2007, http://www.learningace.com/doc/2629844/
ce0901442755af1b46439e4ee6cd269d/pettitt-gutenberg-parenthesis-
paper (accessed 3 March 2015).

Radosavljević, Duška (2013) *Theatre-Making: Interplay Between Text and
Performance in the 21st Century*, Basingstoke: Palgrave.

Radosavljević, Duška (2014a) Interview with Alistair Smith, Editor of the
Stage Newspaper, 21 November.

Radosavljević, Duška (2014b) Interview with Andrzej Lukowski, Editor of
Time Out, 19 December.

Radosavljević, Duška (2015a) Interview with Lyn Gardner, *Guardian* journalist,
31 January.

Radosavljević, Duška (2015b) Interview with Andrew Dickson, former
Theatre Editor, *The Guardian*, 22 January.

Radosavljević, Duška (2015c) Interview with Anne Peter, Editor of *Nachtkritik*,
21 January.

Serres, Michel (2014) *Thumbelina: The Culture and Technology of Millenials*,
London: Rowman & Littlefield International.

Shlain, Leonard (1998) *The Alphabet Versus the Goddess: the Conflict Between
Word and Image*, New York: Penguin/Compass.

Smith, Susan J. (2005) 'Joined-up geographies', *Transactions of the Institute of
British Geographers*, New Series, Vol. 30, No. 4 (Dec.), pp. 389–390.

Sweney, Mark (2012) 'Time Out goes free: London edition of listings
magazine to drop cover price', *The Guardian*, 2 August, http://www.
theguardian.com/media/2012/aug/02/time-out-free-london-edition
(accessed 6 March 2015).

Szilágyi-Gál, Mihály (2014) 'Criticizing the end of criticism: The critical
genre and the internet', *Critical Stages*, February, Issue No. 9. http://
criticalstages9.criticalstages.org/criticizing-the-end-of-criticism-the-
critical-genre-and-the-internet/ (accessed 6 March 2015).

Tripney, Natasha (2015) 'Arts Criticism in the Digital Age', *The Space*, 29
January, http://www.thespace.org/news/view/digital-criticism-feature-
natasha-tripney (accessed 6 March 2015).

Tufekci, Zeynep (2011) 'Why Twitter's oral culture irritates Bill Keller (and why this is an important issue)', http://technosociology.org/?p=431 (accessed 3 March 2015).

Wardle, Irving (1992) *Theatre Criticism*, London and New York: Routledge.

Weinberger, David and Searls, Doc (2015) *New Clues*, http://cluetrain.com/newclues/9 (accessed 6 March 2015).

Worthen, William B. (1997) *Shakespeare and the Authority of Performance*, Cambridge University Press.

Žižek, Slavoj (2012) 'The Revolt of the Salaried Bourgeoisie', *London Review of Books*, Vol. 34 No. 2, 26 January, http://www.lrb.co.uk/v34/n02/slavoj-zizek/the-revolt-of-the-salaried-bourgeoisie (accessed 6 March 2015).

PART I
CONTEXTS AND HISTORIES OF THEATRE CRITICISM

CHAPTER 2
STYLE VERSUS SUBSTANCE: AMERICAN THEATRE CRITICISM SINCE 1945
George Hunka

Tracing the history of American theatre criticism since 1945 provides a lesson about the interrelationship of style and substance. A review of the field in the recent past and its present state reveals a series of landmarks and offers a perspective from which to survey the landscape of this criticism today. As such, it must interpolate a certain amount of the history of contemporary American drama – the art form that inspires that criticism – and consider the many factors pertaining to its generation and dissemination among general, professional, and academic readerships. In the end, it may be concluded that mainstream contemporary American theatre criticism represents the triumph of style over substance. Whether that triumph is merely temporary remains to be seen.

It was not until 1920, with the Broadway premiere of Eugene O'Neill's *Beyond the Horizon* and O'Neill's subsequent Nobel Prize awarded sixteen years later, that both European and American critics recognized the American theatre as a mature form worthy of extended critical examination, notwithstanding the homegrown American drama that emerged from the eighteenth-century American revolution. The first purpose-built playhouses in the colonies dated from the early 1700s, and American dramatists were soon writing for them. But until O'Neill, American plays aspired primarily to entertainment in the form of melodrama, imitation of existing European forms, and farce. These plays attracted the first American audiences and were reviewed by the first American reviewers. Writers as diverse as Washington Irving, Edgar Allan Poe, Walt Whitman, and Henry James, to name only a few, focused on individual theatrical productions in daily newspapers and periodical journals, often written on deadline immediately following attendance at these productions in a process not unlike that of twentieth- and twenty-first-century reviewers and critics. This was, however, not exclusively the case; in 1845 Poe wrote the first extensive essay about drama and theatre in America for the *American Whig Review*, although its very scope, limited to a few now-forgotten American melodramas, renders it of little more than antiquarian interest to the American drama critic of today (Poe 1984).

After O'Neill, things were different. Theatre criticism flourished in America in the years immediately before World War II. Alexander Woollcott, George Jean Nathan, Robert Benchley, Dorothy Parker, H.L. Mencken, Stark Young, and Brooks Atkinson contributed stylish and incisive criticism and reviews about American theatrical productions to high-circulation publications, including newspapers like the *New York Times* and the *New York Herald-Tribune*, magazines like *Life*, the *New Republic*, and the *New Yorker*, and journals such as the *American Mercury*. Collections of their reviews were also regularly issued in book form, especially those of Woollcott and Nathan, testifying to the lasting value of this criticism as deserving of permanent preservation between book covers, implying too that there was a significant readership for these collections. (See Nathan 1942–1951 and Woollcott 1924 for examples.) As stylists, critics like Woollcott, Benchley, and Nathan brought a lively wit to these pages, sometimes at the expense of a more considered perspective on the plays they reviewed, in contrast to the drier evaluations from Young and Atkinson.

After the war: maturity

Within only five years after the end of World War II, three plays that were to shape the future of American drama opened on Broadway: Eugene O'Neill's *The Iceman Cometh* (premiered in 1946), Tennessee Williams' *A Streetcar Named Desire* (1947), and Arthur Miller's *Death of a Salesman* (1949). Away from Broadway, but also in New York, the

American theatre was undergoing additional, more radical shifts in both theme, production, and performance practice. The first performances of Julian Beck and Judith Malina's Living Theatre collective were offered in 1948, and the opening of the Circle in the Square Theatre in Greenwich Village in 1950 established 'off-Broadway' as a force in the evolving American theatre (Little 1972: 16, 59). As American theatre and drama progressed in new directions with the onset of World War II, the journalism and criticism that covered this progress shifted its perspective. The theatre and its criticism together contended with new threats to their place in the culture as forms of both popular and more intellectual entertainment. During the first three decades of the twentieth century, film and radio began to offer inexpensive alternatives to live entertainment, at first affecting theatrical forms like vaudeville but making incursions onto the territory of more 'legitimate' stage entertainment such as evening-length dramas and musicals in New York and other large cities. The emergence of the three major American television networks – ABC, NBC, and CBS – in 1947 brought narrative forms common on the stage into private living rooms. Indeed, playwrights like Paddy Chayevsky and others moved easily between the television studio and the Broadway stage. Ironically, as American drama reached its maturity, the American theatre itself was becoming more marginalized as a form of popular mass entertainment.

At the same time, higher education was further influencing the creation and the critical reception of the new American drama. Although formal degree programs in playwriting were still rare in American colleges and universities, in the 1930s Arthur Miller studied playwriting at the University of Michigan with Kenneth Rowe (Gottfried 2003: 33). During the same period Tennessee Williams attended Washington University in Missouri and The New School in New York, writing his first plays while still a student (Leverich 1995: 177, 346). As playwrights were trained, so were critics – Yale University was home to John Gassner, whose writings and teaching played a central role not only in criticism both before and after the war but continued to influence and inspire future figures in the American theatre as diverse as Joseph Papp and Richard Foreman. Both cited

Gassner as an important influence: he was a critic to whom Papp turned for guidance (see Turan and Papp 2009: 35), and Foreman studied with Gassner at Yale, where he received his MFA in playwriting in 1962 (Gussow 1998: 143).

The most important critical texts that emerged in the immediate postwar theatre were Eric Bentley's *The Playwright as Thinker*, Robert Brustein's *The Theatre of Revolt*, and Richard Gilman's *The Making of Modern Drama*. All three books were influential on several generations of critics, especially in the classroom. Ironically, the most significant contribution to American theatre criticism at that time was the British, Oxford-educated Bentley's *The Playwright as Thinker*, published in 1946 by a mainstream publisher (Reynal & Hitchcock) rather than an academic publisher (it was republished by the mainstream publisher Harcourt Brace in 1987). Bentley, who began teaching at Columbia University in 1953 and joined the Harvard faculty in 1960, had an influence on American drama criticism that cannot be over-estimated. While many of the playwrights that Bentley studied in the book (Ibsen, Strindberg, Shaw, Chekhov, Pirandello, Sartre, and Brecht) enjoyed New York and even Broadway premieres in the years before World War II, Bentley was the first to gather these writers under a broader critical rubric for a book-length study. His study examined these playwrights through close readings engendered by the New Criticism, a critical paradigm founded by T.S. Eliot and other Modernist critics in the pre-war years and taken up by academic literature departments in America after 1945, led by Americans such as John Crowe Ransom (who appears in the acknowledgements to *The Playwright as Thinker*). Though Bentley approached the texts primarily as literary documents rather than texts to be staged, he did not elevate himself to the ivory towers of academe. Bentley, Brustein, and Gilman all also spent time in the journalistic trenches, writing theatre reviews regularly for such national periodicals as *The New Republic*, *The Nation*, and *Newsweek*. These reviews were extensions of their long-form critical work.

It is necessary to acknowledge the importance of the *New York Times* to the history of American drama criticism after 1945, as influential in popular culture and daily theatrical journalism as

Bentley et al. were influential in the academy. After the closure of the *New York Herald-Tribune* in 1967, the *Times* remained New York City's single – and oldest, having been founded in 1851 – broadsheet newspaper. As a factor in the development of both American theatre and American drama criticism, the *New York Times* was uniquely situated. In the 1960s, Broadway was, as it is today, the most visible manifestation of theatre in America. More than a New York thoroughfare, it is an idea, a concept, perhaps most obviously manifested in the Tony Awards, awarded by the American Theatre Wing and the Broadway League, broadcast every year on a national television network and celebrating Broadway excellence. (Only marginal attention is paid to off-Broadway and regional theatres.) Broadway is also American theatre's most commercial manifestation. Broadway producers have always been uniquely dependent upon daily newspapers like the *Times*, not only for reviews, but also as a marketing, publicity, and advertising outlet. In the 1950s and 1960s, with the closure of several newspapers as electronic news outlets and as television and radio replaced the newspaper as sources of information, this dependence concentrated itself upon fewer and fewer newspapers.

In the immediate post-war period, *Times* reviewers like Brooks Atkinson (1894–1984) and Walter Kerr (1913–1996) were believed to have the ability to 'make or break' a show, and whether one defines this as 'power' or 'influence', a distinction with little practical difference, this perception coloured the approach of *Times* editors and critics to the work under review. Regional theatres would look to its pages for new plays to programme into their seasons, and the *Times*, as one of the few 'national' newspapers in the United States (distributed in all fifty states, unlike newspapers in other regions and cities), is still in the twenty-first century a unique source of information about current trends in New York and American theatre. New York theatregoers read *Times* reviews not primarily for critical insight into a given work but for objective information about a given production – as an aid in determining which shows to see and, in some cases, which to avoid. But Bentley, Brustein, and other critics published not in the *New York Times*, but in journals of political opinion like the *New Republic* and the *Nation*, enjoying more space and more time in which to elucidate their opinions. It may be simplistic to say that the *New York Times* and other newspapers published reviews and feature articles, and these other journals published criticism and essays, but this opposition can be compellingly argued.

In New York, the alternative press provided an additional, less mainstream critical perspective. In 1955, the *Village Voice* was founded in New York's Greenwich Village just as the off-off-Broadway movement was launched with the opening of the Caffe Cino on Cornelia Street in 1958 and Ellen Stewart's La MaMa Experimental Theatre Club on West Fourth Street in 1961. The *Voice*'s first publishers, Dan Wolf, Ed Fancher, and Norman Mailer, hoped to introduce 'free-form, high-spirited and passionate journalism into the public discourse [in the form of] no-holds-barred reporting and criticism' (*Village Voice* website). Jerry Tallmer, the *Voice*'s first theatre critic, established the *Voice*'s Obie awards in 1956 to recognize achievements in an off-Broadway and off-off-Broadway theatre less dependent upon commercial considerations and private investment for its success, and its theatre section in the 1960s and 1970s grew to form a substantial part of the *Voice*'s arts coverage. Under the editorship of writers and academics like Erika Munk and Michael Feingold, the *Voice*'s theatre section served a readership of a more progressive cultural perspective, more likely to assess a work's content based upon its formal aesthetic rather than entertainment value.

Drama at the *Times*

In 1966, the *New York Times* attempted to broaden its perspective and integrate some of the more nuanced critical writing found in weekly magazines and journals, hiring the *New Republic*'s film critic Stanley Kauffmann for an eighteen month period. When hired by the *Times*, Kauffmann had been writing about film for the *New Republic* for eight years, but he was uniquely qualified, professionally and academically, for his new post. He had spent four years studying theatre at New York University, and ten years in a repertory company devoted to the classics. He was himself a published playwright, and for three years preceding his employment by the *Times* had been the drama critic for Channel 13, New York's non-profit, educational television station.

In part, Kauffmann's hiring was influenced by the changing American culture of the 1960s. The GI Bill and the greater access to institutions of higher learning, as well as the surge of affluence in America after World War II, had created a theatre-going public which, *Times* editors told Kauffmann, would welcome this more nuanced criticism in the pages of the newspaper. According to Kauffmann, the *Times* was interested in more carefully approaching the art as well as the business of American theatre; editors were becoming restless with reviews that were 'couched in glib journalese and buoyed on hollow, dubiously knowledgeable generalities' (Kauffmann 1967: 37). While Kauffmann (and those managers) claimed to have 'relatively little naïveté about the *Times* job' when he took it, neither Kauffmann nor his editors expected the vociferous negative reaction from the newspaper's readership, comprising theatre professionals and general readers:

> From the start my mail was huge, much larger, I was told, than my predecessor's; and from the start there were many letters of commendation, some of them from very flattering sources inside and outside the theater. But the majority of the letters opposed me with a heat (I confess) that was shocking. The criticism I was writing – to me, essentially a continuation of the kind I always had written – absolutely enraged many people in this new context.... [The] letters all wanted essentially a reviewer who was a kind of shopping service and not too fussy.... I particularly cherished the communiqués from an anonymous backer of *Sweet Charity*, a musical I had disliked. Every week he sent me a copy of the box-office receipts as reported in *Variety*, accompanied by an obscene scrawl.
>
> Kauffmann 1967: 37

He lasted for eight months. When the last of the *Times'* broadsheet competitors, the *New York Herald-Tribune*, closed in August 1966, Kauffmann was replaced by the *Herald-Tribune's* Walter Kerr.

Kauffmann's brief tenure at the *Times* resulted in 'Drama on the *Times*', his brief memoir and analysis of his time at the *Times*, which appeared in the *New American Review* in 1967. This essay remains an insightful discussion of the dynamics that continue to shape *New York Times* drama coverage – 'the junction of power and seriousness in theater criticism' (Kauffmann 1967: 35) – as well as that of American dramatic criticism in daily newspapers in general.

Kauffmann understood that professional American drama was still a form of art dependent upon commercial success rather than national subsidy, and this affected the criticism printed in newspapers. Unlike the visual arts or classical music, American theatre was still considered a form of commercial entertainment like film or television; readers wanted guidance as to where to spend their hard-earned dollars, not insights into aesthetic concerns. Kauffmann and his editors were unpleasantly surprised by the intensity with which both theatregoers and theatre professionals defended this distinction.

The character of American drama criticism for newspapers as Kauffmann described it in 1967 has remained rather the same, privileging style and efficiency over substance: '[The] standard in criticism – as anyone can see in almost any newspaper anywhere – is not quality but readability. The writer who can supply bright readable copy, and supply it quickly, is an acceptable critic' (Kauffmann 1967: 36).

The rise of the 'blurb whore'

In the autumn of 2002, American critic Jonathan Kalb delivered a speech to students at Barnard College and New York University entitled 'The Death (and Life) of American Theater Criticism: Advice to a Young Critic'. Surveying the field, and referencing Kauffmann's 1967 essay as 'still the most important piece written about theater criticism in America' (Kalb 2003: 7), he noted that there were only a 'handful' of 'real critics' working in the daily and weekly print media: Michael Feingold at the *Village Voice*, Robert Brustein at the *New Republic*, John Heilpern at the *New York Observer* – 'a small, embattled, and aging group' (Kalb 2003: 9). Feingold was laid off from the *Village*

Voice in 2013, leaving *Voice* theatre coverage, however scaled down from its 1970s heyday, to freelance reviewers and critics, including Tom Sellar, Alexis Soloski, Miriam Felton-Dansky, and Jacob Gallagher-Ross. Heilpern left the *Observer* in 2009, and Brustein now writes about theatre only occasionally for the *New Republic*. It is notable that the names of critics for the *New York Times* and other mainstream publications do not appear in Kalb's list of 'real' critics, raising the question of what constitutes a 'real' critic after all. This question haunts the history of American theatre and drama criticism as well.

Kalb launched his own online journal, *Hot Review*, in 2003. The emergence of the World Wide Web as a forum for independent drama criticism is the subject of other chapters of this book, and the establishment of *Hot Review* and other blogs and online magazines provided a hoped-for alternative to mainstream press coverage, coverage that he noted was at something of a nadir, taking care to differentiate between a 'stylist' and a 'critic': 'A stylist is a caretaker of recycled culture, a blind monster that feeds on itself. A critic is an independent human being with open eyes, who knows what and where to eat' (Kalb 2003: 19).

Over a decade later, along with the *Village Voice*, the three print publications of most influence in New York theatre are *The New York Times* and *Time Out New York*. (The only national magazine devoted to American drama and theatre, *American Theater*, is published by the non-profit Theater Communications Group, a service organization for non-profit theatres; it is more of a trade journal, offering feature stories and industry overviews rather than criticism or reviews, which it does not carry.) The tone and quality of the Sunday Styles section of the *Times* that Kalb references have slowly spread to the rest of the paper, manifesting in lifestyle sections like 'Home' and 'Dining' that appear each day in the *Times* (and sometimes two of these a day), so that the Arts section and these new Style sections have become almost indistinguishable. One needn't point to more than the puffy interviews with young playwrights and detailed diaries of drama critics' junkets to London and Washington to demonstrate that the theatre pages remain in the hands of the 'stylists'.

The same tone and style affects the arts coverage in *Time Out New York* as well. The tone that crosses over all its coverage of the arts participates in the same trendy consumerism and sexual/materialistic titillation that sells products in ordinary advertising. That some New York drama reviewers and critics like myself have written for both. Both *Times* coverage and *Time Out New York* theatre coverage is affected by the same imbalance of style over substance.

The theatre blogosphere of the early 2000s was thought to possess the potential to provide a genuine alternative. Some theatres, such as Lincoln Center Theatre, instituted what were called 'Bloggers' Nights', for which independent writers not associated with print publications were provided with free tickets in anticipation of additional publicity and reviews. But early on bloggers were ghettoized – the 'Bloggers' Nights' were rarely the same as the nights on which print reviewers were invited – and, in the worst cases, demonstrated the same concern with 'style' as the print medium. And the bloggers ghettoized themselves: if anything, the producers who went along with these 'Bloggers' Nights' further eviscerated the blogosphere from the mainstream media, underscoring the amateur status of these writers. The bloggers themselves acquiesced in this marginalization instead of demanding that they be invited to the same press openings as the print and broadcast media. When the Nights themselves failed to produce the desired publicity stir for these productions, they were phased out.

Many bloggers now have moved to other social media like Twitter and Facebook, which in 140-character tweets and status updates are more amenable to the desire to become, as Kalb describes them, 'blurb whores' – 'the pseudoreviewer[s] bribed with perks to say flattering things that can be quoted in ads':

> This movie-world creature is admittedly rare in the humbler environs of the theater, but its cynical spirit pervades the theater field as well. The corruption of the annual theater awards systems, the shameless journalistic fawning over productions with large budgets, the cozy relationships between high-profile critics and stars: opinions are all clearly for sale,

so who can care deeply about anyone's thoughts? 'Whatever', 'Get over it', 'Not even' — all these generational catchphrases capture the essence of the leveling effect, which, curiously enough, was already apparent to Horkheimer and Adorno in the 1940s.

Kalb 2003: 8

The blogosphere unlike Twitter and Facebook has no 140-character limit and blog posts do not disappear down the bottom of a long column of 14- and 15-word fragmentary comments. It's just possible, though unlikely, that somebody out there is tweeting, 140 letters at a time, the next *Playwright as Thinker*.

In the past several decades there have been few critical voices as simultaneously graceful and authoritative as Bentley, Brustein, Gilman, or Kauffmann. Nor, would these voices desire to be heard, are there arenas for their work, certainly not in daily newspapers or general interest magazines; even the journals of opinion like the *Nation* and the *New Republic* disdain the interest they previously displayed in the art of drama and the stage. The damage this has done to the economic model of criticism is extensive: with fewer outlets, there is less reward for the kind of nuanced criticism that used to be produced by Kauffmann and others. Serious critics must eat just as reviewers do, and although many have found homes in academia, their own criticism must take a backseat to the demands of their scholarly and academic responsibilities. But American drama criticism has a long and vibrant history, and some of its best writing has occurred relatively late in its development. The past is prelude to the present, as well as to the future; while pessimism is warranted, the tide may turn again.

Acknowledgements

This chapter has benefitted enormously from the editorial advice of Duška Radosavljević and Marilyn Nonken. I owe them a large debt of thanks.

Works cited

Benchley, Robert (1985) *Benchley at the Theatre: Dramatic Criticism, 1920–1940*, Ipswich, MA: Ipswich Press.

Bentley, Eric (1946) *The Playwright as Thinker: A Study of Drama in Modern Times*, New York: Reynal and Hitchcock.

Brustein, Robert (1964) *The Theatre of Revolt: An Approach to the Modern Drama*, New York: Little, Brown, and Company.

Gilman, Richard (1974) *The Making of Modern Drama; A Study of Büchner, Ibsen, Strindberg, Chekhov, Pirandello, Brecht, Beckett, Handke*, New York: Farrar, Straus, and Giroux.

Gottfried, Martin (2003) *Arthur Miller: His Life and Work*, New York: Da Capo Press.

Gussow, Mel (1998) *Theatre on the Edge: New Visions, New Voices*, New York: Applause Books.

Kalb, Jonathan (2003) *Play by Play: Theater Essays and Reviews, 1993–2002*, New York: Limelight Editions.

Kauffmann, Stanley (1967) 'Drama on the *Times*', in Theodore Solotaroff (ed), *New American Review #1*, New York: New American Library.

Leverich, Lyle (1995) *Tom: The Unknown Tennessee Williams*, New York: Crown Publishers, Inc.

Little, Stuart W. (1972) *Off-Broadway: The Prophetic Theater*, New York: Coward, McCann & Geoghegan, Inc.

Nathan, George Jean (1942–1951) *The Theatre Book of the Year*, annual series, New York: Alfred A. Knopf.

Poe, Edgar Allan (1984) 'The American Drama', in G.R. Thompson (ed), *Edgar Allan Poe: Essays and Reviews*, New York: Library of America.

Turan, Kenneth and Papp, Joseph (2009) *Free for All: Joe Papp, the Public, and the Greatest Theater Story Ever Told*, New York: Doubleday.

Woollcott, Alexander (1924) *Enchanted Aisles*, New York: G.P. Putnam's Sons.

'About Us', The *Village Voice*, http://www.villagevoice.com/about/index/ (accessed 20 January 2015).

http://www.hotreview.org (accessed 20 January 2015).

CHAPTER 3
THE PROBLEM OF RELIABILITY: THEATRE CRITICISM IN LATVIA
Valda Čakare

On June 2014, Latvian critic Maija Uzula-Petrovska reviewed a performance devised by a group of young theatre artists. Set during the war in Afghanistan, the performance deals with the specific episode of two Latvian soldiers killed in action. Maija Uzula-Petrovska's review, published in the online magazine *kroders.lv*, does not use one unambiguous term to designate the Latvian soldiers: she refers to them as 'mercenaries' and, metaphorically, as 'heavy metal'. Thus the reviewer draws the reader's attention to the fact that the Latvian soldiers in Afghanistan can be categorized in different ways depending on the viewpoint. Since they are not fighting for Latvia, they are perceived as tools in the hands of foreign political forces, hence the use of the term 'mercenaries'. On the other hand, they are tough and reliable on the battlefield and therefore referred to as 'heavy metal' by their American colleagues.

In this article, I examine the way in which Latvian theatre critics articulate their views and clarify social and individual contexts which have propelled their choices. I propose and develop the following thesis: reviews as historical records of theatre performances are unreliable due to the fact that reviewers are subjected to historical and ideological, as well as personal and institutional, influences. At the same time, reviews are fairly reliable as historical records of the critics' perception of a theatre performance.

Following a short introduction about the current critical landscape, the article engages in a close analysis of the use of language by the Soviet Latvian critics in the monthly journal *Karogs* (*The Banner*) between 1945 and 1955, before it returns to a discussion of some contemporary critical writing. Concrete issues are discussed to reveal how critical vocabulary undergoes various degrees of metamorphosis due to historical changes.

The theoretical framework used for the analysis is drawn from Hayden White, Violetta Gudkova, Nathan Constantine, Zita Nuñes and Pierre Bourdieu. For the analysis of reviews from the Soviet. period, White's conception of historical writing as a reflection of literary narrative is significant. Gudkova's typology of protagonists and plots of Soviet drama and Constantine and Nuñes's studies on cannibalism proved helpful in accounting for the strategies and vocabulary chosen by the Soviet Latvian critics. Bourdieu's views about writers being subjected to the 'web of power' prompted closer examination of the critics' freedom in post-Soviet Latvia.

Contemporary context

Latvia's total population is less than two million and the number of people engaged in writing about theatre does not exceed thirty. Under such circumstances, it is quite natural that in Latvia theatre criticism has never been separated from theatre research. The same persons who do theatre research write reviews of shows for newspapers and magazines, and at present, also for websites.

However, with the advent of capitalism in Latvia following its independence from the Soviet Union in 1991, the situation has been changing gradually. Writers have to make their own choice of priorities – either engage in research and give up criticism, or vice versa – it has become next to impossible to combine both callings. Daily newspapers like *Diena* (*The Day*) and *Neatkarīgā Rīta Avīze* (*The Independent Morning Paper*) have started to demand overnight reviewing to outpace other newspapers with exciting news about theatre openings and to promote shows. The internet is another agent that speeds everything up.

On the other hand, theatre research carried out under the auspices of the Latvian Academy of Sciences has never been a profitable occupation to earn one's living. So writers choose to pursue academic careers at higher educational establishments, work as dramaturgs in theatres, become office workers at state institutions like ministries, or else – find some other job that enables them to take part in theatre research projects on a more or less regular basis.

Newspaper theatre criticism in Latvia, meanwhile, is becoming more and more journalistic: bearing strong resemblance to news, merging facts and comments and acquiring a certain market value. Yet, these are not the ultimate changes caused by the advent of the market economy.

After the fall of the Iron Curtain, Latvia faced the same problems as many other Eastern European countries. First, opportunities to publish articles about theatre became scarce – the weekly newspaper *Literatūra un Māksla* (*Literature and Art*) and the yearbook *Teātris un Dzīve* (*Theatre and Life*), which dealt exclusively with the issues of Latvian theatre, ceased to exist due to the hardships caused by the economic transition. The state subsidies were first cut and eventually taken away. The only publication that continued to print more in-depth articles on the theatre was *Teātra Vēstnesis* (*Theatre Herald*), however, the frequency of its publication was gradually reduced from twelve to six, and then to four times a year.

The most efficacious attempt to compensate for the loss of space in printed media was *kroders.lv* – a website which came about in 2011. It was named after one of the most talented and respected Latvian stage directors of the twentieth century – Oļģerts Kroders (1921–2012) and his father – a well-known theatre researcher and critic Roberts Kroders (1892–1956). Kroders' name has acquired a symbolic meaning in the theatre circles of Latvia – it has always been associated with creativity and freedom from outdated aesthetic traditions and canons. The project was funded by the Culture Capital Endowment of Latvia. As *kroders.lv* was concerned with current processes in Latvian theatre from the outset, it took over the reviewing of the main shows from the printed media.

When discussing the ways in which theatre critics in Latvia name phenomena and processes I want to mostly concentrate on examples taken from *kroders.lv*. Chief among the reasons is the fact that this website is one of the two specialized platforms that produce insight into the theatre of Latvia, and the only one that is concerned with quality criticism. The other specialized edition – the magazine *Teātra Vēstnesis* (*Theatre Herald*) comes out four times a year and therefore, turns to reviewing very selectively, mostly favouring research papers and analysis of theatre process. Weekly or daily newspapers, in turn, prefer shorter notices containing a verdict on whether or not the show is worth seeing.

A glimpse of the Soviet past

Like in the rest of the Soviet Union, Stanislavskian psychological realism was officially institutionalized in Latvian theatre after the Second World War. At the time, public discourse about theatre was about its effect within the sociopolitical domain. To illustrate, I will offer an insight into writings on theatre printed in *Karogs* – a literary, arts, and sociopolitical monthly, issued by the Writers' Union of Soviet Latvia.[1] In the first post-war decade very few articles on theatre were published by *Karogs* – between four articles per year in 1947 and thirteen in 1952. It should be noted that before 1953 – the year of Stalin's death – theatre criticism in the sense of evaluation of plays according to the accepted aesthetic principles of socialist realism is absent. Likewise, theatre criticism featuring descriptions of the cast, plot, and technical aspects, or evaluation according to the reviewer's personal taste is not practised. Instead, one can find mere announcements of new productions, or short articles on theatre history. Much more space is allotted to addressing political issues declared urgent by the Soviet system, such as exposition of American imperialism, bankruptcy of the capitalist society, the necessity to consolidate progressive forces to fight warmongers and the like.

However, the issue of March 1953, in which Latvian writers and poets lament over the deceased leader of the Communist Party and the Soviet Union, becomes a turning point. It does not mean that the writers start refraining from political slogans from then on, but some minor changes are observable: specifically, issues such as the spatial and temporal framing of the performance, organization of the fictional world and the contribution of actors are now allotted more space and discussed in greater detail. Subsequent issues of *Karogs* already demonstrate new approaches and a more varied vocabulary, although never transgressing the line of demarcation drawn by the Soviet ideologues.

In 1959, Jānis Kalniņš, an authoritative prose writer and a literary and theatre critic of the postwar period, argued that 'inadmissible allowances' were being made on account of 'the artistic value of performances':

> if the idea of the artwork is acceptable, it's as if we close our eyes and say that we have benefited from this artwork despite the fact that its artistic language is weak. However, the weakness of the artistic language means that the idea of the artwork speaks to us ineffectively as well.
>
> 1959: 114[2]

Before 1953, it would have been unthinkable to claim that stylistic devices are as important as the idea of an artwork and apply terms such as 'mood', 'subtext' or 'understatement', which compromised the clarity and ideological certainty of the Soviet stage art. It is worth mentioning that this relative freedom of expression decreased after 1964 when Leonid Brezhnev became the leader of the Soviet Union and the system became more rigid again.

In April 1953, a new section 'In Theatres and Concert Halls' was introduced by the journal. Among other informative texts it contained some theatre reviews. Anonymous at the beginning, they soon became personalized and oriented towards evaluation according to the aesthetic principles of socialist realism. It should be noted that most of the critics writing for *Karogs* and other periodicals in the initial post-war decades originally came from bourgeois backgrounds, so they had to adopt the principles of socialist realism imposed on all artistic and critical practice in the Soviet Union.

According to the contemporary Latvian critic Guntis Berelis:

> this term [socialist realism] was used more than frequently, yet no-one knew what it was, critics and theoreticians just kept

quoting one another and Stalin in addition [. . .]. The 'recipe' was as follows: the guidelines were produced in Moscow, then – through the committees of the Communist Party – they were forwarded to Riga and supplemented with an anonymous home-produced text in a similar manner.

Berelis 2010: 4

Texts dealing with theatre, just like many other texts, illustrate the control of language by the Soviet system. Reading theatre reviews from the period therefore appears to be a dual experience: the texts seem frightening and at the same time – amusing. One might quite enjoy the ornate style of the poet Jānis Sudrabkalns in his essay dedicated to the Drama Theatre – 'Only now, in the sunshine of Stalin's Constitution, the wreath of the Latvian theatre art is glittering in all colours of the rainbow' (Sudrabkalns 1949: 248) – or even have a laugh at an unidentified reviewer's attempt to draw an analogy between animal characters in a children's matinee and the enemies of the working-class: 'Through the characters of the Mole and the Toad the directors have disclosed relations among the imperialist vultures of today's world' (1952c: 1426).

However, despite the efforts of the theatre critics to be politically correct, in the following example, the supposed analysis of their writings seems menacing:

The cornfield of our theatre criticism has become weedy. [. . .] [Some theatre critics'] output expresses the same villainous cosmopolitanism, formalism, bourgeois aestheticism and snobbery, the same sullenness and hatred disguised as criticism against the best works of the Soviet drama and theatre, the same derogation of these works and deceitfulness that is present in the writings of Yuzovsky[3] and his gang.

Pelše 1949: 371

This kind of direct attack in the official press was followed by consequences as a rule: prohibition from getting published, or in the worst case – arrest and deportation.

Construction of meaning

Are these texts reliable and historically authentic? Taking into account that the reviewer is subjected to the constraints of cultural tradition, current fashions, his or her own taste – and in this particular case, the ideology of the impersonal system of power – it seems worth considering how theatre reviews define the content of performance and help to decipher or to hide its meaning.

The American cultural historian Hayden White, who plays an important part in reconsidering the principles of historiography points out:

The historian shapes his materials if not in accordance with what Popper calls (and criticizes as) a 'framework of preconceived ideas', then in response to the imperatives of narrative discourse in general.

White 1985: 102

Given that past events cannot be verified, it is only possible to compare various interpretations of past events and determine the criteria for selecting the most convincing narrative. Therefore, according to White, history has to pay attention to language, the traditions of historical writing, and the genres employed in order to create a convincing version of the past:

[I]n the very language that the historian uses to describe his object of study, prior to any effort he may make formally to explain or interpret it, he subjects that object of study to the kind of distortion that historicists impose upon their materials in a more explicit and formal way.

White 1985: 102

In the period under discussion, the way of expression is distinctly prescriptive – the principles of the socialist realism have to be studied and cultivated. The way of thinking is schematized and arranged in clear-cut opposition: one's own people/enemies, good/bad, right/wrong.

The articles in *Karogs* of the post-war decades provide an eloquent material to demonstrate how meanings are constructed through language. The following excerpts are taken from the text 'The Representation of the Revolutionary Struggle on the Stage' written by an anonymous reviewer:

> Observing the life of working people in their shabby barracks, following their discussions about the necessity of strikes in order to improve their unbearable condition, listening to their hearty song, one is moved by their artlessness, mutual friendship and openness, their dreams and hope for a happy, respectable human life.
>
> 1952b: 1302

According to an unwritten law, this paragraph, saturated with compassion and optimistic future expectations for proletarians is immediately followed by a sharply contrasting one:

> In the enemies' camp on the contrary we can see real beasts of prey. No matter if they put on a worried face or a flattering grin, they cannot hide the fangs of a bloodthirsty wolf; though they may be wearing white gloves, their claws poised for a fierce clasp are visible.
>
> Ibid

Or another similar example, showing meaning being formed through binary opposition:

> [O]n the one hand – admirable heroism, the fascination of creating a new better life, the hardening and growth of man in struggle; on the other – moral degradation of the defeated bourgeoisie, the hopeless and miserable resistance of desperate individuals to the triumph of revolutionary forces.
>
> Ibid: 1304

Being shaped as a formal construction, both instances demonstrate recurrent narrative designs, patterns of action and character types which allow us to assume that the texts have been created in response to the 'imperatives of narrative discourse'. Complementarily to Hayden White, Russian literary critic Violetta Gudkova has offered a sharper method of analysis. According to her study of archetypes in Soviet literature, both above-mentioned examples demonstrate the mythologising feature of the Soviet culture.

The hero is the most dynamic figure of the myth. He is the constructor of a new life but at the same time, he can be a victim. It means that, not infrequently, Soviet plots combine two myths – that of a hero and that of a victim – thus creating one new Soviet myth.[4] Along with Soviet literature and art, the theatre reviews in *Karogs* also testify to the subversion of pre-Soviet myths and creation of new ones.

The new dimension is occasionally manifested in fairy-tale images. Most often they are deployed when the heroes' opponents are discussed. Dissecting the stage version of the classical novel *The Green Land*, the reviewer Roberts Pelše emphasizes that the central figure – the wealthy farmer Vanags 'is an extremely vivid representative of the rural bourgeoisie. [. . .] He is hypocritical and deceitful: he talks to his farm labourers, makes jokes, treats them to a glass of vodka and even gives one of them a pair of worn-out jack boots as a gift. In reality, he is a greedy wolf with a fox-tail' (Pelše 1950: 978).

However, the most suggestive and interesting is the trope of cannibalism which is amply employed in diversiform variations. The review of *The Green Land* ends with a generalizing statement that communists 'have nothing in common with the capitalist imperialist world of man-eaters and the cannibals *trumans* and *churchills*' (ibid, 983). Similarly, an unidentified reviewer, commenting on the representation of the revolutionary struggle on the Latvian stage, remarks that the recent productions 'turn against the reactionary forces – the bloodsuckers that threaten to drown all humanity and civilization in bloodshed' (1952b: 1301).

One possible explanation why the metaphor of cannibalism is favoured by the Soviet writers can be derived from Zita Nuñes' study of the metaphor's circulation through the work of a number of American writers. Nuñes rightly observes that the metaphor of cannibalism calls attention to struggle, because the source and the target of the metaphor – the eater and the eaten – cannot be the same (2008: xvii). As struggle is an essential concept for the Soviet ideologues of class relations, the metaphor of cannibalism serves as a powerful device. Furthermore, the process of eating presupposes a remainder, a residue that can be deferred into the future as unresolvable, or repressed to emerge as a threat (ibid: 13). The implied message of the representation of the class enemies as cannibals is a warning to them that the proletariat will never perish, even if temporarily defeated.

One more important aspect is highlighted by Nathan Constantine in his study of the history of cannibalism. Constantine argues that there are three essential reasons for it – duty, desperation and desire (2006: 1). Duty is based on the assumption that eating of one's own kind will keep the world going, despair motivates cannibalism in a situation which has no solution, and desire is rooted in some sexual dysfunction of the human body.

Obviously, picturing the class enemy as a cannibal helps theatre reviewers to maintain the ambivalence of the Soviet archetypes. They point out that working people implement the triumph of the revolution and at the same time they are threatened by the imperialist bloodsuckers. Cannibalism possesses the features of ritual, where the makers of sacrifice, as well as those who were sacrificed, have a firm conviction that the ritual is indispensable to keep up the order of the world.

To sum up the discussion thus far: The dominating rhetoric in the theatre reviews of the 1940s and 1950s testifies to the fact that theatre was regarded as a platform for Soviet ideology, and theatre critics – willingly or against their own will – fulfilled the function of watchdogs or even disseminators of this ideology. For that reason, their criticism can be considered reliable in registering the sociopolitical climate of Soviet Latvia – in the sense that it illuminates a way of thinking about life. However, it is not reliable in terms of documenting theatre art and its form.

In this aspect critical commentaries are reduced to a fixed formula – a plot summary, a statement for or against the show, followed by lists of actors and lists of adjectives, either positive or negative. Nothing else can be expected and nothing else is possible, because theatre-makers are compelled to follow already existing standards: '*Lyubov Yarovaya* shows strict and strong scenic traditions, which relieve the director and actors of hard work – they do not need to consider the interpretation, or the inner and outer traits of the characters' (Anonymous, 1952b: 1304).

Latvian theatre practice in the twenty-first century

Browsing the collection of reviews that has accumulated on the website *kroders.lv* since its founding in 2011, it becomes evident that the language and the tradition of writing have undergone considerable changes. The above-mentioned examples testify to the fact that sixty years ago, critics imposed class view upon performance even if it was a love story, and deployed myths fostered by the Soviet system to analyse its structure.

At first sight, the contributors to *kroders.lv* seem to enjoy freedom from these kinds of restrictions. They engage in performance analysis focusing on the performance itself and the way the production is created; they discuss issues regarding the production as a finished aesthetic product, not a platform for ideological statements; they reflect on the interaction between the auditorium and the stage.

Nevertheless, they are 'immersed' in what Pierre Bourdieu calls their own 'natural location' determined by cultural tradition and current trends of fashion and – they are subjected to the 'web of power'. Bourdieu emphasizes that

in a field[5] still being constituted, the internal positions must first of all be understood as so many specifications of the generic position of writers in the field of power, or, if you like, as so many particular forms of the relationship objectively established between writers as a whole and temporal power.

1992: 71

Traces of these specifications can be detected in the theatre reviews. Since the spectrum of critical texts is quite broad, I shall focus on one particular and relatively small part of it – reviews of political performances. First, because they are thematically related to the reviews printed in *Karogs* of the 1950s – the time when all issues tackled by theatre-makers were considered political – second, the change of approach in comparison with the Soviet theatre criticism is here the most evident.

It should be noted that after the fall of the Iron Curtain, in the aftermath of the perestroika or rebuilding, Latvian stage directors, with very few exceptions, demonstrated a total lack of interest in making sociopolitical commentaries on current affairs. Contrary to the 1990s, the years before regaining independence were dominated by the work of rebellious directors who were in their forties at the time – Valentīns Maculēvičs (born in 1950) and Valdis Lūriņš (born in 1951) being the most prominent of them – who maintained faith in the theatre's community-building power and were eager to engage the critical agency of the spectator. They turned radically away from prescriptive socialist realism in order to develop anti-illusionist staging methods, such as direct audience address and presentational play. There was a strong agitprop element in their work, and, for many critics, their capability for addressing urgent political issues and bridging the gap between the stage and the spectators marked the high point of the Latvian theatre in the period of the perestroika.

In the 1990s, the new world of uncertainty, the continuously changing perspective, the unpredictable indeterminacy and multiplicity of worldviews rendered this kind of theatre obsolete. Directors acquainted themselves with Western practices and experimented by freely mixing techniques and trying to create new worlds of their own. They were more concerned with the inner processes of the individual.

In the twenty-first century, Latvian theatre has recovered its interest in social processes. Very likely, this change has taken place with the arrival of a new generation of theatre artists in recent years. They feel more at ease with the diversity of practices in arts funding and management, they privilege their freedom of artistic expression and right to experiment over the safety offered by the state-subsidized repertoire theatres and, most importantly, they have recovered their faith in theatre that fulfills its mission if it is in the forefront of the social and political struggle.

Not only does a theatre review confirm something that was visible during the performance, but it also forms a notion of something we cannot see at all. This 'something' is the underlying meaning associated with the social processes and the cultural context. Consider this example:

> The rules of the game put forward by the director Viesturs Meikšāns are clear from the very first moment. The time of action – now, the place of action – here. Richard III performed by Artūrs Skrastiņš is a politician, not a soldier. His long 'winter of discontent', is, let us say, a burdensome pre-election campaign, an inter-factional struggle and a formation of government; there is nothing of the bloody battle of the royal families on the battlefield. In short, politics are the true spatial and temporal characteristics of the performance.
>
> Tišheizere 2014

This is the theatre critic Edīte Tišheizere trying to supply an objective account of a production of *Richard III* by naming what is available for all to see on the stage. Definitely, the act of naming is an important means of apprehending reality, however, the staging of this production does not initially give much ground for the assumption that the Duke of Gloucester is a politician rather than a soldier. The performance space is divided into separate sections with the help of transparent sliding glass doors enabling the audience to see a wall that is used as a video-screen at times. Potentially, this arrangement may mean anything from an office room to a large public space. Another indication that can be interpreted in different ways is supplied by the actor's garment – a smart suit that fits like a glove – and his body language, which demonstrates the poise and perfect self-control of a mannerly middle-class man.

Commentaries are meaningless without facts, but the facts that the critic comments upon in this case seem to be hiding outside the walls of the theatre. The critic's assumption that Richard is a politician, not a soldier is informed as much by the political situation in Latvia at the time as it is by the visual signs transmitted from the stage.

Richard III was premiered on the main stage of the Daile (Art) theatre on 16 May 2014. The twelfth elections of Saeima or the Parliament of Latvia were already envisaged at the time for 4 October 2014. Tišheizere's review was published on July 4, when the election campaign was in full swing and one could not escape the pictures of smiling politicians on public transport. Thus, the review, in a sense, turns out to be partly true, partly false. In this particular case the critic's imagination fills in the gaps and gives an insight into what is seen on the stage while simultaneously giving an insight into the political reality of Latvia in 2014.

Yet, along with the very concrete reading that is prompted by the urgent political reality, the reviewer analyses Viesturs Meikšāns' production as a cultural performance through which one might understand that the society of Latvia conceives of itself as deceived in its hopes for the future after regaining independence:

> [Director Viesturs Meikšāns] has tried to force a door open to break the news that is known to everyone – democracy has been overestimated. Politicians are bastards and the smartest of them are demagogues; the public are sheep, forever making the same stupid mistakes; and our potential protectors – senile invalids. Well, yes ... So what?

> Tišheizere, 2014

Conclusion

What differs in the comparison between the 1950s and 2010s? The post-war critics were former bourgeoisie who had to learn the precepts of socialist realism, the contemporary critics, Edīte Tišheizere and Maija Uzula-Petrovska quoted earlier, are less likely than the mid-twentieth century critics to assume that one ideological and aesthetic framework can be established for all theatre. Despite the fact that they belong to different generations – Tišheizere is in her early sixties, Uzula-Petrovska in her early thirties – both of them insist on doing justice to what artists are up to in the twenty-first century.

The vocabulary used by theatre reviewers in the 1950s was indicative of political thinking, so is the vocabulary used by the Latvian theatre reviewers in the twenty-first century. However, it is obvious that today Latvian critics try to avoid a codified set of standards. Even if they do not engage a variety of contemporary critical theories, they mostly give a more or less accurate account of what is going on, keeping in mind that they can at best make the nature of the ideological form partly visible and trace a kernel of the real in it. The critics are well aware that the ways they examine and interpret a theatre performance can be re-shaped by new concerns at any moment. The performance-makers are continuously 'throwing a new ration of food for the audience to digest', as noted by Uzula-Petrovska (2014). Pierre Bourdieu's suggestion that the value that determines the significance of a work of art is the result of social processes – although it is not a direct expression of the social stance of its creator – is relevant to the case of Latvian stage art. As for reliability, the reviews of today, just like those of the mid-twentieth century, have to be read with reference to the influence of the sociopolitical and cultural context, bearing in mind that in the twenty-first century this context is much less fixed than it used to be.

Notes

1. Its first issue appeared in the early days of the Soviet occupation in September 1940, however, its editorial policies were developed after the war. *Karogs* continued to be the only literary and arts edition until 1945 when weekly newspaper *Litertūra un Māksla* (*Literature and Art*) was issued.

2. All quotations from Latvian and Russian sources are translated by the author unless otherwise stated.

3. Yuzovsky, Yosiph (Yuri) (1902–1964) – one of the leading Russian Soviet theatre and literary critics. After being accused of cosmopolitanism and bourgeois aestheticism he was deprived of being published and was dismissed from the position of the Senior Researcher at the Institute of the World Literature in Moscow.

4. A perfect example of such an emblematic character is Pavel Korchagin in Nikolay Ostrovsky's novel *How the Steel was Tempered*. A soldier of the

Red Army and a Komsomol leader, he is wounded several times, suffers from a series of illnesses, and eventually loses his mobility and his sight.

5. Bourdieu speaks of the literary field, however, it is applicable to theatre criticism as well.

Works cited

Anonymous (1952a) 'Par dažiem jaunākajiem inscenējumiem', *Karogs*, No.5, pp. 535–537.

Anonymous (1952b) 'Revolucionārās cīņas atspoguļojums uz skatuves', *Karogs*, No.11, pp. 1301–1304.

Anonymous (1952c) 'Saistoša un audzinoša izrāde bērniem', *Karogs*, No.12, pp. 1426–1427.

Berelis, Guntis (2010) 'Cienījama vecuma', *Karogs*. https://berelis.wordpress.com/2010/12/10cienijama-vecuma-karogs/ (accessed 29 January 2015).

Bourdieu, Pierre (1992) *The Rules of Art: Genesis and Structure of the Literary Field*, translated by Susan Emanuel, Stanford: Stanford University Press.

Constantine, Nathan (2006) *A History of Cannibalism: From Ancient Cultures to Survival Stories and Modern Psychopaths*, London: Arcturus.

Gudkova, Violetta (2008) *Rozhdenie sovyetskih syuzhetov: Tipologiya otechestvennoy dramy 1920-h nachala 1930h godov*, Moskva: novoye literaturnoye obozreniye. [Гудкова, Виолетта (2008) *Рождение советских сюжетов: Типология отечественной драмы 1920-х – начала 1930- х годов*, Москва: новое литературное обозрение.]

Kalniņš, Jānis (1959) 'Pa pārāk līkumotu ceļu', *Karogs*, No.12, pp. 112–118.

Nikolajevs-Bergins, Nikolajs (1947) 'K.S. Staņislavskis – teātra mākslas novators', *Karogs*, No.12, pp. 1362–1367.

Nuñes, Zita (2008) *Cannibal Democracy: Race and Representation in the Literature of the Americas*, Minneapolis and London: University of Minnesota Press.

Ozols, Arturs (1951) 'Buržuazisko koncepciju kritika latviešu literārās valodas normu jautājumā', *Karogs*, No.7, p. 650.

Pelše, Arvīds (1949) 'Imperiālistiskās reakcijas ideoloģiskā agresija un antipatriotiskā teātra kritika', *Karogs*, No.4, pp. 367–374.

Pelše, Roberts (1950) 'Drūmās pagātnes ainas', *Karogs*, No.10. pp. 977–984.

Sēja, Austra (1948) 'Ko padomju tauta gaida no latviešu valodniekiem?' *Karogs*, No.12, p. 1217.

Sudrabkalns, Jānis (1949) 'Valsts Dramas teātra ceļš', *Karogs*, No.3, pp. 243–248.

Tišheizere, Edīte (2014) 'Ričards III un . . .' *kroders.lv*, 4 July, www.kroders.lv/verte/493 (accessed 29 January 2015).

Uzula-Petrovska, Maija (2014) 'Platforma pārdomām', *kroders.lv*, 2 June, www.kroders.lv/verte/472 (accessed 29 January 2015).

White, Hayden (1985) *Tropics of Discourse: Essays in Cultural Criticism,* Baltimore: Johns Hopkins University Press.

Zeltiņa, Guna (ed.) (2012) *Theatre in Latvia,* translated by Maija Veide, Riga: Institute of Literature, Folklore and Art, University of Latvia.

CHAPTER 4
FROM THE UNCRITICAL CERTAINTIES OF MODERNISM TO THE CRITICAL UNCERTAINTIES OF POSTMODERNISM: REVIEWING THEATRE IN GREECE

Savas Patsalidis

In English one encounters two terms to describe the act of theatre criticism. One is 'review', which concentrates on a particular performance – it is not very analytical (given the space restrictions and time pressure) and it is published in the press (and now the internet) shortly after the performance. The other is 'academic critique/ criticism' which offers a more analytical reading, and focuses more on the text itself (for more see Palmer 1998). In Greek there is only one word to describe both, *kritiki*. Depending on the medium in which the piece is published, one understands the style and purpose of writing (academic, high or low journalism).

Starting with the hypothesis that politics, economics, popular culture, aesthetics and personal preferences affect reviews, I intend to explore the institutional and ideological conditions that shaped Greek theatre reviewing in newspapers from the mid-1970s to the present, after providing a brief historical survey in order for the reader to have a clearer idea of its trajectory.

Historical survey

What is remarkable is that, despite the substantial body of theatre reviewing in Greece, there is very little written on its history; nor is there any theoretical discourse to provide the necessary tools to deal with changing theatre trends. According to theatre scholar Dimitris Spathis (1986), theatre reviewing in Greece appeared sporadically in the nineteenth century, after the country's War of Independence from Ottoman rule, with the writings of Michael Schinas (?–1870), Emmanuel Roidis (1836–1904) – both advocates of the idea of the Enlightenment – and Angelos Vlachos (1838–1920), and more systematically at the beginning of the twentieth century, and the years in-between the two big wars, with Gregorios Xenopoulos (1867–1951), Nikolaos Laskaratos (1868–1945), Georgios Vlachos (1886–1951) and Leon Koukoulas (1894–1967). It was born basically in newspapers and literary journals[1] more or less at the same time the first travelling troupes and professional companies began making their presence more felt and stable.

One of the issues hotly debated among early critics was the role of theatre and theatre reviewing. Kostis Palamas (1859–1943), for example, a major poet of Greek modernism and writer of the verse play *Trisevgeni*, claimed that the critic's mission is to refine public taste and that the dramatic text does not need the stage to prove its value (for more see Papazoglou 2014) – an idea voiced a few years later (1929) by another important cultural figure, Fotos Politis (1890–1934), a critic himself and the first artistic director of the National Theatre, who confessed that with his reviews he was trying to manipulate the 'uneducated mass' and turn it into a knowledgeable theatre audience (1983: 51, vol. B). Politis believed that modern Greeks lacked artistic perception and that it is the critic's job to help them develop it (1983: 42–48, vol. A).

At a time when Greece, as a young state entity, needed evidence to support its national uniqueness (*hellinikoteta*-Greekness), ancient Greek drama in particular proved to be a useful and also a very sensitive arena on which reviewers fought out their ideas and certainties about theatre, authenticity, continuity and legitimation. Politis, for one, encouraged fellow artists and scholars to look for inspiration from their native soil whenever they revisited the classics; 'nativism', he argued, judges and examines the individual that acquired his/her personality 'from the conditions of national life, its history and tradition, its ancient customs, [...] and national physiognomy' (Politis 1928).[2]

Of course not everybody agreed. There were critics who declared the 'alienness of tragedy' and instead of authenticity and fixity 'prioritized artistic creativity' (Papazoglou 2014: 211). Xenopoulos, for example, the 'father' of modern Greek drama, and the first modern critic, claimed that 'the revival of ancient drama is like trying to square the circle. It is against the law of nature. What dies cannot come back to life' (1903: 86; for more see Papazoglou 2014: 209–228). Also Alkis Thrylos (1896–1971), another established critic and major cultural figure, warned against the critics' eclecticism, their unchecked and unconditional worshipping of the past. 'We, modern Greeks,' she writes, 'belong to a different civilization. In-between the ancients and us too many things were lost, vital for the exact revival of the classics. We have changed. The Olympian gods are dead' (1947/1978: 357–58); and then she goes on to say: 'I wonder how come that theatre people do not understand that there are plays which cannot be staged in their original form [...] they have to be readjusted' (1980: 294).

Yet the vast majority of theatre critics and directors cultivated from the beginning a xenophobic attitude, a 'syndrome of oneiric idolatry', according to Stathis Gourgouris (1996: 31), that set the rules of reviewing for many years to come. Especially with the inauguration of the Epidaurus Festival in the mid-1950s and the productions of the National Theatre of Athens, its exclusive user for about twenty years, reviewers found ample ground to promote their own 'structures of inclusion and exclusion' of the kind Foucault discusses in his *Madness and Civilization* (1965), and at the same time determine which style was held to be a legitimate form of reviving the classics. As Papazoglou correctly observes, the National Theatre's recycling of neoclassicist interpretative and performative model 'ritualized its own "continuity" which was gradually established as the authentic performative code, one that was "faithful" to the original texts, meanings, heroes etc' (2014: 209–10). The site of 'now', the celebrated substance of live performance, did not seriously enter most reviewers' discourse. Nor did the ties to industry, capital, power, politics or institutions. It was quite self-contradictory that, although they promoted the everlasting beauty of ancient drama, reviewers did not treat it as a living organism but as a monument which had to remain intact. They were content to look at the Festival as the 'sacralized site' which provided the 'umbilical cord', that somehow naturalized the idea of continuity from the Athenian democracy to the present day (Ioannidou 2008: 14–30 and 2010: 385–403).

For the vast majority of critics (in both academia and in newspapers) reviewing was not so much a job (it never paid well, anyway),[3] but a mission grounded upon the premise of Greek exclusivism and exceptionalism. As director Karolos Koun, a major figure of Greek modernism, put the case, 'What has always been stimulating to us is the Greekness of ancient drama and the privilege, we, as Greeks, had to reach back to its sources ...' (1994: 141). This idealization of Greek tragedy, along with the call for the preservation and continuity of Greek classical heritage, became the founding principles upon which most local reviewers, strangely enough young as well as old, developed their absolutist discourse and their ranking criteria in the decades to come. Their 'colonizing' views (rave or pan) not only affected people's ideas about theatre but had a serious impact on the box office, especially when there was a kind of unanimous approval or disapproval.

The utopia of the post-dictatorship years

The collapse of the seven-year long Dictatorship of the Colonels (1967–1974) opened a new chapter in Greece's national life. The reestablishment of democracy has brought forward ideological conflicts, as well as dreams and desire for change; and so did the entry into the European Union a few years later (1981), followed by the election of a socialist government led by Andreas Papandreou (PASOK) shortly after (1983). At the same time, the collapse of the Soviet Bloc in 1990 brought to Greece thousands of economic immigrants (mainly from Albania and other neighbouring countries), creating yet another front for heated debates, this time directly related to the question of citizenship (and Greekness).

The problem is that not many people could see that joining the Union meant more things than passport-free travelling and security. Not many seriously reflected on the fact that entering the Union meant embracing a vision of a counter image of the static state order, 'an institutionalized "more and further"' (Beck & Grande 2007: 6); it meant beating people's archival memory, recasting documents, reconsidering maps, re-examining literary texts, archaelogical remains and all other items resistant to change in the name of a boundless 'moreness'. A most telling example of the prevailing atmosphere was the change of Epidaurus' Festival policy.

After years of hosting just the productions of the National Theatre of Athens, the Festival finally opened its doors first to local companies (in the mid 1970s) and a few years later to foreign companies,[4] a shift of policy which caused endless debates, continuing to the present day, among reviewers on whether Epidaurus should also host foreign or experimental shows.

What is striking in all this is that despite the leftist rhetoric that dominated political discourse in the post-dictatorship years (1970s and 1980s), local reviewing continued propagating a kind of a xenophobic superego, which, more or less, claimed that, by right of language and birth, Greeks are supposed to know more and better what the ancient texts mean. A most telling example is Karolos Koun again, who claimed that as the 'sole beneficiaries of the ancient past', Greeks know better than other Westerners who, without 'the sense of tragedy that we [have], are led astray' (1994: 156). Others supported the idea that Epidaurus should be closed to all those who did not respect the integrity of the classical tradition (Lignatis 1988: 138). Even younger critics, like Varveris, were in favour of this Hellenist exclusivism, claiming that Epidaurus is not a place for 'international theatre acrobatics' (1985: 148). Most of these reviewers were responding to the more adventurous theatre readings not only of foreign artists but also (and mainly) of local innovative artists who at first hesitatingly, and later far more confidently, started embracing more unconventional and poststructuralist ideas, which disrupted the claims to stable meaning, characterization, everlasting truth, authenticity, uniqueness, closure and sacredness in favour of absence, deferral, play and openness. By reversing standard trajectories, in such productions as *Bacchae* (dir. Thodoros Terzopoulos, 1986), *The Frogs* (dir. Yannis Kakleas, 1989), *Medea* (dir. Michael Marmarinos, 1991), among others, artists-*auteurs*, most of them in their mid-thirties, pushed the reading of theatre, especially the classics, from an assumed homogeneity of identity and praxis towards an endlessly proliferating heterogeneity. They introduced newer paradigms of presentation, involving visual, somatic, multimedia, multilingual and multicultural elements, paradigms more self-referential, drawing attention not just to their own modes of representation but also to the audience's acts of perception. These stage re-readings of the classics tested the limits of traditional aesthetic approaches and perspectives. They operated as platforms for the liberation of historical moments, sensations and affinities. Excavating the past was not only an act of just reviewing the past but also bringing the past to the present moment of performance.

This shift of perspective in theatre practice, although most useful, met the approval of just a handful of theatre critics who spoke to the need for a more flexible, more understanding, less idealized and politically more engaged theatre discourse. Yet, as mentioned earlier, when the classics were at stake, strange as it may sound, young and old critics, leftists and rightists, more or less continued to share the same belief in the innate Greekness of the old texts and felt that their staging should affirm the links with the past; that is, cement the idea of national identity. For them the favourite word was 'revival', for it underlined a kind of connection with something beautiful and everlasting (for more see Bien 2005: 226). Quite revealing of the prevailing attitude is the debate caused by Mattias Langhoff's radical *Bacchae* (State Theatre of Northern Greece, 1997). Most critics found the reconceptualization of Euripides' text scandalous, totally egocentric and unrelated to the original. They did not really

see his work as a form of fair appropriation but rather as [...] an example of an arrogant 'neo-imperialism' hastily disguised as an aesthetic pursuit; [...] What mattered most to local critics was not the fact that Langhoff used the text of Euripides, but that he trivialized it, draining it of its source culture through an

> arbitrary, ill-informed, non-negotiated, and essentially one-sided mode of transportation. ... [T]hey feel that a totally open and unprotected text is in danger of being expropriated by a stronger, 'imperial text,' and particularly by the globalizing mechanisms and complexities of the market.
>
> Patsalidis and Sakellaridou 1999: 16, 17

Similar reactions followed other productions, like the Greek-Turkish *Persians* presented in the Festival of Epidaurus in 2006, in collaboration with Istanbul's Festival, and Dimiter Goetscheff's *The Persians* (a production of the National Theatre of Athens, 2009), among others.

From utopia to dystopia: enter depression culture

Despite local debates and quarrels, things looked relatively promising till the Athens Olympics in 2004. As far as theatre was concerned, the economic development, the unchecked growth of the television industry and the proliferation of drama schools in the private sector, side by side with the vanity or inflated aspirations of many artists for glory and big money, helped create a buoyant market hungry for more products. At no point in Greece's history has there been such a hectic theatre activity as in the years between 1990 and 2010. The more affluent local society grew, the more theatre it consumed. Theatre, low and high, gradually became the ideal lifestyle of the whole society.

Like all fairytales, however, this one had to end sometime, somehow. It is a well-known story: when people are doing well nobody cares, nobody recognizes the fundamental sickness of the system or the bubble that sustains it. And that is what happened in Greece. People, either willingly or out of ignorance, turned a blind eye to the 'real' dominated by speculative businesses and settled for the chimera of the 'hyperreal'. The hedonistic ethic which for well over thirty years had dominated a big part of Greek society created a generation of shoppers, whose main concern was to consume more and more. Thus the sudden economic slump in 2009 was inevitable to ground everybody very violently, dramatically changing their mentality and their morale. Overnight a whole nation entered the 'real world' via a shocking crisis which created a rupture between the individual and the collective conception of the nation and its ideologies. From the comforting certainties of modernism people passed to the discomforting openness (and uncertainties) of postmodernism that called for painful redefinitions and new poetics of representation. Identity politics went hand in hand with an identity crisis: Who am I? Who are they? Why me? People wanted to know who to blame: the politicians, the malfunctioning system, the State, the Bankers (or Banksters), the International Monetary Fund, Europeanization, Globalization or themselves for their unconfessed wrongdoings – their over-borrowing and overspending?

We know that when societies are confronted with situations which threaten their customs and beliefs, they have the tendency to turn to the past, looking either for certainties and/or new ways to re-examine its legacy. A telling example of this return to the past is the repertory of both the National Theatre in Athens and the State Theatre of Northern Greece in Thessaloniki for the period 2010–2013. The two biggest theatre organizations of the country, shortly after the crisis broke, abandoned their earlier plans and turned the question 'What is a motherland?' into the governing principle of their policy. What they were after was mainly grassroot plays that touched upon issues which had to do with the component parts of the nation, its national character, its historical process, its folk traditions and current problems. By emphasizing the centrality of the nation they wanted to show to people that they had a mission not only to represent the nation and its pressing concerns, but also to be an inspiring force of nation re-building. At no time in their recent history were the two national theatres so overwhelmingly visible and dominating as they have been in the period between 2010 and 2014.

Theatre economics: the meltdown

Theatre is an important sector of the Greek workforce and economy – probably one of the largest business communities, with 3000 registered actors (Equity members) and as many unregistered, and well over 300 theatre companies. Although deeply affected by the ongoing economic crisis, Greek theatre gives the impression that, in some miraculous way, it is sailing pretty clear of many of the worst financial problems. Otherwise, how can we explain the fact that in the heart of the depression we've been having more new plays and productions than we could have thought possible a decade back? It suffices to say that for 2014–2015, in Athens alone, about 1000 new professional productions were scheduled according to press releases (Loverdou 2014), a number well above the average production volume of the period between 2000 and 2010 (400–500 per year). New audiences, people who might not have considered theatre as part of their cultural life, show up now, tempted by the special prices offered or by the fact that theatre is much cheaper than other entertainment venues. And what is remarkable is that audiences keep coming, so according to the law of supply and demand, things look good: people want theatre and they get it. But are things really what they seem? On the surface yes, but not underneath.

The economic slump is now taking its toll. The scarcity of money in the business sector, in combination with the absence of state funding have led to huge debts, deeper cuts, unpaid rent, difficulty in meeting staff payroll. Until 2010 state support amounted to a mere three and a half million euros for theatre. Applications for state funding varied from 170 to 200 every year. From my experience as a member of the selection committee (2006–2009), less than 40 per cent of the applications were approved. Big repertory companies used to get up to 250,000 euros per year, mid-size companies between 50 and 100,000 and small companies no more than 30,000 euros – not enough to cover expenses but psychologically important as it provided a kind of security blanket. In 2015, with no state funding at all, their future remains bleak and uncertain. Most actors work with no pay or are paid per performance (between 30 and 50 euros). Many shows are announced but equally many do not see the light of day. They are postponed, which means they drift permanently off the map. Even companies like Piramatiki Skini, Aplo Theatre, and Amphi-Theatro, which for many years managed to maintain impressive standards, have run out of steam and terminated their operation.

Regardless of size, all playhouses have introduced a series of preemptive measures to stave off a total financial meltdown. They offer special prices for the unemployed, the students and those hit the hardest by the economic situation. In many cases spectators are asked to give what they want or can afford. The State Theatre of Northern Greece went a step further. For certain productions (all accommodated under the umbrella term 'Theatrestore') instead of cash (normally something between 10–20 euros), people could hand over food at the ticket booth, which would later on be donated to poorhouses or children's charity organizations. As Sotiris Hatzakis, the artistic director of the State Theatre of Northern Greece (2009–2013), put it in a press conference in 2012: 'We are creating a solidarity network [...] which works in terms of direct democracy'. This is not to say that a big state theatre like this, that lives on state money, has turned radical all of a sudden. What I am arguing here is that radical social changes sometimes trigger equally inventive ways to inspire the audiences, engage the communities and also discuss burning national issues that directly affect their lives. In other words, by choosing to appeal directly to the audience, the State Theatre of Northern Greece targeted a more 'active culture', an active relation to theatre that Dan Rebellato refers to as 'a rehearsal for active citizenship' (2009: 54).

Even so, very few shows run long enough to recoup their initial investment and hope for profit afterwards. And the reason is not just the crisis. There are too many shows competing for the audience's disposable income and that makes the repertory choices very risky business. At the periphery of the local theatre activity, about two hundred smaller and younger companies, although hit the hardest by the economic downturn, still soldier on in an increasingly disheartening environment, most of them with no money. Young artists and ensembles like Vasistas, Simio Miden, Blitz, Choros, among others, instead of running away, seem to be emboldened by the economic slump and insist on searching for the dark, the advanced, the difficult. They search for a renewed contract with the audience, by exploring different acting styles and communication tactics. They want to reflect on the experience of the crisis by undoing the ideological platform of earlier practitioners and by putting the nation and its narratives under the microscope. Their aim is to conceive its national diversity and unsettle the narrative of its homogeneity with shows which go beyond the tight confines of dramatic theatre, such as site specific, devised, improvisational theatre, docudrama and physical theatre. *Dance me to the End of Greece* by Kyriaki Spanou (2012), *Telemachus: Should I Stay or Should I Go* by Prodromos Tsinikoris (2012), *Polis* by the group Kanigunda (2013) are just three recent productions that attracted the critics' attention, who saw them as an attempt to ascribe sense to the present; an attempt to keep theatre central to the public discourse and social interaction.

Surprising as it may sound, it is not only the young who participate in this deconstructive renewal. The Hellenic Festival, which was for many years the platform for the maintenance of national identity through the celebration of the classics, has now, under the leadership of its last artistic director Yorgos Loukos (2006–), managed to challenge the long-established practices and notions regarding legitimacy, textual integrity and local identity. Opening up the Festival to international collaborations and, more recently, to very young local artists, has generated a new dynamic that made many critics, particularly of the older generation, really furious since it upset their traditionalist notion that the symbiosis of the classical text with contemporary cultural texts most of the time does not do justice to the original.

I am not arguing that the overcrowded theatre community in Greece is all that successful. Yet even if many attempts fail, by simply trying, they bring into the field a forward-looking energy.

The critics and the crisis

Thirty years ago, when I first entered the reviewing business, critics were in a position to affect theatre affairs, to promote or even close down shows. Not any more. A Gallup poll published in the Greek newspaper *Eleftherotypia* (Marinou 2009) has shown that 64.3 per cent of those who plan their evening entertainment (which includes theatre as well) primarily take the recommendations of friends and relatives (word of mouth). Other sources of information include the commercials on television, the posters on the streets and of course the internet. As for newspapers, although we do know the number of readers of each newspaper, we do not know how many are review readers. Also, we do not know how many review readers of one newspaper are readers of another. What we do know, however, is the number of productions reviewed, and that can tell us things about the level of interest among the readership habits of the general public and the readership of particular newspapers. From my experience, I know that the greater the quantity of reviews, the lower the damage both to ticket sales and morale. Unless all reviews are extremely bad, then it is very possible that readers, irrespective of their regular source of information, will think twice before they go to see a show. If all reviews strongly recommend a show, then the positive impact is also strongly felt.[5] Yet, what is worth noting is that the most successful commercial shows of the last ten years, by popular stand-up comedians like Lakis Lazopoulos and Markos Seferlis, have in fact received bad reviews. This means that one must take into account a wider range of variables which affect audience attendance, like aggressive PR and other marketing campaigns, advanced-sale ticket packages, special offers and mainly ordinary theatregoers blasting their opinions through social media.

It is quite obvious that the arrival of the internet has made all those involved in the traditional press industry very nervous. Since the 1980s and well into the 2000s, there were more than 30 daily newspapers in Athens alone, most of them carrying their own theatre column. In 2015 there were less than ten left. With the exception of four that still manage to maintain a relatively viable circulation,[6] all others are vulnerable to closure.

I am among those very few critics who still writes for a daily newspaper (*Anggelioforos*), 850 words every Sunday. I also used to write for *Eleftherotypia*, the third largest newspaper in the country in terms of readership, which, as of December 2014, is no longer in circulation. When the crisis broke, the message from both managements was clear: I could hang on if I wished (with no pay anymore) or walk out. I decided to stay in the game, working long hours for free, just like most of my colleagues. That's always been the problem for Greek critics – whether established or aspiring. As mentioned earlier, writing about theatre in Greece means you need a regular job to support your writing, unless you are rich enough and you do not care, or you find ways to use your title 'critic' as a way to enter the larger theatre market (as a dramaturg, repertory consultant, etc.). The truth of the matter is that the advent of the internet has made the economic model of the full-time critic totally unviable. At present there are fewer than ten regular newspaper theatre critics all over the country and some say that in a decade or so there will be none left. They may be right. Having been in the centre of the local theatre life once, critics are now ironically either 'authorities' on the margins or just critics among hundreds of other critics who use the web.[7]

The times when a few spoke for the many is certainly over. As Esther Slevogt, one of the founders of the web journal *nachtkritik*, claims, 'the critic is no longer protected by the discourse power of the publication for which he is writing. Rather, he becomes part of a public discussion that is organizing itself anew' (2014). And what is most worrisome is that even artists themselves are less and less eager to find out what experienced newspaper critics have to say. They are gradually getting more than enough from easy-to-read free press reports, public relations, and other sources to promote their work.

The critics' (postmodern) role

A good part of the world is at the threshold of a second modernity, quite distinct from the nation-state of modernity; and that makes me think more and more about the critics' position within (global) culture and how their writing relates to the ordinary commerce of society. How is their work used and how do they lend themselves to these uses? How do they manage to survive in a militarized economy, which leaves them with no other option but to serve it? As far as I am concerned, having a stable university career, I had no motivation to cross-examine my position in all this. Yet what this economic crisis has brought to the surface is the persistence of these questions. In the midst of a landscape of uncertainties, where the foundation stones of the Greek welfare system are gradually dismantled, along with many forms of social protection, the unemployment rate – especially among young people – going up, and the arts-funding going down, I realize how important it is that theatre critics, no matter for which medium they write, also reconsider their critical tools and their social responsibilities: i.e. widen their understanding by reshuffling all past knowledge of drama, of the world and of course, their audiences. It is not enough to be appealing to familiar customers anymore. In order to be part of what is going on or what comes after this crisis is over, one has to learn to adapt. There is no return to the certainties and fixities of the old days. There is too much fluidity now. One cannot ignore the fact that in the last few years Greece has experienced such an inflow of immigrants that according to the 2012 census, up to 10 per cent of the local population is of non-Greek origin. The population change will sooner or later bring changes to the physiognomy of reviews and of theatre consumers. Unlike earlier days, consumers are no longer identifiable either by race or religion or colour or shared memory banks. Nor do they belong to a national group that necessarily carries attributes, beliefs, symbols and myths that describe the defining content of group identity. The cross-cuttings of our post-industrial era have displaced lots of old cultural and philosophical beliefs. We do not live in isolated uniformed sections anymore but in polychromatic intersections, where races, nations, languages and cultures meet, and this means that reviewers have to develop a critical discourse which would accommodate changing social, cultural, and economic conditions, ranging from globalization to migration, identity politics, multiculturalism, hybrid cultures, transnational cultural traffic, that is a discourse able to balance between particularities (and certainties) of places, characters, aesthetics and ideologies, and macro-interdependencies (and uncertainties).

In short, going through this crisis I have seen more clearly what Jim Merod meant when he said back in 1987 that we are in need of criticism that is more practical without losing clarity and analytic skill, more democratic (or democratically useful) and not evasive, more historical and not authoritative, and finally more disruptive rather than unifying, in the sense of being able to create the anomalous arguments that would widen and deepen the critics' as well as the artists' responsibility and people's awareness in a world immersed in consumer junk and drowning in images of false liberation (1987: 89, 63).

Concluding remark

The traces, the uncertainties and the trauma of this crisis will not go away that easily. What I can tell at this point is that whenever there is crisis there will always be someone to turn it into drama and someone to tell us whether this drama is good or not; and this can be done effectively only when one is ready to immerse in life's intensity and openness. That is, find ways to reactivate the word activism and make it mean something substantial. If s/he does so, then the act of reviewing, whether it is on the internet or in a traditional newspaper, will not be just doing business with shows but also doing business with the world.

Notes

1. Like *Proodos, Panathenea, Akropolis, Demikratia, Eleftheros Logos, Eleftheros Vema, Noumas* among others.

2. All quotations from sources published in Greek have been translated into English by myself.

3. It is important to note that most critics were basically middle and upper class, educated people (many studied abroad – France and Germany) who earned their living as lawyers, historians, state officials, diplomats, and translators, or had enough family resources to support unpaid activities, like writing for the theatre.

4. The State Theatre of Northern Greece was the first to enter in 1975 with Sophocles' *Electra*, followed by Theatro Technis (Athens, 1976), Cyprus State Theatre (1980) and Amphi-Theatre (Athens, 1980). *Oresteia*, directed by Tony Harrison and produced by the National Theatre of Great Britain, was the first foreign production to enter Epidaurus' site in 1982.

5. For a more detailed account of this point see Senior's interesting article (1988: 65–69).

6. *Ta Nea*, *To Vema*, *Real News* and *To Thema*.

7. Realizing that there is no more future for theatre reviewing in newspapers, as of January 2015 I also began writing for a web journal (http://parallaximag.gr) that covers mostly cultural matters, just like most of my colleagues, whose newspapers have closed down, did. And as far as I know, no-one gets paid.

Works cited

Beck, Ulrich and Grande, Edgar (2007) *Cosmopolitan Europe*, translated by Ciaran Cronin, Cambridge: Polity.

Bien, Peter (2005) 'Inventing Greece', *Journal of Modern Greek Studies*, 23: 217–34.

Foucault, Michel (1965) *Madness and Civilization,* translated by Richard Howard, New York: Vintage.

Gourgouris, Stathis (1996) *Dream Nation: Enlightenment, Colonization, and the Institution of Modern Greece*, Stanford CA: Stanford University Press.

Ioannidou, Eleftheria (2008) 'Monumental Texts: Greek Tragedy in Greece and Michael Marmarinos's Postmodern Stagings', *New Voices in Classical Reception Studies*, 3: 14–30.

Ioannidou, Eleftheria (2010/11) 'Toward a National Heterotopia: Ancient Theatres and the Cultural Politics of Performing Ancient Drama in Modern Greece', *Comparative Drama*, 44. 4/45.1: 385–403.

Koun, Karolos (1994) *Kanoume theatro yia ten psychi mas*, Athens: Kastaniotis. [Κουν, Κάρολος (1994), Κάνουμε θέατρο για την ψυχή μας, Αθήνα: Καστανιώτης].

Loverdou, Myrto (2014) 'Chilies parastasis sten Athena', Politistiko entheto, *To Vema*, 9 Noemvrios. [Λοβέρδου, Μυρτώ (2014) 'Χίλιες παραστάσεις στην Αθήνα'. Πολιτιστικό ένθετο, *Το Βήμα*, 9 Νοέμβριος].

Marinou, Efi (2009) 'E psychagogia se arithmous'. Epta/7. Politistiko Entheto. *Kyriakatiki Eleftherotypia*, 3 Maios. [Μαρίνου, Έφη (2009) "Η ψυχαγωγία σε αριθμούς". Επτά/7. Πολιτιστικό ένθετο. *Κυριακάτικη Ελευθεροτυπία*, 3 Μάιος].

Merod, Jim (1987) *The Political Responsibility of the Critic*, Ithaca: Cornell University Press.

Palmer, Richard H. (1988) *The Critics' Canon: Standards of Theatrical Reviewing in America,* New York: Greenwood Press.

Papazoglou, Eleni (2014) 'Between Texts and Rituals: Moderns Against Ancients in the Reception of Tragedy in Greece', in Dimitris Tziovas (ed.), *Re-Imagining the Past: Antiquity and Modern Greek Culture,* Oxford: Oxford University Press: 209–28.

Patsalidis, Savas and Sakellaridou, Elizabeth (eds) (1999) *(Dis)Placing Classical Greek Theatre,* Thessaloniki: University Studio Press.

Politis, Fotos (1928) 'Entyposis ke Krisis', *Eleftheron Vema,* 15 Avghustos. [Πολίτης, Φώτος (1928) 'Εντυπώσεις και κρίσεις.' *Ελεύθερον Βήμα,* 15 Αύγουστος].

Politis, Fotos (1984) *Epologi kritikon arthron* vol. A & B, Athens: Ikaros. [Πολίτης, Φώτος (1984), Επιλογή κριτικών άρθρων τομ. Α & Β, Αθήνα: Ίκαρος].

Senior, Ian (2004) 'Theatre Critics and Theatregoing', *Institute of Economic Affairs,* 24. 2: 65–69.

Slevogt, Esther (2014) 'Oncoming Traffic! Theatre Criticism on Line: The German Internet Platform nachtkritik.de', translated by Lucy Powell, *Critical Stages* 9. http://www.criticalstages.org (accessed 30/01/2014).

Spathis, Dimitris (1986) *O diafotismos ke to neoelliniko theatro,* Thessaloniki: University Studio Press. [Σπάθης, Δημήτρης (1986) Ο Διαφωτισμός και το νεοελληνικό θέατρο, Θεσσαλονίκη].

Thrylos, Alkis (1977–1981) *To Elliniko theatro,* ten volumes, Athens: Athens Academy. [Θρύλος, Άλκης (1977–1981) Το ελληνικό θέατρο, δέκα τόμοι, Αθήνα: Ακαδημία Αθηνών].

Varveris, Yannis (1985) *E krisi tou theatrou,* Athens: Kastaniotis. [Βαρβέρης, Γιάννης (1985) Η σκηνή του θεάτρου, Αθήνα: Καστανιώτης].

CHAPTER 5
RUSSIAN THEATRE CRITICISM: IN SEARCH OF CONTEMPORARY RELEVANCE
Kristina Matvienko

Theatre criticism in Russia

To understand the importance of theatre for contemporary Russia one should remember that the artist has always been a highly significant figure in Russian society. During the nineteenth century, Russian literature, for example, was perceived as having a 'messianic' purpose – in the sense of being capable of delivering a message to the audience. After 1917 the importance of the artist was connected with new utopian ideas which were based on the desire to create a 'new human', 'new life' and 'new art'. In the 1920s when the Russian avant-garde theatre achieved its highest level of popularity, theatre art was taken by the state as a substitute for the church; new theatres were built in every provincial town while the churches were being closed and demolished. The critic's role was strongly connected to the importance of art in society and the fate of the artist often depended on the reviews published in the *Pravda* in the decades between the 1930s and 1980s. The Soviet authorities and the professional media officials (*Teatr* magazine, for example) also used so-called 'public opinion' for their own interests. In 1956, for instance, the innovative plays by the debutante author Alexander Volodin faced a cruel attack from the 'ordinary people' who were annoyed by the main characters' language and their immorality. Critics were used by the Communist Party as instruments, which increased their importance, and their impact on real life could even be fatal sometimes.

Following a decline of theatre audiences in Russia in the 1990s, we saw a growth in theatre-going in the early 2000s. This was a time when the younger generation of artists was allowed to access small – and even some big – venues in many Russian cities including Moscow and the more hierarchical St Petersburg, and when relatively free media and free criticism were established. But since the appointment of Vladimir Medinsky as the Russian Minister of Culture under Putin in 2012, a move towards the prohibitory function of criticism has taken place again. To write, to evaluate and to censor – those are the principles of arts criticism in the reformed propagandist media designed to support the official course of the new cultural politics of the Russian state. The power to ban a theatre production – especially in regional communities – has become more and more attractive to the non-professional audience, who, paradoxically, by appealing to the freedom of speech, insist on being irritated or even insulted by art. In early 2015 a production of Wagner's *Tannhauser*, directed by Timofei Kulyabin at the Novosibirsk Opera and Ballet Theatre (the biggest opera house in Russia), caused controversy on a national scale including protests and clashes between the Orthodox community and the liberal intelligentsia. Although the Novosibirsk court dismissed the charges brought against the director by a local senior cleric (Liesowska and Lambie 2015), the dismissal of the general manager of this theatre was nevertheless announced by Medinsky in the aftermath of the trial (*The Siberian Times* reporter, 2015). Thus the power of the neo-conservative propagandist critic is boosted by the public and by the purveyors of official ideology. Furthermore, contemporary arts are traditionally connected with the image of something 'immoral' and destructive. As a result, there is notable neglect of the contemporary arts in Russia today. Given that some artists are facing a real threat of the possibility of being exiled from the professional field due to propaganda pressure, it seems to be increasingly important to consider all of these sociological aspects of theatre life. That is why contemporary Russian criticism sometimes looks like a battlefield between polarised approaches, rather than a spectre of intellectually-founded endeavours: more a case of dichotomy than of diversity. As a result, the polemical genre of the column has become more significant in contemporary Russian theatre media than a classical review.

In considering the critic's responsibility, we should take into account not only the function of advocating for an artist, which is so important in modern Russia, but also the development of professional theoretical tools for exploring the subject matter of contemporary theatre. The latter is a real problem, despite the rich Russian tradition of theatre research. Critics are dealing with an increasingly difficult theatrical language, such as the experimental non-narrative work of the young director Dmitry Volkostrelov or the playwright Pavel Pryazhko. Apart from needing fundamental knowledge of contemporary genres in order to become mediators between the artists and the audience, in dealing with the language of contemporary theatre (Volkostrelov's *Lecture on Nothing* based on John Cage, for example), they take on a double task: to understand it themselves and to help the audience understand it.

While the Arts pages in Russian newspapers have been decreasing in volume year after year, the critics can (and they do) use the public space and open discussion for educating spectators. Particularly popular among the young intellectual audience have been websites such as *Openspace.ru* and *Colta.ru* covering new music, cinema, literature, media and theatre. Some critics such as Pavel Rudnev and John Freedman run popular blogs, or they share opinions about new premieres and the actual problems of contemporary theatre on Facebook. So the lack of publishing opportunities doesn't stop Russian critics from being engaged in this intellectual sphere of work and life.

Former director of the Edinburgh International Festival, Jonathan Mills, has noted: 'At the time when there is ever more need for translation of the context there are evaporating opportunities for serious criticism to translate these contexts' (Mills in Kim 2014). According to Mills, the translation of contexts is a critic's job. But besides this sociological aspect of the critical process whereby the critic's work moves from the sphere of clear aesthetics towards the task of translating social contexts of the performance, there is another more practical one: saving the professional tradition of theatre criticism ensures survival of the instruments of recording and describing contemporary theatre processes and provides a legacy for the future generations of researchers. The main challenge for the critic in this situation of a 'fundamentally shifted paradigm' (ibid) towards a multi-genred (or postdramatic) theatre is how to keep up with the artist, and what tools to deploy in describing, 'translating' and analysing the new type of theatre.

The Russian school of criticism

The Russian school of criticism has deep roots in the eighteenth and nineteenth century. But theatre criticism as a system of methods began in the 1920s when Alexey Gvozdev (1887–1939) became the head of the Theatre section at the Zubovsky Institute of Art History in St Petersburg (currently Art Science Institute on Isaakievskaya square). Gvozdev and his colleagues Vladimir Solovyev, Sergey Mokulsky, Alexander Slonimsky and others researched theatre and drama from a formalist point of view. The Gvozdev method was consequently established as a branch of the Formalist School with the publication of his article 'The results and the aims of scientific theatre history' in 1924.

In his method, Alexey Gvozdev followed the principles of his teacher, the German theatre scholar Max Herrmann (1865–1942), who believed in an artistic, aesthetic – rather than quotidian – logic of theatre. Like his colleague Victor Shklovsky (1893–1984) and others, Gvozdev considered that 'art is not an inscription, but a depiction' (Gvozdev 1919: 139–140). As the critic starts to analyse 'the pattern', he recognizes the meaning of the production in its composition, structure and specifically in its theatrical features such as the acting, stage design, rhythm etc. So through the critic, ephemeral performance finds its flesh and bones – on paper, in a review.

This new system of tools and perspectives on theatre production coincided with the birth of the experimental directing of Vsevolod Meyerhold (1874–1940), who confirmed the ultimate right of the director to be the author of a theatre production. Incidentally Gvozdev was one of the main intellectual partners of Meyerhold's – a natural consequence of his formalist approach to theatre. Meyerhold's productions definitely demanded the kind of analysis that Gvozdev's school proposed and insisted upon. This kind of analysis assumed that theatre art uses its own specific language separate from the language of literature, music, ballet etc; (only architecture could be seen to be similar to the idiom of theatre due to its connection to time and space).

While the new critics of the 1920s fought for the director's authority, the others continued to insist on the priorities of acting and literature. The latter was based on the old Russian conception of theatre as an interpreter of literature or a platform for delivering important ethical lessons to the audience. The status of theatre was linked to the similarly high status of Russian literature, to the messianic potential of art and to a great level of trust in the Orthodox church. The function of spiritual guidance has always been part of the Russian theatre institutions. After the abolition of the church in 1917, theatre (later joined by cinema) acquired the function of an ideological platform, in keeping with Lenin's idea of propaganda.

This has led to an enduring tendency of Russian critics to describe theatre productions from an 'ideological' point of view or, more specifically, from the point of view of the work's intended 'message'. 'What would the director like to tell us from the stage?' is a commonplace question for Soviet and even post-Soviet criticism. 'How did the director transform the play?' And 'what does it mean according to common logic – is it persuasive or not?' As a result, the verbal aspect of theatre has prevailed over such categories as structure, style, type of acting, rhythm and others which Gvozdev's school of theatre research considered to be the most important. Theatre was not an art of interpretation of the text for Gvozdev, and the job of the critic was not limited to decoding the message. Instead, theatre was considered to have its own specific language, structure and technique. The Formalist school was suppressed in the 1930s, and Russian theatre criticism moved to a more literature-oriented, decoding methodology as described above.

More recent Western theatre theories such as the French structuralism and semiotics were never properly accepted into Russian criticism, so Gvozdev's school remained the only one which challenged the dominant critical approach to Russian theatre in the twentieth century.

New theatre theories and their influence on Russian criticism

Changing aesthetic trends in theatre did have an influence on criticism to some extent. Dealing with the narrative theatre of the Soviet neorealism of the mid-1950s, the critics concentrated on acting and the play more than on directing, but when theatre turned to visual experiments as in Lyubimov's *Taganka* in the 1960s, the critics began to pay more attention to composition, style of acting and physical expression. Probably the main challenge for Russian criticism came with Anatoly Vassiliev's innovations in the 1980s. Vassiliev's theatre suggested a new understanding of inner theatre structure and acting, and obliged critics to update the philosophical, sociological and political context of their work.

Maybe even more important was the fact that Russian criticism had to accept and legitimize those kinds of theatre which were considered to be paratheatrical such as happenings or street-theatre actions created by the underground companies of St Petersburg at the end of the 1980s/beginning of the 1990s, such as Anton Adasinsky's *Derevo* and Andrey Moguchy's *Formalny Teatr*. The problem was that Russia, the homeland of the 1920s avant-garde theatre, had no real history of post-war theatre experiment and, as a consequence, no habit of analysing experimental art.

Meanwhile, theatre in Western Europe had already begun to escape the traditional theatre space towards the borderlands of contemporary art in the 1960s. Broadly speaking, theatre attempted a renewal by returning to its non-dramatic roots, with artists Antonin Artaud and, later, Jerzy Grotowski and Peter Brook looking for the artistic energy in ritual. As the notion of 'performance' was developed in the USA and the Actionists came out onto the streets of Vienna, the need for new critical approaches to theatre manifested itself with greater urgency. These new artistic practices provoked the expansion of the critical and scholarly tools in the West and influenced a new understanding of what theatre is. In comparison with the older conception of theatre as straight drama, the 1960s made Western critics accept the polyphonic and multi-faceted nature of theatre. Russian critics, meanwhile – at least those who favoured Meyerhold's way of working – had to keep their silence or, alternatively, change their topic and write about Soviet dramaturgy and socialist realism. So Konstantin Rudnitsky, eminent theatre researcher and the author of the first book about Meyerhold (issued in 1968), was writing in the late 1950s and early 1960s about mainstream social realist playwrights such as Nikolay Pogodin and Vladimir Bill-Belotserkovsky. Nevertheless, during the period of 'Soviet neorealism', or the 'Thaw' in the 1960s, a new generation of fine young critics such as Maya Turovskaya emerged in the world of contemporary theatre and cinema.

Following the end of Communism, the Russian situation changed significantly in the 1990s and 2000s when some new theatre ideas started to travel around the professional communities of both the practitioners and the theoreticians. The works of Peter Szondi or Julia Kristeva had never been translated into Russian because of a lack of funding but also because they were not known in the context of theatre study. Some individual critics might have had a chance to read their works in foreign languages – but this theoretical knowledge did not spread among the professional community. A unique exception was *Dictionary of the Theatre* by Patrice Pavis, published in Russia in 1991, which had a remarkable impact upon scholars, students and practitioners of theatre. Another example of a widely influential book was the Russian edition of *Postdramatic Theatre* by Hans-Thies Lehmann, which was translated and published in 2013 with the support of the Anatoly Vassiliev Fund. This book generated much discussion in Russia, attempting to evaluate the real scientific value of Lehmann's work. Theatre professionals mostly argued about whether Lehmann's view of contemporary theatre was new or not. Two camps emerged: those who doubted Lehmann's novelty and relevance for contemporary theatre, and those who believed that he offered real tools for exploration and – more importantly for Russia today – acceptance of new forms of theatre.

How was new theatre of the 2000s perceived by Russian critics?

The 2000s brought about new changes in Russian theatre. A new generation of playwrights came to the attention of the audience creating what became known as 'Novaya drama' – New Drama (see Kovalskaya and Matvienko 2008). Additionally this decade was marked by the young directors' use of multimedia and generic cross-semination, and the young choreographers' exploration of new theatre spaces. This ranged from the experimental work of contemporary dance artists such as Sasha Pepelyaev or Gennady Abramov in the 1990s, to the open-air and multimedia creations of Andrey Moguchy; and to the more recent experiments of Filipp Grigoryan in the 2000s, using the aesthetics of happening and multimedia at the same time. Russian critics often didn't know how to deal with these changes, debating whether they represented amateurism, or genuine reform of the mainstream. It was not easy for many critics to accept this new generation because of a tradition of strong and strict concern with 'professionalism', rooted in the nineteenth century struggles of the theatre figures such as Alexander Ostrovsky and Konstantin Stanislavsky to raise the standards of theatre production in Russia by distinguishing the field of professional theatre from amateur and non-professional endeavours. The idea of professionalism became crucial to the pedagogical approach of Konstantin Stanislavsky – who had himself started out as an amateur actor – and, by extension, to the Russian theatre education system as a whole. As a professional, one is equipped with the appropriate tools for creating 'action' on stage correctly, for example, and so on.

In the 2000s, Russian contemporary artists also became involved in social activity and began to create socially responsible projects dealing with repressed communities (the disabled, the blind, the deaf, or those dealing with drug addiction) in order to help with their socialisation. As part of these projects, artists took the opportunity to become involved in real social work. The playwrights from Teatr.doc, for example, worked with women prisoners on the 2002 production of *Crimes of Passion* (directed by Galina Sinkina).[1] Similarly the 2012 Liquid Theatre project *While You Are Here* (directed by Andrei Smirnov) was a result of working with patients recovering from alcoholism. The problem is that productions of this kind have been excluded from the professional sphere by the critics who think that they look like amateur theatre and that, while they might be good as social work, they could not be taken seriously by the professional theatre community. Initially perceived as humanitarian actions, these socially engaged theatre works are nevertheless being embraced with increasing enthusiasm by the younger generations of theatre managers and especially by the audience. In the last five years there have been many good examples of the genre and some of them have received important awards. *Akyn-Opera* (2013) made by Vsevolod Lisovsky for Teatr.doc and featuring highly educated Tajiik immigrants who otherwise work as cleaners in Moscow, received a major award at the country's most prestigious festival The Golden Mask in 2014. Following this recognition by the jury which consisted of critics, directors and actors, Russian critics have become more accepting of social theatre as part of the professional sphere.

New Russian Drama has also had a long and hard history of acceptance among critics at home (Beumers and Lipovetsky 2008, 2009). Partly its success was connected with the fact that a lot of the young playwrights of the 2000s such as Vassily Sigarev, Maxim Kurochkin, Pavel Pryazhko, Michail and Vyacheslav Durnenkovy, Yury Klavdiev, Yaroslava Pulinovich and others had no professional roots or theatre training. They didn't know the theatre world and insisted on a licence to ignore theatre tradition, aware of the fact that it was becoming old-fashioned.

There was one more serious reason why Russian critics neglected New Drama – its reputation as a 'dark art' (depressive, gloomy, hyper-realistic plays with marginal heroes and dark stories). New Drama was perceived as being aligned with the 'pro-Western' exploitation of new artistic stereotypes generated by the British tradition of new writing, specifically Mark Ravenhill and Sarah Kane. In fact, the past decade in Russian theatre is characterized by a polyphonic chaos of new and old styles, so in reality these 'stereotypes' don't apply. But they were successful enough in creating a niche interest, so that the reputation of 'dark' Russian theatre keeps feeding external discussions and even some theatre research. New Drama has been blamed by the critics and even researchers for a negative representation of the contemporary Russian reality. The most frequent charge has been that the reality is so dark by itself that the theatre should help distract the public attention from it.

Thus, the critics often analysed the early productions of Teatr.doc or other independent companies as they had always done, using the methodology of 'message interpretation' – in other words, they evaluated whether the playwrights gave a positive or a negative image of the world, and whether they suggested hope at the end. The authors of those reviews refused to analyse the style or the innovative use of language in these plays and – crucially – omitted commenting on the documentary nature of acting and directing, borne out of the demands of these texts.

Although various international festivals such as the New European Festival, International Chekhov's Festival and New Drama Festival in Moscow as well as Baltic House Festival in St. Petersburg did present different kinds of new theatre, Russian criticism generally remained blind to them. New texts by the Belorussian author Pavel Pryazhko, the minimalistic productions by Dmitry Volkostrelov, the political and documentary experiments of Teatr.doc, the poetic non-verbal compositions of Dmitry Krymov, the provocative large-audience works by Konstantin Bogomolov certainly demanded new tools for analysis, and some critics like Alyona Karas, Dina Goder and Marina Davydova responded to these demands in a very deep and systematic way. New plays, written in a non-traditional style, with fragmented structure, reflected current social and political changes introducing the trend of 'post-catastrophic' theatre. An example of this was *Three Days in Hell* (Theatre of Nations, 2013) directed by Volkostrelov and based on Pryazhko's play, featuring a combination of non-verbal scenes in which the author shows several days from the everyday life of his hero. The spectators were seated in separate camps and could not see each other during the whole show – although in the end they did meet, and ate a meal of potatoes together in the theatre foyer. New storylines, issues and acting styles could be conceived, developed and destroyed within the lifetime of a single performance. As a result it has gradually become impossible for critics to keep up with the changes using the 'message interpretation' model of criticism. The 'here and now' of live performance, the actors' physicality and presence on the stage, the texture of the sound and music used in production, the communication between the performer and a specific spectator (as opposed to the audience in general) have become more important as criteria than the verbal message itself. Open structures are replacing the completeness and narrowness of the previous ones. So, considering all these parameters, we can acknowledge that interpreting the 'author's (director's) idea or message' is no longer a sufficient mode of criticism in Russia.

As the theatre researcher Lidia Tilga observes, the main function of the modern critic is to determine the contact between the show and the spectator, but not on the basis of its literary value (2013: 175). With the theatre art becoming increasingly sophisticated, the audience requires more expert help. This demands the skill of permanent self-reinvention on behalf of the critic and an open-mindedness to new types of theatre. And the need for new coping skills does not concern theatre alone, now that the political situation is becoming more challenging: the Russian state is applying a more aggressive approach to theatre, trying to cleanse the stage by propagating myths which reinforce conservative values, patriotism and a non-Western style of development for the Russian society. So we are in a situation partly similar to the Hungarian one[2] where the theatre professionals really need the critics' support and intellectual solidarity.

Contemporary Russian criticism – summary

There are two types of theatre criticism in Russia at present. The first one is oriented towards sociological aspects of theatre, similar to the columns in *The Guardian* or the *Financial Times*. As noted above, Russian culture is in a controversial situation where the professional community is split into opposing camps due to the new state politics: one of them is trying to preserve traditional approaches to classical art (which really belong in museums, not in theatres), the other is fighting for freedom of expression in contemporary art even when it is funded by the Ministry of Culture. This sociological type of theatre criticism is often written for loudspeaking and aimed at tackling specific problems – as was done on the website *www.openspace.ru*.[3] Marina Davydova is one of the important representatives of this style of writing.

The other type of theatre criticism is focusing on theatre from within a wider context of other arts, as exemplified by Zara Abdullaeva of the monthly magazine *Iskusstvo Kino* (*The Art of Cinema*) www.filmart.ru. Abdullaeva writes about cross-disciplinary performance such as, for example, Brett Bailey's *Exhibit B* which was shown at the Territory Festival in Moscow (2014), or Katie Mitchell's *Atmen* in Schaubuhne am Leniner Platz (2014) or Volkostrelov's *Russian Songs* in the Theatre of Nations (2014) etc. The particular value of her reviews is contained in her ability to specify the artistic method used via the wider interdisciplinary context. Her review of *Exhibit B* (Abdullaeva 2014) was a good example of the critic's comprehension of both the social responsibility and the language of contemporary art at the same time. Additionally, also important is the fact that the critic succeeded in fixing her own position as an audience member and she represents this position every time she writes about a show. The more we get to know about communication (or its absence) the better we may understand the artistic principles of theatre production.

Nowadays we are witnessing the arrival of a new generation of Russian theatre critics graduating from GITIS or St Petersburg Theatre Arts Academy. They paradoxically have opportunities for regular work (both paid as in *Vedomosti*, *Afisha*, *Gazeta.ru*, and non-paid on the blog of *Theatre Magazine*). Nevertheless, this is not about having a salary – only the editor of *Afisha*'s theatre section is salaried, the rest are freelancers. Young critics have much more experience of visiting international festivals – so their background, in spite of their age, is usually much more diverse than was the case with the previous generation at the same age. At the same time we come to realize how the level of trust towards – and even the need for – theatre criticism is declining from year to year. The demand for the voice of good professional criticism has diminished significantly since the last century. However, people are still reading the print media, and they are interested in cultural commentary. The above-mentioned protests of the Orthodox community against *Tannhauser* in Novosibirsk led in turn to a rare example of solidarity among the theatre community, facilitated further by social media. Initiated by one of the main Russian critics, Roman

Dolzhansky (curator of the New European Theatre Festival in Moscow), a campaign for the freedom of expression was supported by the Novosibirsk cultural community and then spread further through Facebook, Colta.ru and other social media. Probably the ultimate mission of Russian critics in 2015 is to inspire this kind of solidarity – or we might face a total disappearance of contemporary arts in Russia.

Notes

1. The production is discussed in some detail in Beumers and Lipovetsky (2009: 217).

2. In 2012 Hungarian director Arpad Schilling and his famous theatre Kretakor was deprived of state financial support because the new conservative and nationalistic government considered this kind of message too radical.

3. The website was established as a sociopolitical publication in 2008 focusing on culture only and featuring various interesting columnists. It closed in 2013 due to financial problems.

Works cited

Abdullaeva, Zara (2014) 'Proisshestvie' [Абдуллаева, Зара 'Происшествие'], 17 October, http://www.colta.ru/articles/theatre/5060 (accessed 20 March 2015).

Beumers, Birgit and Lipovetsky, Mark (2009) *Performing Violence: Literary and Theatrical Experiments of New Russian Drama,* Bristol and Chicago: Intellect.

Gvozdev, A. (1919) 'Kino kak iskusstvo', *Zhizn iskusstva,* № 139–140. S. 15–27. [Гвоздев А. (1919) 'Кино как искусство', *Жизнь искусства,* № 139–140. С. 15–27.]

Gvozdev, Alexey (1987) *Teatralnaya kritika,* Leningrad: Iskusstvo. [Гвоздев А. (1987) *Театральная критика.* Ленинград: Искусство.]

Gvozdev, Alexey (1924) 'Itogi i zadachi nauchnoy istorii teatra', *Zadachi i metody izucheniya iskusstv,* Petrograd: Academia. [Гвоздев А. (1924) 'Итоги и задачи научной истории театра', *Задачи и методы изучения искусств,* Петроград: Academia.]

Gvozdev, Alexey (1926) 'O smene teatralnyh system', *O teatre: Vremennik Otdela istorii i teorii teatra Gosudarstvennogo institute istorii iskusstv,*

Leningrad: Academia. S. 7–37. [Гвоздев А.А. (1926) 'О смене театральных систем', *О театре: Временник Отдела истории и теории театра Государственного института истории искусств*, Ленинград.: Academia. С. 7–37.]

Kim, Yun-Cheol (2014) 'Interview with Jonathan Mills, director of Edinburgh International Festival', *Critical Stages*, Issue 10, October http://www.criticalstages.org/interview-with-jonathan-mills-director-of-edinburgh-international-festival/ (accessed 20 March 2015).

Kovalskaya, Elena and Matvienko, Kristina (sostaviteli) (2008) *Novaya drama*, Sankt-Peterburg: Seans. [Ковальская, Е. и Матвиенко, К. (составители) (2008) *Новая драма*, Санкт-Петербург: Сеанс.]

Lehmann, Hans-Thies (2013) *Postdramatichesky teatr*, per. s nemetskogo, vstupitelnaya statya i kommentaryi Natali Isayevoy, Moskva: Izdatelskaya programma Fonda razvitia iskusstva dramaticheskogo teatre rezhissera i pedagoga Anatolia Vassilieva. [Леман Х.-Т. (2013) *Постдраматический театр*, пер. с немецкого, вступительная статья и комментарии Натали Исаевой, Москва: Издательская программа Фонда развития искусства драматического театра режиссера и педагога Анатолия Васильева.]

Liesowska, Anna and Lambie, Derek (2015) 'Court throws out claims Novosibirsk opera offended Orthodox believers', *The Siberian Times*, 13 March, http://siberiantimes.com/culture/theatre/news/n0150-court-throws-out-claims-novosibirsk-opera-offended-orthodox-believers/ (accessed 11April 2015).

Pavis, Patrice (1991) *Slovar teatra*, pod redakciey Kirilla Razlogova, Moskva: Progress. [Пави П. (1991) *Словарь театра*, Под редакцией Кирилла Разлогова, Москва: Прогресс.]

Rudnitsky, Konstantin (1969) *Rezhisser Meyerhold*, Москва: Nauka. [Рудницкий К. (1969) *Режиссер Мейерхольд*, Москва: Наука.]

The Siberian Times reporter (2015) 'Director of Novosibirsk Opera and Ballet Theatre fired in religious backlash', *The Siberian Times*, 29 March, http://siberiantimes.com/culture/theatre/news/n0169-director-of-novosibirsk-opera-and-ballet-theatre-fired-in-religious-backlash/ (accessed 11 April 2015).

Tilga, Lidia (2013) Recenzia// *Seminar po teatralnoy kritike*, Sankt-Peterburg: Izdatelstvo Sankt-Peterburgskoy gosudarstvennoy Academii teatralnoy iskusstva. [Тильга Л. (2013) Рецензия// *Семинар по театральной критике*, Санкт-Петербург: Издательство Санкт-Петербургской государственной Академии театрального искусства.]

CHAPTER 6
HOW TO GET YOUR HANDS DIRTY: OLD AND NEW MODELS OF 'MILITANT' THEATRE CRITICISM IN ITALY

Margherita Laera

In the popular imagination, what theatre critics do is little more than pompous fault-finding and, less often, needless flattery. Administering praise and blame from the privileged seclusion of an ivory tower, rather than actively participating in theatrical life, this dinosaur of a professional figure is seen as a censorious chronicler whose experience of the theatre never exceeds sitting in the stalls on opening nights. But a close look at the history of this profession in Italy reveals that the image of the theatre critic as a desk-based intellectual could not be further from the truth. Since the second half of the nineteenth century, Italian critics have never entirely conformed to the 'ivory tower' model.[1] However, participation in theatre making, steering and organizing became the *pièce de résistance* of a new breed of Italian theatre critics in the 1960s, who brought their involvement in practice to an entirely new level.

This group of young thinkers, who later became known as *critici militanti* ('militant critics') or *Nuova Critica* (New Criticism, not to be confused with the formalist literary movement), organized an important conference in Ivrea in 1967, which is often referred to as the founding act of Italy's experimental theatre scene of the late 1960s and 1970s, although of course theatre experimentation preceded this date. In truth, Ivrea was also the symbolic birthplace of a new model for theatre criticism advocated by the 'militants', which would later become popularized as the 'get-your-hands-dirty' paradigm.[2] This was an actively engaged approach whereby, instead of observing and judging from a distance, critics took to the field to influence theatre's course and trends, shifting the traditional deontology, which had hitherto been based on distance from the object of inquiry. For the 'militants', criticism was a creative endeavour.

The 'militant', hands-on approach of Italian theatre criticism in the 1960s was a pioneering experiment in our field, which prefigured postmodern attitudes to criticism by theorizing the positioning of the critic inside its field of inquiry, rather than outside, and characterizing him/her as an immanent participant to, rather than an authoritative transcendental observer of, theatre and performance.[3] The general stance of 1960s revolutionaries was one of challenging of authority, and in this climate the traditional role of the critic, which had so far been seen as an authoritative external observer and an objective interpreter of his/her field of inquiry, came into question. Poststructuralist and deconstructive approaches to hermeneutics appeared concurrently with the work of these Italian critics: it was in 1967, the same year of the Ivrea conference, that Derrida published his seminal work *On Grammatology*, in which he asserted that 'there is no outside-text' (1998: 158), challenging the very notion of the critical 'vantage point'.

New ideas and practices that emerged in the 1960s, particularly the 'militant criticism' model, still influence the way contemporary Italian critics practice the profession and perceive its ethics today. However, so far, this pivotal phase of Italian theatre criticism and its legacy has received little scholarly attention outside of Italy. The present essay therefore seeks to present it to a wide international readership, arguing that the 'militant' approach still matters today outside of the immediate national context out of which it emerged. The notion of 'creative criticism', for instance, was proposed by the 'militant critics' and continues to prove fruitful in practice to date: for instance, in his 2005 edited collection *After Criticism*, Gavin Butt and his contributors make an ample case for continuing to position arts criticism as 'a kind of cultural participation in its own right', whereby 'the theorist, rather than being remote from that which he or she surveys, is [. . .] enmeshed in the very, perhaps even "creative", production of the cultural fabric itself' (Butt 2005: 3).

In the first part of my essay I discuss the 'get-your-hands-dirty' modus operandi with reference to some of the most influential exponents of this group. The second part of this chapter examines the legacy this model has had on new paradigms recently evolved in Italy in the internet era. Throughout the second part, I also report on the results of an internet survey I designed to map out the state of the profession in Italy today. One of the key issues explored in the chapter is deontology: what did the 'militant critics' consider to be ethical in their profession? What consequences did the 1960s 'get-your-hands-dirty' approach have on current perceptions of ethics in relation to the profession? What kind of ethical code underpins the practice of twenty-first-century Italian theatre critics? My argument accepts that the power accumulation enabled by developments of the 1960s 'militant' model had reached excessive and detrimental levels in certain cases. But while I acknowledge that a minority of Italian theatre critics have responded to these excesses by demanding a stricter deontological code for the profession, I do not see the latter as a viable or productive position in line with its times and the material conditions which the profession is facing. I maintain that the way the majority of Italian theatre critics currently practice the profession is influenced by at least two major factors: firstly, the on-going legacy of the 'get-your-hands-dirty', 'creative' approach of the 1960s and its conformity with attitudes that would later be popularized by postmodernist criticism, and secondly, the material conditions of employment and the lack of viable business models for online and print journalism. These conditions, I argue, make the 'get-your-hands-dirty' model, whereby critics engage creatively with theatre practice, a necessity.

Dirty hands and militancy: creative criticism

In the autumn of 1966, prompted by what they viewed as the stagnant and lethargic state of theatrical arts in Italy, theatre scholars Ettore

Capriolo and Roberto Lerici, writers Corrado Augias and Giuliano Scabia, theatre critics Giuseppe Bartolucci, Edoardo Fadini and Franco Quadri met up in Milan and started to write a manifesto entitled '*Per un convegno sul nuovo teatro*' ('For a conference on new theatre'), which would set out their position on the current state of theatre in Italy, and function as a call for participants to a conference in Ivrea, near Turin, the following summer. After months of discussion, a version of the manifesto was published in the theatre review *Sipario* (issue 247, November 1966), then edited by Quadri, and was signed by a group of twenty carefully selected theatre practitioners, who had been invited to add their name to the call for participants by the core group. Among the invited signatories were some of the most experimental artists of the period, who would later become pillars of Italian theatre history, such as Carmelo Bene, Leo de Berardinis, Liliana Cavani, Antonio Calenda and Luca Ronconi.[4]

A few months later, in June 1967, a heterogeneous group of theatre practitioners, critics, directors, musicians, set designers, technicians and writers attended the Ivrea conference to discuss the role of what had unimaginatively been labelled 'New Theatre', that is, the work of Italy's politically engaged experimental theatre practitioners.[5] Among the participants were also important artists who had not signed the manifesto, such as Dario Fo and Eugenio Barba, for whom this occasion marked a turning point in practice and discourse. According to Fo, 'that colloquium was a point of departure, in Ivrea we met for the first time and talked, we clarified our different positions [...] It was the first time that we discussed avant-garde theatre, and what it meant to make political theatre' (Bono 2007, my translation).[6]

The manifesto authors lamented the withering of contemporary theatre in Italy, its subservience to the powers that be and its lack of experimentation in the context of more theatrically advanced European countries, where the stage had long been developing new languages and techniques. The manifesto advocated a new struggle for a theatre that 'would be able to express absolute and total dissent', against 'official' theatre and its inability to establish a dialogue with international developments in other arts (Augias et al.1966). Crucially, the Ivrea manifesto also took issue with the conventions and current practices in theatre criticism, especially the profession's inability to challenge the status quo:

> Instead of performing a function of provocation and stimulation vis-à-vis this general situation [of decline], traditional theatre criticism contributed to the maintenance of the status quo and was too easily aligned with official positions, anchoring its methods and language to out-dated models, renouncing its most important tasks of research and interpretation.
>
> Augias et al. 1966

Surfing the new wave of revolutionary ideologies, the 'militant critics' aimed to subvert current hierarchies and ultimately change society through theatre. In order to achieve this goal, the 'militants' proposed a much more involved, 'insider' and partisan role for criticism, one that would dare to take the field and promote New Theatre over the 'old', assume responsibility for the course of Italian theatre and, as Andrea Porcheddu and Roberta Ferraresi put it, 'claim ownership over theatre-as-object and determine its existence and possibilities' (2010: 41). The manifesto emphasized the necessary work to be done 'to elicit, gather, add value to and defend new forces and trends in the theatre' (Augias et al. 1966). Ultimately, the manifesto, and to a greater extent later publications (see Bartolucci et al. 1968), put forward the idea of a collapse of distance between the critic and its object, the theatre, championing direct intervention. Their position raised questions about professional ethics: can an overtly partisan critic be credible? Can a critic be actively involved in promoting a certain aesthetic? Is the critic's role to influence public taste and artistic practice? The 'militants' believed that it was experimental theatre itself that demanded this sort of engaged criticism, as I discuss below.

During a conference promoted by the National Association of Theatre Critics (ANCT) in 1969, 'militant' Fadini clashed with Nicola Chiaromonte, a colleague who did not share the Ivrea group's views. During the conference, Chiaromonte argued for the critic's political independence and expressed disapproval towards the growing trend for image and physical theatre to the detriment of text and literature, which he understood as a fashion for the 'spectacular' denying the rationality of the spoken word (Chiaromonte, 1971: 54–58). Chiaromonte's intervention was dubbed 'reactionary' by the 'militant' Fadini, who accused him of grossly misunderstanding avant-gardes and supporting the status quo (Fadini 1971: 73). It was a war of two worlds.

At the ANCT conference, Fadini maintained that recent developments of experimentation in Italy and abroad demanded a precise type of engagement from critics. He claimed that current theatrical research trends in Italy could be divided into two main strands: 'action theatre' and 'estrangement or negation theatre' (1971: 76). The former could be described as straightforward political theatre, a theatre of class struggle; the latter marked a distancing of the theatre maker vis-à-vis the audience – that is, the bourgeoisie – by shifting away from bourgeois conventions and norms, unveiling bourgeois mystification and manipulation of reality. Both strands, according to Fadini, implied a specific response from the theatre critic: the former prompted direct sociopolitical action, while the latter 'involve[d] the critic in the process of estrangement enacted by the theatre-maker' (1971: 77).

Fadini's view was that New Theatre was engaged in an act of repudiation of its relation to the bourgeois system, its only remit being that of establishing a rapport with the working classes. It is in the political aesthetics of Nuovo Teatro that the reasons for a new kind of 'militant' criticism were to be found. Criticism '[was] not possible unless exclusively within the function defined by theatrical research' (1971: 77). This position was echoed in fellow 'militant' Giuseppe Bartolucci's view that 'criticism is constructed by performances, so one's mode of making criticism ought to change when performances change' (1970: 92). The critic's mission was therefore 'creative' for Fadini, in the sense that she or he was an active participant in the 'formation of a revolutionary conscience' that experimental theatre was trying to achieve (1971: 77).

Among the most notable 'militant' theatre critics of this period were of course Ivrea group founders Bartolucci and Fadini, but also 'outsiders' such as Gerardo Guerrieri. Bartolucci (1923–96) was not only a critic and scholar, but also a fervent theatre organizer, artistic director, founder of theatre reviews and prizes, mastermind of symposia and conferences and, later, an advocate/theorist of what he called Italian 'post-avant-garde theatre', such as that of Societas Raffaello Sanzio, Toni Servillo and Giorgio Barberio Corsetti. Fadini, a co-founder with Bartolucci and Ettore Capriolo of the magazine *Teatro* and also a champion of Italian avant-garde theatre, was the orchestrator behind the Turin-based experimental venue Cabaret Voltaire (1975–94), introducing artists such as John Cage, Richard Schechner, Peter Schumann and the Living Theatre to an Italian audience (see Fadini and Quartucci 1976). Guerrieri (1920–86), a theorist, dramaturg, translator and director, had been similarly involved in organizing theatre in his Teatro Club in Rome, which he founded in the late 1950s, inviting the likes of Tadeusz Kantor, Antoine Vitez and Peter Brook.

But the most prominent exponent of the 'get-your-hands-dirty' approach, and arguably the most influential Italian theatre critic of all time, is Franco Quadri (1936–2011), or 'the father of us all', as critic Andrea Porcheddu referred to him in an interview I carried out with him in 2014. Throughout his long career, Quadri worked as editor and founder of magazines, artistic director of festivals, judge of theatre prizes, essayist, artistic consultant, translator, organizer of acting seminars, dramaturg and publisher, exercising all of these professions at once, not without conflicts of interest. He is best known for founding and editing the influential theatre yearbook *Patalogo* and for his work as the chief critic of Italy's leading left-leaning newspaper *La Repubblica* (1987–2011). He also established a publishing company specializing in theatre, Ubulibri, in 1977, and authored scholarly books on Italian and European avant-gardes. Also in 1977, Quadri founded the Italian theatre 'Oscars', the Premio Ubu, the jury of which he presided. Concurrently he was artistic director of the Venice Biennale of Theatre from 1983 to 86, and later he directed several other festivals. It is relevant to note that his 'get-your-hands-dirty' approach led him to acquire an unprecedented level of authority and influence, leading many to question the deontological robustness of his practice. Can a practicing theatre critic work as artistic director of a festival and avoid favouritism? Can a critic also run a publishing business that will overtly benefit from its authors being promoted by the critic himself through his articles in the national press and his work as artistic director? Can a critic/publisher/artistic director also lead the jury for the most prestigious annual theatre prize without preventing fair competition from critics holding alternative views?

Quadri was a feared and revered arbiter of taste, and there was a time in which his reviews could make the box office success or failure of any production. His seal of approval turned theatre material into gold. One of the many examples of this is Rodrigo García (Mello 2014, 52 per cent, Location 2676–85 of 5217). As a result of Quadri's favourable review of García's work in Avignon, he went from being virtually unknown in Italy in 2002 to being the darling of the experimental scene in 2003, having his texts published with Ubulibri and winning an Ubu Prize in 2004 for his adaptation of *Agamemnon*. Although the Ubu Prize is awarded through a rigorous voting process by over sixty jury members, it is undeniable that Quadri's reviews, the decision to include him in the 2002 edition of the *Patalogo* (issue 25) and to speed up the publication of his texts by Ubulibri in 2003 influenced the visibility and significance García acquired among theatre critics and organisers, who subsequently awarded him the prize. A similar story could be told of Rafael Spregelburd, who was little known until Quadri 'discovered' him and included him in the *Patalogo* (issue 31), published his texts and made him an instant celebrity. Spregelburd went on to win the Ubu Prize for best play in 2010 and 2011 (Mello 2014, 52 per cent, Location 2702 of 5217).

Anna Bandettini, Quadri's colleague at *La Repubblica*, highlights how he did not simply want to be 'a magnifying glass', but above all 'change the audience's taste' (2014, 28 per cent, Location 1400 of 5217). Andrea Porcheddu stressed how Quadri's dominance had reached unprecedented levels in the second half of his career: 'At a certain moment of our history, Quadri was the Artistic Director of Italian theatre, so to speak, and nothing moved unless he said so' (Laera 2014b). Although admittedly Ubulibri never managed to become a sustainable business and always ran at a loss, Quadri's conflicts of interest in working simultaneously as critic, artistic director, translator, prize judge and publisher were not negligible.[7] What is relevant to our discussion here is that the power conglomerate he was able to amass in his own hands was a direct consequence of his 'militant', 'get-your-hands-dirty' brand of theatre criticism, and not only of his indubitable talent and commitment to the profession. Today, contemporary theatre critics are still coming to terms with his and his fellow 'militants' legacy, especially on matters of deontology.

Dirty hands after the 1980s: from political statement to material necessity

By the mid-1980s, while the ideological beliefs underpinning the 'militant' approach deflated, critics started to question their partisanship and efforts to steer practice towards a specific aesthetics. Where the belief in the power of theatre to change society had made 'militant' critics 'get their hands dirty' in practice, one could argue that the disillusionment with theatre's powers over society had a distancing effect on the role that the critic played in the theatre system. The air had changed: governmental funds for the theatre (known as Fondo Unico per lo Spettacolo, or FUS) had begun to shrink, and they would continue to do so as a percentage of Italian GDP well into the twenty-first century, going from 0.0832 per cent of GDP in 1985 to 0.0263 per cent in 2012 (Ministero dei Beni e delle Attività Culturali e del Turismo 2012: 17).[8] Spaces for theatre reviews in local and national print press were reduced, and the few jobs that were available at newspapers around the country became even fewer.[9] Rather than actively and declaredly trying to legitimize certain kinds of theatre over others on the basis of their political or ideological allegiances, those who could still call themselves theatre critics despite this crisis began to defend theatre as a whole, both experimental and classical, perhaps against the growing predominance of television as a medium of mass communication in Italy.[10]

In an interview published in 2008, *Corriere della Sera* critic Franco Cordelli, who had been a 'militant' in his youth, was asked whether he thought the 'get-your-hands-dirty' approach of the 1960s was still viable (Anonymous 2008). Cordelli rejected the partisanship of that model, or as he puts it, its 'sectarianism', adding that the methodology he adopted after rejecting that paradigm can still be called 'militant', albeit becoming more 'conservative' in attempting to be more broadly inclusive of the variety and heterogeneity of the Italian theatrical offering. While Cordelli is far from dismissing his ideological investment and engagement in the 1960s, he argued for a less prejudiced approach that aims at a more comprehensive championing of stage arts.

In the same interview, *Il Sole 24 Ore* critic Antonio Audino usefully distinguished between 'getting one's hands dirty' and getting compromised (ibid). While he argued that the work of the critic always involves the act of 'getting one's hands dirty', specifically by publicizing new or unknown work that is worthy of attention, he drew a line between this type of partisanship and more serious kinds of lobbying, which he saw as affecting the Italian theatre system as a result of the 'militant' approach. Both Cordelli and Audino, although distancing themselves from the typical 1960s model, are keen to keep the terminology in place: the former by declaring himself a 'militant', and the latter by advocating a new, more deontologically sound 'dirty-your-hands' paradigm. It would appear that, while in the 1960s a 'militant' critic would work to defend 'New Theatre' against the 'old', towards the end of the twentieth century 'militancy' in theatre criticism came to designate the more generic, combative resilience of those who realize they are defending a not-so-popular, not-so-well-funded, declining art form from oblivion. If 'getting one's hands dirty' once meant to actively work to establish a new age of experimental, anti-bourgeois theatre for the masses, forty years on this phrase has become synonymous with getting involved in the practice of theatre, exercising the profession in full acknowledgement of one's political role and influence or, in its negative acceptation, doing so and having a conflict of interest.

It is interesting to note that the use of this terminology still divides theatre critics in Italy. In the internet-based survey I carried out in 2014, I asked the question, 'What does it mean for critics to "get their hands dirty" today?' Of 144 respondents, only 39 (27 per cent) thought the phrase was out-dated and belonged to a different time, and even less, 25 (17 per cent), thought it meant 'to work in the field of theatre, not just as a theatre critic, and face conflicts of interest'.[11] The larger proportion of respondents, 52 (36 per cent) thought the phrase suggested simply 'to work in the field of theatre, not just as a critic'. The overall majority of the respondents, therefore, thought the phrase displayed a positive or at least neutral meaning, and that 'getting one's hands dirty' did not necessarily come hand in hand with conflicts of interest. This is relevant to our discussion of the legacy of the 'militant' critics in that, as the survey suggests through other questions, most contemporary theatre critics in 2014 were also involved in theatre practice in different ways.

The question, 'What other profession(s) do you practice?', was particularly revealing in this sense. Out of 148 people who replied, only 7 (5 per cent) declared they had no other profession, 53 (36 per cent) declared they worked in the theatre field, 46 (31 per cent) declared they taught or studied theatre, 22 (15 per cent) declared they taught or studied a discipline other than theatre, while 63 (43 per cent) declared they worked in a field different from theatre.[12] The answer to the question, 'Have you ever been involved in theatre in a practical way?', confirmed one of the main arguments of this essay: only 27 of 146 (18 per cent) stated they had never been involved in the practice of theatre, neither on stage nor back stage. 55 (37 per cent) stated they practiced theatre 'regularly' (either on or back stage), while 64 (43 per cent) did so 'occasionally'. Of the respondents who formulated their own answer, 4 had practiced theatre in the past and 7 continued to do so in 2014.

Of the many theatrical professions Italian theatre critics practice, the most popular are 'organizing conferences and symposia' (59 out of 146 respondents), 'dramaturgy' (52), 'acting' (46), 'directing' (35), 'artistic direction of festivals' (28), 'artistic consultancies' (32), 'production' (20), 'translation' (20) and 'audio, video, sound, light design' (14). Attitudes towards critics getting involved in theatre practice are also generally positive: of 146 people, only 12 stated that they viewed the fact that some colleagues get involved in theatre practice as a negative thing, because 'it inevitably entails a conflict of interest'. By contrast, 54 declared they thought it was a positive thing, because 'it enabled them to widen their knowledge of theatre', and 74 viewed it as 'either a negative or positive thing, depending on how each critic is able to manage possible conflicts of interest'. These results demonstrate how open contemporary theatre critics in Italy are towards the practice of 'creativity' in the profession.

During a round table discussion on Italian theatre criticism in Milan in March 2014, theatre director Corrado d'Elia asked a panel of critics whether they considered themselves 'militant' and whether they 'got their hands dirty' in doing their job. Among his respondents were *Hystrio* Editor-in-Chief Claudia Cannella and freelance critic, lecturer and writer Andrea Porcheddu.[13] Cannella, who like Porcheddu was born in the 1960s and started work in the 1990s when the strictly 'militant', 'get-your-hands-dirty' approach had already gone out of fashion, argued that it was no longer relevant to talk about 'militancy', whatever that meant. What was required in this day and age was a more cogent deontological code for Italian theatre critics. As the editor of the quarterly print magazine *Hystrio*, Cannella recounted the countless times in which she is contacted by aspiring theatre critics wanting to review their friends' or relatives' work, which she always turns down as a matter of principle. Evidently, she implied, such 'unsound' practices are endemic to the profession.

In a 2011 issue of *Hystrio* on the state of theatre criticism in Italy, Cannella had addressed the matter of deontology by publishing a 'Charter of the Rights and Duties of the Critic' which she compiled with the editorial office and freelance collaborators of the magazine (2011: 53). *Hystrio*'s Charter represents a break with the traditionally blasé attitude of Italian critics towards conflicts of interest. Cannella believes that while it is a critic's right to 'get her hands dirty' by being involved in theatre practice, it is her duty not to get tangled in conflicts of interest by reviewing shows in which friends or family are involved (Cannella 2011: 53). Cannella also denounces the increasingly popular practice of critics being employed by a theatre festival to write or blog about the festival itself (Laera 2014a). *Hystrio*'s Charter strives for a balance to be struck between 'critical detachment and participation in theatre's community', implying that critical judgement cannot operate freely when one's relationship with the parties involved has been pre-determined by professional or personal connections (Cannella 2011: 53).

As suggested by the results of my survey, Cannella's arguments characterize the thinking of a minority of Italian critics. In answer to the question, 'Would you review a show in which a friend or relative is involved?', only 18 out of 146 (12 per cent) declared 'No, because I would have a conflict of interest', while 55 (38 per cent) said 'Yes, because I can exercise my judgement objectively' and 67 (46 per cent) declared 'Generally, yes, but I would consider case by case following my professional conscience'. When questioned about the particulars of possible conflicts of interest, only 7 (5 per cent) out of 146 declared they would not accept a producer to cover their travel and accommodation expenses if they were reviewing a show, while 68 (47 per cent) would not review a show if the producer of the show was also the commissioner of the review. 49 (34 per cent) would refuse to review a show in which a friend had taken part, while 108 (74 per cent) would decline an offer to review a show in which they were themselves involved. Lastly, only 16 (11 per cent) would not accept the position of artistic director of a festival if still working as a theatre critic elsewhere.

In an interview I carried out with her, Cannella revealed she rated most highly those collaborators whose main day job was in a field other than theatre, as in her view this ensured critical distance from the object in question (Laera 2014a). It is interesting to note that Cannella's argument, if taken at face value, implies that theatre critics who are not paid for their job are better placed than those who are paid to carry out their critical work. Paradoxically, therefore, Cannella's ideal critic is an 'amateur'. By 'amateur' I do not mean someone who practices the profession less than skilfully, but someone who is not paid to practice it – mainly doing it out of 'love' – and whose main business and social connections are probably located in a field other than theatre. Cannella's views, though mitigated by exposure to postmodern discourse, appear to propose an outdated model in which the critic would return to its role of external observer. On the matter of whether Italian critics feel they are observers or participants, the survey results again contradict Cannella: in response to the question, 'What do you consider yourself to be vis-à-vis the world of theatre?', only 19 out of 146 (13 per cent) stated they felt 'external observers', while 82 (56 per cent) declared they felt 'participant observers', and 48 (33 per cent) considered themselves 'internal participants'. Additionally, when asked about their relationships to theatre-makers and producers, the vast majority declared they frequently spend time in an informal and para-professional fashion with both artists and organizers, demonstrating how most Italian theatre critics don't shy away from taking part in the theatre community.

Also prompted by D'Elia during the round table in Milan, Andrea Porcheddu maintained that 'keeping one's hands clean' is not always achievable, and perhaps not even desirable in the current economic climate, where very few people are paid for their work as theatre critics. In an interview I carried out with him, Porcheddu acknowledged the legacy of the 'militant' critics in the way his generation practices criticism, stating that 'we try to avoid the excesses of 'militant' critics and their conflicts of interest' (Laera 2014b), while also 'refuting the ivory tower model' (ibid). Porcheddu suggested that, if the 'ivory tower model' were the thesis phase of theatre criticism, and the 'militants' the antithesis, his generation represents the synthesis. In my view, however, the fundamental distinction between how the 'militant' critics of the 1960s practiced theatre and the way this engagement is carried out by contemporary critics in the twenty-first century is to be found in the current economic circumstances and conditions of labour. For instance, since the 1990s, Italian theatre practitioners, such as artistic directors and theatre companies, recognized that the profession was in danger of disappearing, and started to employ theatre critics directly, without the mediation of the press.[14] This is, in my opinion, a positive model for collaboration between critics and practitioners which offers new opportunities for disseminating discourses on theatre: it would be misguided to oppose it on the grounds of its non-conformance with anachronistic ethical standards.

Given the general employment conditions in late capitalism, but also the ongoing difficulties of developing a sustainable business model for print and online journalism, most critics are no longer paid for their work, or they are not paid enough to live off criticism alone. Lack of remuneration was highlighted in the survey, according to which only 2 of 152 (1 per cent) revealed they earn 100 per cent of their income through theatre criticism alone. 99 (65 per cent) revealed they earned 0 per cent of their overall income through theatre criticism, 28 (18 per cent) between 1 per cent and 10 per cent, 13 between 10 per cent and 50 per cent, and 10 between 50 per cent and 99 per cent. The precariousness of employment terms was evidenced by the fact that only 3 out of 152 respondents (2 per cent) declared they had a permanent contract as theatre critics. It could be argued, therefore, that the current 'get-your-hands-dirty' model, whereby contemporary critics get involved in theatre practice, constitutes a new type of 'militancy': 'getting one's hands dirty' has turned from a political statement to a material necessity, a necessity to 'diversify'. For Italian critics who want to support themselves through this profession, covering different roles in theatre practice is a choice dictated by the precarious conditions of employment in arts journalism. In the words of Porcheddu:

We make theatre without making theatre. We make theatre by writing about it. It is a new mode of 'militancy', as you say. Our mode of making criticism is transposed into a myriad types (*sic*) of interventions: books, articles, lectures, workshops, seminars, symposia, consultancies, artistic directions, dramaturgies. All of this can be classified as criticism: perhaps this is the biggest and most influential lesson that Franco Quadri left us.

Laera 2014b

The way contemporary critics get involved in theatre practice constitutes a new mode of 'militancy', which one might call 'militancy out of necessity'. 'Getting one's hands dirty' is no longer a political statement for contemporary theatre critics, but a way to continue to engage creatively with the theatre community and make a living out of a profession that has seen remuneration, number of full-time posts and job security levels plummet in the past few decades. It is undeniable, however, that the legacy of the 1960s 'militants' has provided a model for creativity to contemporary theatre critics in Italy and beyond.

Notes

1. Italian theatre critics of the nineteenth and early twentieth centuries rarely exercised this profession exclusively, with creative writing featuring among the most popular complementary line of work. For a history of theatre criticism in Italy, see Antonucci (1995), although the volume's scholarship is sketchy and biased against the 'militant' model.

2. It is difficult to define the origin of these phrases. Neither 'militant critic' (in Italian, *critico militante*), nor 'get one's hands dirty' (in Italian, *sporcarsi le mani*) were labels employed by the Ivrea critics themselves. They became popular years later and were retrospectively employed to refer to the Ivrea critics, their followers and their *modus operandi*.

3. It is important to remember, however, that similar moves had been taking place in Italian visual arts criticism, where critics/curators, such as Germano Celant and Achille Bonito Oliva, proposed a model of 'creative criticism' which refuses the role of simple 'mediator' between the work of art and the public.

4. The manifesto was signed by Corrado Augias, Giuseppe Bartolucci, Marco Bellocchio, Carmelo Bene, Cathy Berberian, Sylvano Bussotti, Antonio Calenda, Virginio Gazzolo, Ettore Capriolo, Liliana Cavani, Leo De Berardinis, Massimo De Vita, Nuccio Ambrosino, Edoardo Fadini, Roberto Guicciardini, Roberto Lerici, Sergio Liberovici, Emanuele Luzzati, Franco Nonnis, Franco Quadri, Carlo Quartucci and Teatrogruppo, Luca Ronconi, Giuliano Scabia, and Aldo Trionfo.

5. For a more detailed discussion of the Ivrea conference, see Visone 2010: 227–57.

6. All translations from Italian in this chapter are mine unless otherwise stated.

7. It must be said that conflicts of interest were never entirely absent from the profession. In the first half of the twentieth century, that is before the 'militants' came about, critics would translate plays and be paid substantial royalties; they would write programme notes in exchange for a fee; they would be members of prize juries and artistic committees, both paid positions at the time; and they would be put up in luxury hotels to review summer festivals. Thanks to Oliviero Ponte di Pino for pointing this out.

8. The FUS are governmental funds paid out by the Ministry of Culture, to which funds from the Regional, Provincial and City budgets are added each year. But while the FUS diminished in value, the gap left was never made up by 'local' funds.

9. For instance, Quadri's reviews went from 6,000–7,500 characters twice a week in the 1970s to 1,200 characters once a week in the 2000s. (See Marino 2014, 18 per cent, Location 899–1041 of 5217).

10. Berlusconi founded his first private commercial channel, Canale 5, in 1980.

11. In the autumn of 2014, I launched an internet survey consisting of thirty-seven questions, on the state of theatre criticism in Italy. Questions were developed in collaboration with Oliviero Ponte di Pino, Professor of Theatre at the Brera Academy of Fine Arts, theatre critic and founding editor of Ateatro.it, one of the oldest and most respected online theatre magazines in Italy. The survey was completed by 223 people, 126 of whom answered all of the questions. Given the current de-professionalization of theatre criticism, the survey was open to all those who regularly write about the theatre, including those who only do so part-time and without pay. I discuss the full results of the survey in an article in Italian for Ateatro.it, available at <http://www.ateatro. it/webzine/2014/12/30/14153/> [accessed 3 February 2015]. For more information on those who practice theatre criticism in Italy, see Ponte di Pino (2012a; 2012b).

12. Respondents could select not only one, but multiple responses from the list provided.

13. The event was part of *Festival della Regia* (Festival of Directing), which took place from 24 to 26 March 2014.

14. This happened in the 1990s with the publication of the journal of Santarcangelo Festival by Leo de Berardinis and the journal of ETI (Ente Teatrale Italiano). In the 2000s and 2010s, several blogs have appeared that regularly collaborate with festivals or companies/artists by editing publications, journals and programme notes in print and online, curating talks, symposia and public events, and offering training opportunities for aspiring critics: www.altrevelocita.it, www.fattiditeatro. it, www.iltamburodikattrin.com, www.ateatro.it, amongst others. Effectively then, blogs function as service providers for venues, festivals, companies and artists.

Works cited

Anonymous (28 July 2008), 'Punti di vista #1', in *La Differenza*, Issue 1.29, <http://www.differenza.org/articolo.asp?sezione=archivio&ID=322> (accessed 6 June 2014).

Antonucci, Giovanni (1995) *Storia della critica teatrale*, Rome: Studium.

Augias, Corrado, et al., 'Per un convegno sul nuovo teatro', *Sipario*, issue 247, November 1966, pp. 1–2, transcribed in a special issue of *Ateatro. it*, 44.4 (28 October 2002) http://www.ateatro.org/mostranotizie2bis. asp?num=44&ord=4 (accessed 2 December 2014).

Bandettini, Anna (2014) 'L'Approdo a Repubblica', in Renata M. Molinari and Jacopo Quadri, *Panta*, special issue on Franco Quadri, Milan: Bompiani, e-book.

Bartolucci, Giuseppe (1970) 'Al di là di una critica tecnico-formale', in *Teatro-corpo: Teatro- immagine*, Padua: Marsilio.

Bartolucci, Giuseppe, Capriolo, Ettore and Fadini, Edoardo (eds) (1968) *Teatro: Rassegna trimestrale di ricerca teatrale*, issue 3/4, summer/autumn.

Bono, Francesco (4 July 2007), 'Dossier Ivrea 1967: Le opinioni di chi partecipò', in Ateatro.it, <http://www.ateatro.org/mostranotizie2bis. asp?num=108&ord=11> (accessed 11 June 2014).

Butt, Gavin (ed.) (2005) *After Criticism: New Responses to Art and Performance*, Oxford: Blackwell.

Cannella et al. (2011) 'Per una carta dei diritti e dei doveri del critico', *Hystrio*, 24.2.

Chiaromonte, Nicola (1971) 'Parola, scena, critica', in *Biblioteca Teatrale: Il mestiere del critico: dagli atti del convegno 'Situazione e funzione della critica teatrale'*, Rome: Bulzioni, pp. 54–58.

Derrida, Jacques (1998) *Of Grammatology*, translated by Gayatri Chakravorty Spivak, Baltimore: Johns Hopkins University Press.

Fadini, Edoardo (1971) 'Al di là della critica tecnico-formale', in *Biblioteca Teatrale: Il mestiere del critico: dagli atti del convegno 'Situazione e funzione della critica teatrale'*, Rome: Bulzioni, pp. 72–78.

Laera, Margherita (2014a) Interview with Claudia Cannella, carried out on 3 April 2014.

Laera, Margherita (2014b) Interview with Andrea Porcheddu, carried out on 19 August 2014.

Marino, Massimo (2014) 'Franco Quadri critico militante', in Renata M. Molinari and Jacopo Quadri, *Panta*, special issue on Franco Quadri, Milan: Bompiani, e-book.

Mello, Leonardo (2014) 'Franco Quadri fa scoprire all'Italia *hispanidad*: Il caso di Rodrigo García e Rafael Spregelburg', in Renata M. Molinari and Jacopo Quadri, *Panta*, special issue on Franco Quadri, Milan: Bompiani, e-book.

Ministero dei Beni e delle Attività Culturali e del Turismo (2012), 'Relazione sull'utilizzo del Fondo Unico per lo Spettacolo', p. 17, available at <http://www.spettacolodalvivo.beniculturali.it/index.php/download-relazioni-al-parlamento> (accessed 6 June 2014).

Ponte di Pino, Oliviero (2012), 'The Italian Critical Web: A Virtual Resurrection of Theatre Criticism?', *Ateatro.it*, <http://www.ateatro.it/webzine/2012/10/20/dossier-larte-dello-spettatore-the-italian-critical-web-a-virtual-resurrection-of-theatre-criticism/> (accessed 3 November 2013).

Ponte di Pino, Oliviero (2012), 'Il teatro al tempo di TripAdvisor', *Ateatro.it*, <http://www.ateatro.it/webzine/2012/10/25/dossier-larte-dello-spettatore-points-of-interest-il-teatro-al-tempo-di-tripadvisor/> (accessed 3 November 2013).

Porcheddu Andrea, and Ferraresi, Roberta (2010) *Questo fantasma: Il critico a teatro*, Pisa: Titivillus.

Visone, Daniela (2010) *La nascita del Nuovo Teatro in Italia. 1959–1967*, Pisa: Titivillus.

CHAPTER 7
WHAT GERMAN THEATRE CRITICS THINK AND WHAT THEIR READERS EXPECT: AN EMPIRICAL ANALYSIS OF MISUNDERSTANDINGS

Vasco Boenisch

Theatre criticism in Germany

Since its appearance in the mid-eighteenth century, the development of German theatre criticism[1] has always been closely linked to the changes in theatre production itself. In the late eighteenth and early nineteenth century the reviews became entertaining and more personal, emphasizing the individual impression a performance had on the critic rather than evaluation against strict norms. The newspaper industry grew considerably at the time, and modern journalism replaced the academic critiques of the past with witty, tartly polemic, fluently written feuilletons. Society, politics, theatre, art – all belonged together in a newspaper and found their ways into the reviews. The critic was no longer an author who occasionally wrote a review, but became a highly esteemed professional, sometimes even a figurehead of the newspaper. Competition between newspapers rose and, thus, also the pressure on the critics: they needed to be distinctive and fast. Two names in German theatre criticism have kept their legendary aura to the present day: Herbert Jhering (1888–1977) and his – even more famous – antagonist Alfred Kerr (1867–1948). Their names were known far beyond theatre circles, their verdicts were both dreaded and highly respected, and they could make and destroy careers with a single review. Furthermore, theatre criticism substitutionally participated in the ideological battles of that time: between conservatives and left-wing intellectuals, between realism and naturalism, between bourgeoisie and the rising social activists.

Theatre criticism has been of certain relevance even after the Second World War as part of the newly-created intellectual scene in the country. Theatre was a factor in the development of the intellectual elite. Serious newspapers cultivated theatre reviews, and critics could distinguish themselves by writing sharp and smart articles. Günther Rühle (1924–) and Georg Hensel (1923–1996) of *Frankfurter Allgemeine Zeitung*, Joachim Kaiser (1928–) and Benjamin Henrichs (1946–) of *Süddeutsche Zeitung*, as well as Peter Iden (1938–) of *Frankfurter Rundschau*, Gerhard Stadelmaier (1950–) of *Frankfurter Allgemeine Zeitung* and C. Bernd Sucher of *Süddeutsche Zeitung* are considered to be probably the last so-called 'Großkritiker' (great critics) of our time. Of course they owe their reputation to the radical theatre directors of the 1970s, whose works demanded explanation and were, at least for a while, the talk of the nation.

Since then, theatre has lost its unique voice in society's discourse and has to compete for audiences with many other spare-time activities. On the other hand, theatre practice has diversified. This should make the need for professional evaluation even more urgent (and simultaneously the requirements on the critics themselves much more demanding). However, newspaper circulation numbers have dropped, space for reviews is being cut down, and most of the critics can no longer be critics only but have to take on other tasks or jobs.

The study

What is a theatre review today? What should it be? How do critics see their job? What are their views on what they do – and, conversely, what do their readers expect from them? These were some of the questions at the heart of my doctoral research project (Boenisch 2008) investigating the working conditions, reception habits and, specifically, the practical expectations concerning the function of theatre reviews in the context of mass media communications in Germany.

In 2007, I interviewed 27 professional German theatre critics, all of them working for daily newspapers – regional and supraregional newspapers were equally represented and so were women and men. Some of the leading German critics were among the interviewees, including Christine Dössel, Till Briegleb, Jürgen Berger and Peter Laudenbach from *Süddeutsche Zeitung (SZ)*, Teresa Grenzmann and Eberhard Rathgeb from *Frankfurter Allgemeine Zeitung (FAZ)*, Peter Michalzik and Anke Dürr from *Frankfurter Rundschau*, Matthias Heine from *Die Welt* and Esther Slevogt from *die tageszeitung*.

For the purpose of comparison, readers of newspaper reviews were also interviewed through a questionnaire containing 55 topics with an overall amount of 130 questions. 227 readers took part in the study. They came from different parts of Germany: Bavaria (Munich and Nuremberg), North-Rhine-Westfalia (Bochum, Recklinghausen, Dusseldorf) and from Berlin. Two thirds of them are women, one third are men; half of them usually read regional, the other half supraregional newspapers.

It is important to note that all newspapers in Germany were founded from a regional standpoint; some of them then gained nationwide importance, but they still have a regional supplement like the *Frankfurter Allgemeine Zeitung (FAZ)* for Frankfurt, or the *Süddeutsche Zeitung (SZ)* for Munich – that is why in Germany they are called 'supraregional' rather than 'national' papers.

The study did not make a newspaper content analysis but an analysis of communication between journalists and readers. In general it can be said that regional reviews are shorter, and even in supraregional papers the lengths vary between 50 and 250 lines. At the time of the survey, a standard theatre review in the supraregional *SZ* had 140–150 lines (with 40 characters per line): shorter if not so important – 120 lines, very short if nearly unimportant – 80 lines, 170–180 if the performance was important and good, and very rarely more than 200 lines if the performance was extraordinary. (Already in 2015, 140–150 lines is unusual, the standard length in the *SZ* is 120 lines.) But this information is based on personal experience rather than scientific analysis.

The critics

Self-conception and target groups of German theatre critics

In response to Alfred Kerr's often quoted classification of criticism as a literary genre, there has always been a debate among German theatre critics on whether they see themselves as authors or as journalists. In our study 60 per cent of the critics consider their work part of arts journalism. The other 35 per cent emphasize more strongly the literary aspect of their work and professional self-conception. As one of them puts it: 'Amongst the journalists we are the artists' (Ronald Meyer-Arlt, *Hannoversche Allgemeine*). In this respect, an interesting differentiation emerged: critics of smaller, regional newspapers more broadly see themselves as journalists rather than writers (75 per cent to 20 per cent), whereas only half of the critics of the big renowned papers consider their work as journalistic (45 per cent to 45 per cent).

What role do the critics give themselves in mediating between theatres, artists, audiences and readers? Only 20 per cent of the supraregional critics say that they clearly belong to the audience in the stalls, whereas at least 60 per cent of the regional papers' critics see themselves that way. The supraregional critics dispute possible association with either of the two poles of 'theatre' and 'audience', and see themselves as being somewhere in-between: 'Of course I am no theatre artist, but surely more than a common viewer', says Simone Kaempf of *die tageszeitung*. That leads to the effect that only a quarter of the supraregional critics think that their job should be the role of a mediator between theatre and audience, whereas more than half of the regional critics think so; altogether the 'mediators' make up 40 per cent.

Most of the critics, therefore, stand on the audience's side but from a theatre perspective. They consider this to be the most appropriate position as far as their knowledge and sense of belonging (to a kind of theatre spirit) is concerned on the one hand, and their journalistic responsibility on the other. This area of potential conflict of allegiance can surely lead to confusion and that is why some critics seek to remain outsiders: 'I do not belong to any of the sides, I stand on my own', says Jürgen Berger of *SZ*. Or according to his colleague Till Briegleb: 'You have to protect your distance from all participants in order to trust your own judgement'. Well-renowned critic Peter Michalzik of supraregional *Frankfurter Rundschau* concludes:

> There is an honest and a dishonest answer. The dishonest but correct answer is: of course I am a representative of the audience. Actually, this should be the only legitimate answer. But, the part of our readership that reacts most emphatically to what we write belongs to theatre. And after a certain time you also get to know all these people personally. In this respect you cannot avoid writing for theatre people, too. You will not get those people out of your mind. It is a group – of professionals – you cannot leave aside, in fact.[2]

It is striking that, in contrast to the regional critics, supraregional critics often do not have a clear idea of who their target readers are – or at least, they do not give much thought to the question. Consequently, they seldom know who they are writing for. The reason for this is that potential readership of a supraregional newspaper is not only larger than a regional one, but also more complex and diverse. Whereas supraregional critics abstractly speak of 'readers interested in theatre', most of the regional critics (75 per cent) explain that they address potential theatregoers. This is an important aspect since it reveals a central function of theatre reviews. Christine Dössel (*SZ*) claims she wants to do all her readers – both theatre professionals and people interested in theatre – justice by 'writing coherently, clearly and wittily and not too intellectually and sophisticatedly'. Other supraregional critics are more pessimistic. Anke Dürr (*Frankfurter Rundschau*):

> It is not possible to write completely without preconceptions. I cannot explain over and over again what the fourth wall is or what 'speaking against the text' means. I seek to write in such a way that as many readers as possible will understand it, but one

should not cherish the illusion that our reviews are read by everyone.

The more vague the idea of a target group, the more difficult it gets to estimate its pre-knowledge. Thus, regional critics have an edge over their supraregional colleagues. They have a more precise understanding of their readers' knowledge, and their group of addressees is more homogenous.

Functions of theatre reviews – from the critics' perspective

This research has shown that German theatre critics assume the central functions of theatre reviews to be to inform and to provide an evaluation; although the understanding of the term 'to inform' can vary significantly. Furthermore they all agree that analysis as well as explanation inevitably belong in a review. Contextualizing the artists' work is a function which half of the supraregional critics believe to be important whereas only a quarter of their regional colleagues do. On the other hand, half of them – and nearly none of the supraregional critics – assume decision-guidance as part of their task. Entertainment is a factor which twice as many supraregional as regional critics assume to be the function of a theatre review.

Not surprisingly, *information* is considered to be the most important function. '[A] review should fulfil the trivial task of describing a theatre performance in such a manner that readers can at least approximately envisage what has happened on stage', says Peter Laudenbach (*SZ*). However, in reading the critics' statements, one can get the impression that supraregional critics seek to put the performances through a subjective filter and therefore describe them differently: 'You need to find your own expression for the artistic idea of the performance', says Eberhard Ratgeb (*FAZ*). Simone Kaempf (*tageszeitung*) adds: 'The function of describing has become more complex. It is no longer a valid objective to say how many actors perform the text. There is so much more to it. One therefore responds with one's own imagery or puts up a thesis'. In this case, accompanying description is also a matter of interpretation and even inspiration.

For German theatre critics, *description* needs to be accompanied by *interpretation*: 'Plain description is dreadful', says Christine Dössel (*SZ*) while Bettina Schulte (*Badische Zeitung*) emphasizes that description is not enough for most readers: 'The aim is to convey aesthetic concepts'. It can therefore be observed that regional critics want to stay closer to the concrete action on stage when giving information than their supraregional colleagues.

The tasks of *explanation* and *interpretation* grow out of the process of providing information and are closely linked to it. Both regional and supraregional critics consider these functions to be essential – and more important than in the past. According to Matthias Heine (*Die Welt*):

> We all pay more attention to explaining than we did in the past. The times when you did not need to tell people what *Hamlet* is about are over. Nowadays you need to explain more and more the context of a play or why a director has chosen this or that interpretation.

This function of *contextualizing* (in German: *einordnen*) cannot be translated precisely though it is a function of reviewing most often mentioned by German theatre critics. It aims at explaining contexts: of a subject matter, of an artistic style, of a person, of political circumstances etc. Supraregional critics (70 per cent) pay particular attention to it (compared to 35 per cent of regional critics). This might be related to the fact that they have more opportunities as well as more need to compare performances, artists, themes and styles with each other.

Most of the critics emphasize how important evaluation or *judgement* within a theatre review is: 'People want to know quite distinctly: is it good or bad', says Matthias Heine (*Die Welt*). Teresa Grenzmann (*FAZ*) specifies: 'A theatre review should present a clear opinion and take up a position for or against – or: for and against'. Till Briegleb (*SZ*) mentions an important aspect of this: 'A good review differs from a bad review in as far as it makes transparent why it comes to its conclusion'. And Peter Laudenbach (*SZ*) adds: 'I like reviews where I totally disagree but can follow the critic's argument'.

Nearly all regional theatre critics see their work as being of *service* to the readers – specifically as decision guidance – whereas only one third of the supraregional critics agree. This might be because of a different self-conception and understanding of their work, but it is also related to the fact that most of the readers of supraregional reviews will rarely have a chance to travel to performances reviewed by their critics. The critics are noticing a trend whereby 'more service is expected from theatre reviews' (Jenny Schmetz, *Aachener Zeitung*).

There is probably no theatre critic who wants to bore his or her readers. Supraregional critics emphasize the task of offering reading pleasure far more (90 per cent) than the regional critics (35 per cent). They often claim that the *entertainment* factor of their reviews is supposed to be one of the most important reasons why people actually read their texts: 'In a supraregional newspaper a theatre review should be interesting for itself', says Matthias Heine (*Die Welt*). And his colleague Anke Dürr (*Frankfurter Rundschau*) adds: 'A theatre review – more than any other newspaper article – must not bore because it is under threat and has to fight for its space in the paper more than ever before'.

Concerning other possible functions of theatre reviews proposed to the critics in the survey, being an annalist of theatre life was of importance to very few. The function of offering an analysis of society, reflecting social questions and how the production relates to them was of interest mostly to the supraregional critics, but less so to their regional counterparts.

Ultimately, it is obvious that German theatre critics today bear in mind the – assumed – needs and wishes of their readers more strongly and are more willing to fulfil them than might have been the case in the past. They are much more understood to serve certain demands of the readers. But, of course, there are different groups of readers and different views on how the described tasks are best fulfilled. Regional critics see themselves predominantly as service providers and reporters, whereas their supraregional colleagues see themselves rather as entertainers and analysts. As far as the concrete composition of a review is concerned, the overall views differ, too.

Components of a theatre review

Due to the often-emphasized absence of strict rules, it is almost a provocation to ask the critics what kind of information should occur in a review. The critics therefore usually come up with a catalogue of minimum requirements. Nearly all German critics (95 per cent) find it indispensable to name the venue and the title of the production, as well as the name of the director. After that, the consensus dissipates. The name of the stage designer is only compulsory for one third of the critics, most of them regional. The name of the costume designer is only a must for one quarter of the regional critics and for none of the supraregional.

Only 58 per cent of German theatre critics think that one should mention the name of the main actor(s) or actress(es) with a major gap between the two groups: 30 per cent of the supraregional and 90 per cent of regional critics hold this view. For the latter this seems to be compulsory regardless of the acting quality, and some even think that a regional review should mention all actors by name. On the other hand, supraregional critics prefer to mention actors only if their performance was in some way outstanding – one reason for that is the assumption that their names are usually unknown in a supraregional context anyway.

How much detail a review should provide concerning the plot is, of course, a decision to be made on a case-by-case basis. In simple terms: the more unknown the play the more detailed the information on its plot should be. Bettina Schulte (*Badische Zeitung*) reports she devotes about half of her text to the plot when reviewing the first performance of a new play, for example. This is also important since, in such cases, the review has to judge the play's literary quality as well as the production's achievements.

But what about the classics? According to Sabine Leucht (*die tageszeitung*):

Actually you should not assume any knowledge at all, but then you think: probably no one would read a theatre review in a supraregional newspaper about a performance in another city if he or she did not have at least a bit of previous knowledge about plays and theatre.

Other critics are less attentive as implied by Eberhard Ratgeb (*FAZ*): 'I am not willing to explain how *Hamlet* works. [...] It would take too much space'. Similarly, regional critic Günter Ott (*Augsburger Allgemeine*) proffers: 'It is not the purpose of a theatre review to re-narrate a play for those who are too lazy to inform themselves'.

On the other hand there are voices who emphasize the need to explain: 'You are well advised to write what those plays are about even when it comes to *Hamlet* or *Othello*', says supraregional critic Peter Michalzik (*Frankfurter Rundschau*). His colleague Christine Dössel (*SZ*) adds: 'You cannot assume that everyone reading theatre reviews is aware of the plot, even if we talk about very famous plays'.

In short, there is some willingness among German theatre critics to provide their readers with information regarding the plays' plots, although they are not sure and certainly not in complete agreement as to how far this should go.

The duration of a production is necessary information for half of the regional critics, whereas none of the supraregional see this as compulsory – they would only mention it if the length is unusually long or short.

The audience reaction (whether or not in line with the critic's opinion) is of interest to half of the regional critics in any case, whereas only every fifth of their supraregional colleagues agrees.

The Readers

Readers as playgoers and playgoers as readers

Most of the 227 readers in our study are frequent playgoers: about half of them attend theatre performances nine or more times a year; whereas one quarter goes to the theatre more sporadically (a maximum of five productions per year). In other words: every second reader has a broad understanding and knowledge of theatre, plays and playwrights.

Readers of theatre reviews are active newspaper consumers. 91 per cent of the respondents say that they read the paper often or very often (more than three times a week). These people tend to have a broader understanding of and interest in what is going on in the world. The intensity of reading theatre reviews grows with the reader's age: whereas only every third young reader (up to 30 years old) says that he or she reads reviews often or very often, every nine out of ten readers of the over 60-year-olds does so.

When it comes to different genres of theatre journalism, reviews are ranked very high. Two thirds of the readers (67 per cent) name reviews as one of their three most favourite journalistic formats. Second-ranked are preview articles (50 per cent) and third ranked are profile features (49 per cent). They are followed by interviews (45 per cent), essays (26 per cent), background features (23 per cent) and reportage (19 per cent). But results vary between different ages. For the readers aged under 30 the most favourite genres are profiles (59 per cent), followed by reportage (45 per cent) and interviews, previews and reviews (ranked shared third with 38 per cent each). In other words: theatre criticism has an acceptance problem among younger readers.

Customer satisfaction

German readers of theatre reviews judge the critics' work as 'satisfactory'. Every second reader says that he or she is 'largely satisfied' (51 per cent) with the reviews, every third reader is 'somewhat satisfied' (33 per cent), 12 per cent are 'somewhat dissatisfied' and four per cent 'largely dissatisfied'. In other words, merging together the last two groups, which make up 16 per cent, nearly every fifth reader is 'dissatisfied' with the kind of reviews he or she finds in his or her newspaper.

In addressing the question of what the critics could improve, those readers who are only 'somewhat satisfied' should also be included because they too have some points they dislike. So, if we look at those readers who say that they like reviews in general *and* that they are nevertheless not really satisfied with the reviews they find in their papers ('somewhat satisfied', 'somewhat dissatisfied', 'largely dissatisfied'), this intersection makes up 26 per cent of all readers. Thus, every fourth reader likes reviews in general but is 'not really satisfied' – this indicates the potential that could be regained by the critics if they changed their work.

In general, the main reasons for dissatisfaction concerning theatre reviews are: arrogance (mentioned by 59 per cent); lack of information (52 per cent); uninspired writing style (46 per cent); incomprehensibility (45 per cent); boasting with knowledge (42 per cent) and narcissistic writing style (42 per cent). Surprisingly there are nearly no differences between readers of regional and supraregional newspapers in this respect. Only a few aspects are estimated differently: regional readers dislike uninspired writing much more than supraregional readers (52 to 43 per cent), whereas the latter dislike lack of information more strongly than regional readers (32 to 21 per cent). This might have something to do with the fact that supraregional critics presuppose too much knowledge more often than their regional colleagues do.

Functions of theatre reviews – from the readers' perspective

There are various reasons why people read theatre reviews. Both regional and supraregional readers name the intention of going to a certain performance (or at least thinking about it) as the main reason for reading a review (ranked first for 23 per cent and in the top three for 51 per cent). Thus, theatre criticism is closely linked to theatregoing – and this is true for supraregional as well as regional readers, which might be surprising for supraregional critics.

The second main reason for reading a review is interest in the play or subject matter of the performance (ranked first for 16 per cent and in the top three for 50 per cent). All other reasons – like interest in the author, interest in the director or interest in certain actors – are less relevant (only 20 per cent put these reasons in their top three). The reputation of the venue and readers' interest in theatre in general are further reasons that do not play an important role.

As far as *information* is concerned, stating what happens on stage is the central function of a theatre review for all readers. Three quarters of them (73 per cent) think that *description* of actions, props, costumes, light, music etc. is the most important. Again, there is no difference between regional and supraregional readers.

The central demands of all readers can be summarized as follows: A review should be easy to read (84 per cent 'important'), state what one sees on the stage (73 per cent), make clear if it is worth going to see the production (63 per cent), explain the director's concept (54 per cent), contextualize the production (52 per cent), reflect current affairs (49 per cent), convey a clear judgement (48 per cent) and be preferably entertaining (27 per cent).

Coming next after description are *interpretation* and *explanation*. Interestingly, regional readers do not pay as much attention to this function as supraregional readers – 46 as opposed to 61 per cent consider it 'important'. The latter are more interested in the explanation of directors' concepts and intentions (which might be a result of their papers' coverage of more complex productions at the major theatre houses).

Comparing and *contextualizing* is the fifth most important function for readers, according to more than half of the respondents. Thus, German readers expect the critics not only to describe and evaluate a performance but also to explain reference points and deliver information that helps understand the background and context of a production.

Judgement is certainly an indispensable function and the highest rated stimulus for reading a review. But noticeably readers prefer to see how much the critic's view matches their own taste, rather than accepting a critic's judgement as certificate for a high or low artistic quality.

This goes hand in hand with the *service* function. Over two thirds of respondents (73 per cent) say a review should make clear if going to a show is worth it. However, what they mean is that through description and explanation (which are the most important functions of theatre reviews) they want to get an impression that only helps them to come to a decision on their own instead of wanting to adopt the critic's opinion. The reviews should assist indirectly, not advise or patronize.

Last but not least, *entertainment* in the form of witty writing style does not play an important role for the readers. This is true for both regional and supraregional readers, although there are more supraregional readers who find entertainment unimportant than regional readers (44 to 37 per cent).

To sum up: Theatre reviews in German newspapers are mainly read for two reasons – readers want to be informed and they want to be given advice (more indirectly than directly). Information about what is going on on stage is the central function of theatre criticism. Service provision and recommendation is the second central function; both nearly equally important, although for regional newspapers service is somewhat more important. Reflection on current affairs within a review is generally seen as important as explanation, contextualization and judgement, but dips down against the others when compared. Entertainment, on the one hand, is the most, and on the other, the least important function: in terms of writing elegance and comprehensibility, it is seen as the most important and basic function of criticism, but embellishment through witticisms and puns is seen as positively unnecessary.

Components of a theatre review

There are four components that are definitely compulsory for German readers: the names of the production, the author, the venue and the director. They must not be missing in any review. Thus, on the one hand readers are realistic (only four requirements), but on the other they hold up certain standards which must be met, the failure of which will lead to discontentment.

Aspects which the respondents wanted more information about (ranging from 'sometimes' to 'often') included: comparison with other productions (71 per cent); background of the author (63 per cent); director's concept (57 per cent); comparison with other theatres (54 per cent); casting process (50 per cent); plot summary, set design, topicality of the production (47 per cent each). All these aspects represent the wish for more contextualization and explanation. But these are luxury items on the wish-list as they are mainly mentioned by those readers who are satisfied with the reviews.

It is more informative to have a closer look at those components deemed dissatisfactory by the readers. These aspects are (in order of importance): unsatisfying discussion of the actors' performance, stage design, costumes, plot, the critic's interpretation of the production, the production's reference to current affairs, the overall achievements of the theatre venue, music and sound. Supraregional readers want more information on plots whereas regional readers especially miss information on music and the critic's interpretation.

Adding together those aspects that are ranked the highest shows that the three major deficiencies of German theatre reviews are: comparison with other productions (34 per cent of all readers in the top three ranks), the director's concept (28 per cent) and information on the plot summary (24 per cent). Since the lack of information on plot summary is mentioned especially frequently by those readers who are 'dissatisfied' with German theatre reviews, and since it is the case especially for supraregional readers, one can conclude that German theatre critics, especially in the supraregional newspapers, disregard information about plots too much.

It is the same with the actors' performance. The harsh criticism of dissatisfied readers (64 per cent of them miss information about actors, compared to the average 40 per cent) shows that this is an effective lack, too.

We also found that half of the readers sometimes have problems following the critic's judgement due to an insufficient explanatory statement. Every third reader finds the reasoning generally (rather) unelaborate (34 per cent). Especially readers under 30 hold this view (56 per cent). Of the 'dissatisfied' readers 70 per cent report this as a deficiency. Thus, we can conclude that insufficient explanatory judgement statements are seen as a major deficiency of German theatre reviews.

Critics and their readers

The study shows that communication between critics and readers is by no means always successful. It is not surprising that the readers' verdict on the quality of reviews was restrained, having been rated as only 'satisfactory', nothing more, nothing less; and with even poorer ratings from younger readers.

The reasons can be found in considerable differences of expectation between the German critics and their readers. It starts with the critics' self-conception – they do not see themselves as journalists as clearly as their readers expect them to. And it leads to the point where (especially supraregional critics) also try to write for theatre professionals as a target group. It is striking that the supraregional critics address a supraregional target group, which does not exist as such. The everyday function of a review as decision-guidance is obviously underestimated by the critics.

Even if the German theatre critics today respect the information function of theatre criticism more than they did in the past, one has to conclude: this is still not enough. Whereas critics understandably pay much attention to their judgements, their readers prefer to distil decision-guidance from their description, explanation and contextualization – which they would like to find even more of in the reviews. And as far as entertainment is concerned: supraregional critics still attach too much importance to this aspect of writing, especially witticisms and puns.

Generally, it is striking how much more frequently reviews in supraregional newspapers have to confront communication dysfunctions between the critics and their readers than those in regional papers. There are nearly twice as many differences between supraregional critics and their readers than their regional counterparts.

However, given the results of this study, one thing is certain: the readers of theatre reviews do not want to dispense with them. Only 3 per cent of respondents in 2007 said there could be fewer reviews in the daily newspapers; three quarters thought that the amount at the time was just right; and every fourth reader thought that there should be even more reviews. More reviews? More reviews of a different kind, at least.

Notes

1. The terms 'theatre' and 'theatre criticism' in this article refer to drama and plays, rather than operas, musicals or ballets.

2. All quotes are taken from the author's primary research; all translations from German provided by the author.

Work cited

Boenisch, Vasco (2008): *Was soll Theaterkritik? Was Kritiker denken und Leser erwarten. Aufgabe, Arbeitsweise und Rezeption deutscher Theaterkritik im 21. Jahrhundert.* Inaugural-Dissertation zur Erlangung des Doktorgrades der Philosophie an der Ludwig-Maximilians-Universität München.

CHAPTER 8
A BRIEF HISTORY OF ONLINE
THEATRE CRITICISM IN ENGLAND
Andrew Haydon

Although, in principle, I'm all for blogs, I still cherish the idea of
the printed review. The restrictions of space and time are
considerable, but they force one to focus on essentials. A blog is
more like an informal letter.

Michael Billington, 17 September 2007

I couldn't see a future for theatre criticism in newspapers and
suspected that my generation might be the last to review theatre
in newspapers in the traditional way. Now I think that predictions
of my imminent demise were premature. The rise of the internet
and the blogosphere makes me think that theatre criticism may
get a whole new lease of life.

Lyn Gardner, 18 September 2007

The best [blogs] add much of worth to the critical discourse; they
are certainly not a threat to reviews (not yet anyway). Indeed the
growth of blogging as a medium has to date had very little real
effect on the way arts coverage is handled in the mainstream print
press.

Natasha Tripney, 20 September 2007

In September 2007, *The Guardian*'s Theatre Blog ran a series of articles
marking a decisive point in the discussion of writing about theatre
online. The fact that *The Guardian*'s chief theatre critic felt moved to
say anything at all on the subject is significant. When it was published,
his sniffy undermining of 'blogs' felt like a disproportionate attack on

something that wasn't doing him any harm. However, in the years since Billington's blog was posted, the relationship between the print review and online has changed immeasurably. In this chapter I intend to look at the history of British theatre criticism online and attempt to trace what changes and impact it has had on the ecology of theatre criticism at large.

Phase 1

The history of online reviewing starts at least ten years earlier than the above quotes. In 1997, the World Wide Web or internet was still very much in its infancy. Laptops were heavy; desktops, which tended to be standard, were bulky; and the internet was accessed by plugging your computer into a phone socket in the wall and using a dial-up modem. The speed at which web-pages loaded was almost measured in minutes. There was no such thing as Wi-Fi. Indeed, in 1997 the internet was only just starting to be any more than a niche interest. Over the next three years, technology and commerce moved at remarkable speeds so that by 2000, there could be a 'dot.com boom', which turned out to be a 'dot.com bubble', bursting numerically on 10 March 2000. In practice: pre-March 2000, venture capitalists invested in anything calling itself an 'internet start-up'. Then, when the market lost faith that these investments could make a return on their money, the money began to flood out of internet start-ups. This, combined with the terrorist attacks of 9/11 in 2001, led to wiping out within two years $5 trillion in paper wealth on NASDAQ, the stock market on which the shares of many tech companies are traded (Gaither & Chmielewski 2006).

In 1997 two major players in British online theatre reviewing were established: *British Theatre Guide* (*BTG*) and *WhatsOnStage.com* (*WOS*). Both sites are still running and thriving at the time of writing (June 2015). The genesis, business models, aims and objectives of the two sites couldn't be more different, however. Peter Lathan, founder of *BTG*, was a comprehensive school teacher in Sunderland who had started a successful online resource for other drama teachers putting on school plays. Lathan recalls:

Towards the end of 1996 I was approached by New York-based General Internet to create a website for them. They were trading under the name The Mining Company and were setting up a range of websites, each run by an 'expert guide', which would 'mine' the Internet for resources in each subject area.

Lathan 2014

In February 1997 the site went live offering links to specific pages within theatres' websites, feature articles and a news digest. The first review published was of Bob Carlton's touring production of *From a Jack to a King* on 18 June 1997. Over the next couple of years, the Mining Company changed its name to About.com, and About.com was taken over by US media conglomerate Primedia. There were over 900 About sites by the time of the acquisition, but Primedia was only interested in those which were in some way related to a print title. As a result, on 25 September 2001, 300 sites were axed, including About British Theatre. Primedia allowed those who had been operating those sites access to their material, so Lathan, having been persuaded by his site's 4,000-plus subscribers, started the process of rebranding, and British Theatre Guide as we now know it launched on 17 November 2001.

WhatsOnStage.com was started by the magazine publisher EMAP in December 1996. The site's first editor, Terri Paddock explains:

Back in the first internet boom EMAP decided to start an internet division – Emap-online – creating original-content websites separate from their published magazines. There were two joint managing directors, Roger Green and Carol Dukes. Dukes was a keen theatregoer and she had the idea to launch a theatre website, and gave it the name. Initially it was only basic listings, and then they tried to introduce an e-commerce element where, if someone wanted to buy tickets they could hit a button which would send an email to the office and someone at EMAP would call the box office. Pretty basic. And there was no content on it. But that was before online booking was commonplace.

Paddock 2014

The embryonic *WhatsOnStage* advertised for a part-time editor and the job went to Paddock, who joined the site in March 1997 to add unique content. Paddock's first news story as editor was the appointment of Ian Rickson to the artistic directorship of the Royal Court. The site soon added reviews, and shortly after a facility for user reviews. The first was of Ben Elton's *Popcorn*, which was then running in the West End. User reviews were attached to the main articles as they still are. The site also had star-ratings from the very beginning. In 1998 it launched its popular discussion forum. All these features were well ahead of their time, at least as far as theatre coverage was concerned. By the end of 1998, most of the still-familiar elements of WhatsOnStage.com were in place.

As the dot.com bubble expanded, other websites incorporating theatre reviews sprang up. The homepage of *Financial Times* co-chief drama critic and current editor of *Theatre Record*, Ian Shuttleworth, for example, records that he was 'UK Theatre reviewer for www. divento.com (European arts review/listings website run by Vivendi Universal), from its inception in 2000 to its demise in late 2002' (Shuttleworth 'Who am I?'). Indeed, my own reviewing career began in 2000 when I joined the theatre section of the now-defunct (as of 2013) CultureWars.org.uk, the web magazine of The Institute of Ideas.

At this stage, the reviews on these websites reproduced the conventions of the newspaper/print media. The internet was functioning as a less-attractively presented version of a Sunday culture supplement, with a similar set of hierarchies, values and tastes. And while the internet as a whole was still running at a speed slower than it took to turn the page of a newspaper, it was never going to feel more cutting-edge than one.

The website that changed all this was *Encore Theatre Magazine*. Founded anonymously in 2003 by the academic and playwright Dan Rebellato, and suspected of having multiple contributors – all posting under the name 'Theatre Worker' – it changed the game in terms of how theatre was written about in the UK (albeit predominantly concerned with London theatre). *Encore* was combative, irreverent, and anti-establishment. It loved theatre, but was concerned that complacency and idiocy were killing it. It offered challenges to and critiques of the chief theatre critics of the British press. Although not built as 'a blog', *Encore* was the first theatre magazine online that gave some indication of what was to come next.

Phase II

The web log, or 'blog' for short, was one of the elements of Web 2.0. Put simply, Web 2.0 is the name given to the advent of whole websites dedicated to 'user-generated content'. As we see with *WhatsOnStage*, user-generated content pre-existed Web 2.0, but within fixed parameters. With the advent of blogging, platforms like LiveJournal, Blogger, and WordPress gave anyone who wanted it, access to a self-publishing platform from which they could express their thoughts on whatever they liked. A lot of these blogs took the form of unread teenage diaries or lucratively published sex memoirs, but a few dedicated themselves to writing about theatre.

It's difficult to know when the phenomenon of 'the theatre blog' took off in the UK, but there's a strong argument to date it from spring 2006. On 8 March a pair of 'anonymous' bloggers – Andrew and Phil – naming themselves *The West End Whingers*, started a blog to express their disgust at the Old Vic's production of *Resurrection Blues*. The 'review' itself ran to all of 182 words, and the criticism doesn't get more detailed than: 'It was unwatchable. Everyone was terrible. The set was terrible. The costumes were terrible. It cost a fortune.' (West End Whingers 2006). Despite these inauspicious beginnings, by 2010 The West End Whingers had entered *The Times*'s 'Luvvie power list' at number fifty (Bungey 2010). To get there, the Whingers developed a new style of theatre criticism, one almost opposite to the prevailing mainstream British reviewing culture. They had the space to mess about with style and form and did so memorably in, for example, their 'Nigerian scam email' review of Wole Soyinka's *Death and the King's Horsemen* (West End Whingers 2009), their panning of Tony Harrison's *Fram* in rhyming couplets (West End Whingers 2008), and famously when they christened Andrew Lloyd Webber's *Love Never Dies* 'Paint Never Dries' (West End Whingers 2010).

At the opposite end of an imaginary artistic spectrum, on Saturday 13 May 2006, theatre-maker Chris Goode started his blog *Thompson's Bank of Communicable Desire*. For a generation of critics and bloggers, I suspect it is Goode's blog which served as their genesis impulse. Chris Goode is a theatre-maker who has been making work since the late 1990s, gaining recognition for his production of *The Tempest* which performed in audiences' homes on the Edinburgh Fringe in 2000.[1] His blog, rather than reviewing show after show, was more a set of polemics, arguments, engagements, interventions, and thinkings-out-loud. From its inception, it galvanized an entire section of British theatre which might previously have been described as marginal or obscure. At roughly the same time as Goode started *Thompsons Bank of Communicable Desire*, the playwright David Eldridge also began a blog called *One Writer and his Dog*. Annoyingly, following quotes from his blog being used in *The Guardian*'s *Noises Off* blog round-up (Wilkinson 2008), Eldridge redacted the entire thing, so citation is now impossible. Other blogs started around this time include Dan Bye's *Pessimism of the Intellect, Optimism of the Will*, Alex Ferguson's *Persons Unknown*, and Andy Field's *The Arcades Project*. Within a year, I had started my own blog, *Postcards From the Gods*, and a year after that, Matt Trueman began *Carousel of Fantasies*.

There was a world of difference between the reviews blog of the *West End Whingers*, and the far longer, more thoughtful pieces found on *Thompson's Bank of Communicable Desire* and the blogs it inspired. And both these types of blog differed again from online reviews sites, such as *British Theatre Guide*, *CultureWars*, and *WhatsOnStage*, which had editors and multiple critics. Over the following year, the differences between these blogs and sites and their diverse aims and functions were overlooked in a series of 'Bloggers versus Critics' articles, which occurred with depressing regularity, bundling all online writing up into one homogeneous thing, held up as the opposite to 'Professional criticism'. 'Professional' became a frequent stick used to beat the unpaid 'amateur' critic, blogger, or website reviewer. Irrespective of such jibes, from 2006 until about 2008 or 2009, this second wave of writing about theatre online seemed to enjoy a cultural energy and momentum quite beyond anything that had greeted the first gradual and tentative wave of theatre websites.

***

The moment that it became obvious that something big was going on was in the spring of 2007. The American playwright Edward Albee had given an interview to *L.A. Weekly*, in which he had said:

> The big problem is the assumption that writing a play is a collaborative act. It isn't. It's a creative act, and then other people come in. The interpretation should be for the accuracy of what the playwright wrote. Playwrights are expected to have their text changed by actors they never wanted. Directors seem to feel they are as creative as the playwright.

Albee quoted in Goode 2007

The story itself was reported in *The Guardian* (Caines 2007) and might have stopped there in a pre-blog world. Online, however, the story turned into a long, knotty, thoroughgoing debate about what Albee had said, with various practitioners and critics (Chris Goode, George Hunka, Alison Croggan, Andy Field, David Eldridge, et al) arguing as if for the soul of theatre itself. It was an insightful, erudite, fascinating discussion, which seemed to raise as many new questions as it answered. It was also an education. Here was the very stuff that was missing from newspaper criticism and 'features' about theatre. Here were some of the brightest minds making and/or writing about theatre offering new, live debate on a subject that they chose and cared about. I learnt more from following that one discussion and the comment threads under the blogs it generated, than I had in several years of reading mainstream newspaper theatre coverage, because it wasn't neatly packaged as a single article. It was an ongoing negotiation. What this discussion, and countless others like it since, have proved is that there had been a real need for this new venue for discussion and opinion-sharing and -bashing. The 'blogosphere' was making something available that had been lacking in mainstream theatre coverage. It was making it possible for new voices and schools of thought to be widely read, where before a process of gate-keepers ensured that more-or-less a single vision of what theatre was had prevailed since about 1956. There was also something of the punk spirit about it. Just as with punk music – with its ethos that anyone could pick up a guitar, learn three chords and form a band[2] – anyone with access to a computer and the internet could start their own theatre blog, join in the discussion, and if entertaining or thoughtful, would rapidly gain an active, passionate readership.

Something else that was striking about the theatre blogosphere is the way in which it wasn't constrained by national borders. The discussion on the merits or otherwise of Albee's intractable stance (re: how directors should approach plays) took place across three continents (see Croggon 2007). And, while the top tier of the English critical establishment then consisted of old, white, Oxbridge-educated men, this new anti-establishment had women and men, of many nationalities (including a significant proportion of migrants from eastern Europe), who had been educated anywhere from Melbourne to Moscow.

This very diversity added something else to the mixture. It could be argued that British (read: English, read: London) criticism had long since settled on some cosy precepts. The new independent criticism, and the discussions being made available online, questioned these as a matter of course. The nature of the internet, coupled with ever cheaper international travel, and the number of younger critics and theatre-makers turning their eyes toward mainland Europe, meant that this new generation were coming into contact with pre-existing, already-established, proven *other ways of doing things*.[3] This was given an added energy by the fact that (post-2007) several online critics based in the UK or Australia hailed from eastern Europe (notably Diana Damian and Jana Perkovic) and brought with them fresh ideas and a completely different set of assumptions of what writing-about-theatre should look like. The complacency of the mainstream British chief critics was thrown into stark relief. The traditional way of doing things suddenly had challenges and competition.

However, as the piece by Natasha Tripney which I quoted at the start of this chapter makes clear, there wasn't ever anything like a coup being planned. There was a sense of urgency and excitement about new work that was being made and the possibility of there being channels for it to gain coverage, and, at the same time, an impatience with an upper echelon of critics whose Olympian disdain for certain sorts of work on stage seemed as if it was starting to do real damage to British theatre.

***

Throughout 2007, it felt as if the stronghold of mainstream print journalism was being challenged. In March, as the Albee row was rumbling, the National Theatre presented Katie Mitchell's technologically-groundbreaking, incisive, dynamic, adrenaline rush of a production of Martin Crimp's play *Attempts on Her Life*. It was condemned by the print critics who just plain didn't like it. When, later that year, the National Theatre's artistic director, Nicholas Hytner, made the mischievous accusation that Britain's theatre critics were 'Dead White Males' (Hytner 2007) his comments did not come from nowhere. The phrase would not have gained the enormous and immediate traction it did (Shuttleworth 2007) without the widespread feeling Hytner was just the first person to say out loud something a lot of people had been thinking for a long time.[4] The personal tastes of a single critic are an occupational hazard of having theatre reviewed professionally: the problem by 2007 was that the combined personal tastes of *all* the first stringers no longer represented a significant proportion of the theatre-going public. It was because of this that online writing-about-theatre began to gain more notice.

But, as we can see from the above quoted sources, the 'Dead White Males' scandal still took place across the pages of the mainstream press. While the National had been able to publicize Mitchell's *Attempts on Her Life* using online reviews rather than mainstream print ones, there's no evidence to suggest that this strategy had much reach or effect. The readership of online theatre magazines/theatre sections remained niche, and the 'blogosphere', while invaluable to those taking part in it, had yet to consolidate its position.

Phase III

The third wave of online theatre writing begins in 2010. Since 2007 two massive sea changes had taken place on the internet. One is

Facebook, the other is Twitter. Granted, Facebook was founded in 2004, but it was only in 2006/07 that it was being rolled out to a non-USA, non-university-based public. At the beginning of 2010 Facebook had 350 million users, by the end of 2010 that number had nearly doubled to 608 million (Associated Press 2012). Similarly, while Twitter had been launched in 2006, it depended on mass uptake for it to have any effect. The next development, as far as theatre criticism went, however, was the establishment of *Exeunt Magazine* and *A Younger Theatre* – two theatre review-and-comment magazine sites. Within a couple of years both had established their different identities, due in no small part to the possibility of raised visibility through Twitter.

Exeunt was launched in February 2011 by Daniel B. Yates (a brilliant writer, critic and sociologist trained at LSE, with a rare gift for making philosophically-dense prose funny and readable), along with Natasha Tripney (a freelance journalist whose analysis of the relationship between bloggers and critics starts this chapter) and Diana Damian (a Romanian PhD candidate at Royal Holloway). The magazine established a reputation for incisive critical commentary more than capable of holding its own against mainstream competition. *A Younger Theatre* (originally founded as a blog in 2009 and turned into a magazine in 2010), by contrast, was a training ground. There was an age limit of 25 for its reviewers, and its staff – founder, social media genius and digital native Jake Orr, joined not a moment too soon by editor par excellence, Eleanor Turney – created a place where young critics could develop their skills as writers. These developments set the scene for what could be viewed as a defining moment for the theatre blogosphere: the coverage of *Three Kingdoms* in 2012.

Three Kingdoms was a tri-national collaboration between England, Germany and Estonia: a play by British playwright Simon Stephens, directed by his long-term collaborator, Sebastian Nübling, and designed by Estonian Ene-Liis Semper, with performers from the Estonian company No99, members of the Munich Kammerspiele ensemble, and three English actors. The production had already toured to Munich and Tallinn, garnering rave reviews. When it opened in London its mainstream notices might be euphemized as 'mixed'. While the *Standard*, *Time Out* and *Financial Times* politely three-starred it, confessing to varying degrees of bafflement, *The Guardian*, *WhatsOnStage*, and the *Telegraph* all laid into both play and production with savage abandon. For a few days, ticket sales were poor and audiences small. Then something extraordinary happened: thanks to positive reviews from *Exeunt* and various online critics – Catherine Love, Matt Trueman, Dan Hutton, Dan Rebellato, Meg Vaughan, myself – the production gathered momentum, becoming *the* play to see in London. The last few dates completely sold out. Re-reading those reviews even now still conjures something of both the excitement and the combativeness with which these new critics greeted *Three Kingdoms*.[5] A new generation had found their *Look Back in Anger* moment:[6] infuriated by the reaction of the critical establishment, *Three Kingdoms* seemed to cement online criticism's sense of what it was for, how it could operate, and why it was necessary. And, unlike the landscape during Katie Mitchell's production of *Attempts on Her Life*, online criticism now had an infrastructure, a readership and reach. It could sell-out performances of a show that had been panned by the mainstream. The voices of those who disagreed with the mainstream assessment were now part of the ecology.

What was crucial about the experience of *Three Kingdoms* was the way in which it catapulted independent critics to the forefront of the debate; not only in the eyes of their readers, but also in the eyes of theatres. As Duška Radosavljević puts it in the conclusion of her section on *Three Kingdoms* in *Theatre-Making*:

[T]he most important outcome of the controversy around Three Kingdoms' reception [. . .] was the way in which the blogosphere managed to outweigh the mainstream press in the depth of insight and its intellectual inquiry.

Radosavljević 2013: 118

That *Three Kingdoms* represented a paradigm shift is now a commonplace – it is understood that online reviews and Twitter feedback can reverse poor reviews in the mainstream press. Theatres like the Royal Court, under Vicky Featherstone, and the Almeida under Rupert Goold's artistic directorship, can stage plays with non-mainstream appeal and those plays will *find their audience*. Shows like the Almeida's 2014 production of *Mr Burns* sold well off the back of an enthusiastic online reception written by a generation of critics and theatregoers with an appreciation not only of text, but also design and dramaturgy.

Conclusion

At the same time, the mainstream print media itself is changing. In July 2013, the *Independent on Sunday* became the first newspaper to sack all its critics, including Kate Bassett, their theatre critic. The paper now runs an extract from its sister paper's review, supplemented by a few comments copied and pasted from Twitter. Aleks Sierz and Michael Coveney, nominally 'professional critics', are now both writing for online publications: Coveney at *WhatsOnStage* and Sierz for *The Arts Desk*. Similarly, when *The Times* fired Libby Purves from her job as their theatre critic in September 2013 – replacing her with Dominic Maxwell – she took her reviewing online with a theatre blog of her own. The same is also true of Mark Shenton, who, when fired by the *Sunday Express* in December 2013 on the disgraceful pretext that some personal images maliciously posted online by a third party could 'bring the company into disrepute' (Shenton 2013), kept his job blogging for *The Stage* and subsequently, with Terri Paddock, founded *MyTheatreMates.com* in early 2015.[7] On 1 September 2014, Charles Spencer of the Daily Telegraph announced that he was retiring (Singh 2014), leaving Michael Billington as the only 'Dead White Male' from 2007 still standing (Nicholas de Jongh and Benedict Nightingale having respectively been let-go and retired in the interim). In December 2014 the *Sunday Telegraph*'s theatre critic Tim Walker was sacked and not replaced.

At the same time (as of 2015), Natasha Tripney, the 'blogger' and co-founder of *Exeunt*, has been made joint chief critic of *The Stage*, Matt Trueman has a regular position at *WhatsOnStage* and frequently has articles printed on paper, while *Time Out* occupies an interesting (but paid) no-man's-land between print and online, regularly employing many of *Exeunt*'s best critics. Meanwhile, the age and gender diversity of British criticism feels improved, with Lyn Gardner now a de facto joint chief critic at *The Guardian*, Sarah Hemming at the *Financial Times* and Susannah Clapp at the *Observer*, as well as the younger Dominic Maxwell at *The Times*, Dominic Cavendish at the *Telegraph* and Henry Hitchings at the *Evening Standard*.

The 'blogosphere' and online writing-about-theatre continues to be a diverse field, encompassing everything from Canada-based Holger Syme's eloquent reviews and discussions of British and German stagings of classics, or Dan Rebellato's forensic reviews of London theatre through to Meg Vaughan's sense-led impressionism and technological experimentation, by way of everything from Maddy Costa's 10,000-word interrogations of Chris Goode and Company to the thoughtful, polished, often innovative prose of Catherine Love, Stewart Pringle, and Tim Bano.

What seems most vital about the years in this survey is, first, the depth and quality that writing-about-theatre has gained with the addition of online to the coverage of theatre, and, secondly, the massive expansion in available understandings, plurality of viewpoints and coverage of a far greater range of work that has been achieved. Moreover, from the vantage point of 2015, it seems clear that 'the blogosphere' effected real change in the overall landscape of British theatre criticism.

In the midst of the ongoing post-2008 economy, with the newspaper industry in decline and arts funding continuing to suffer successive cuts, it is impossible to predict what the future of the theatre criticism will look like. What the past two decades do demonstrate, however, is that while theatre in its many forms continues to exercise a fascination and a hold over the imaginations of its audiences, it seems likely that people will continue to write about it, read about it, and that the art of criticism will continue to grow, be refined, re-defined, and argued over. What it won't do, it seems, is fade away or die out.

Notes

1. 'I have never seen a Tempest that has been quite such fun or moved me quite so much' (Gardner 2000).

2. The punk fanzine Sideburns once famously featured a front cover picturing three guitar chord diagrams, with the legend: 'this is a chord, this is another, this is a third. Now form a band'.

3. Throughout the chapter, I have used the online convention '*[word]*' to denote emphasis. (The convention originally deriving from MSWord, which (used to?) use asterisks as a keyboard shortcut for bold.)

4. Ian Shuttleworth, for example, wrote in his *Prompt Corner* column for *Theatre Record* two years earlier: 'The number-ones have been around now for a fair old time. In his recent public lecture on the history of *Theatre Record*, my esteemed colleague and predecessor Ian Herbert pointed out that our very first issue in 1981 contained reviews by Michael Billington, Michael Coveney, Nicholas de Jongh, Sheridan Morley and Benedict Nightingale. While Michael B. is the only one still writing for the same publication, the point stands: room is simply not being made for the next generation to come through, in a way that did happen more often for our predecessors.' http://www.compulink.co.uk/~shutters/reviews/05141.htm (accessed 31 August 2014).

5. Megan Vaughan's review perhaps best conveys a snapshot sense of the play and production: 'So there were these two detectives, Iggy and Beardy, and they were investigating the murder of a woman whose head was covered in jizz then sawn off and dumped in the Thames. They followed this porn/sex slavery ring to Germany and then Estonia but none of that really matters. What matters is ALL THE STUFF THAT WAS GOING ON. They say that you shouldn't really notice a show's direction but Three Kingdoms was directed to fuck ... I'm writing this in a coffee shop near Victoria Station right now and when I pay my bill I'm going to flash the waitress then hurl the empty tea pot right through the fucking window. LASST UNS GEHEN UND TATSÄCHLICH LEBEN MEIE FUCKING ELU' (Vaughan 2012).

6. Matt Trueman's review in particular echoes Tynan's famous *Observer* review: 'About halfway through the first half of Three Kingdoms on Tuesday night, probably an hour and fifteen minutes in or so, I scrawled the following in my notebook: "Stop everything. Storm the National Theatre. Tear down the Donmar Warehouse. Torch the Royal Court. Redact the entire history of the RSC and fetch me Trevor Nunn's head on a plate". In retrospect, this was probably an overreaction born in the heat of the moment ... Let's blame the breathlessness and the dizziness; the disbelief and the sheer fucking thrill. I was putty. I was windswept. I was in love' (Trueman 2012).

7. On 30 April 2015, *The Stage* posted a searching article by Megan Vaughan critiquing the MyTheatreMates concept: 'My Theatre Mates syndicates

content posted independently, and promises nothing but the vague possibility of additional web traffic that might lead to that Holy Grail: "supplemental revenue"[...] Exactly how are bloggers chosen for the site? What criteria are they using? Who gets to decide which opinion matters? Turns out My Theatre Mates is just as in thrall to the system (*anarchy face*) as any mainstream publication. All syndicate 'Mates' must "provide three recognised theatre PRs or publicists as referees" [...] This is not a readership finding its own niches within a democratic critical conversation. This isn't even the "authority" that Mark has been searching for this whole time' (Vaughan 2015).

Works cited

Associated Press (2012) 'Number of active users at Facebook over the years', Yahoo Finance, 23 October, http://finance.yahoo.com/news/number-active-users-facebook-over-years-214600186--finance.html (accessed 19 June 2015).

Billington, Michael (2007); 'Who needs reviews?', *The Guardian*, 17 September, http://www.theguardian.com/stage/theatreblog/2007/sep/17/whoneedsreviews (accessed 30 August 2014).

Bungey, John (2010) 'Luvvie Power List', *The Times*, 15 December, http://www.thetimes.co.uk/tto/arts/stage/theatre/article2844309.ece (accessed 30 August 2014).

Caines, Michael (2007) Why does Edward Albee hate directors? *The Guardian*, 02 March, http://www.theguardian.com/stage/theatreblog/2007/mar/02/whydoesedwardalbeehatedir (accessed 30 August 2014).

Costa, Maddy (2012) 'Three Kingdoms', The *Guardian*, 16 May, http://www.theguardian.com/stage/theatreblog/2012/may/16/three-kingdoms-shapebritish-theatre-or-flop (accessed 30 August 2014).

Croggan, Alison (2007) 'The Playwright as King', 03 March, http://theatrenotes.blogspot.co.uk/2007/03/playwright-as-king.html (accessed 30 August 2014).

Gaither, Chris & Chmielewski, Dawn C (2006), 'Fears of Dot-Com Crash, Version 2.0', *L.A. Times*, 16 July, http://articles.latimes.com/2006/jul/16/business/fi-overheat16 (accessed 19 June 2015).

Gardner, Lyn (2000) 'All the flat's a stage', *The Guardian*, 8 August, http://www.theguardian.com/culture/2000/aug/08/artsfeatures.edinburghfestival2000 (accessed 30 August 2014).

Gardner, Lyn (2007) 'Blogging saved critics from extinction', *Guardian Blog*, 18 September, http://www.theguardian.com/stage/theatreblog/2007/sep/18/bloggingsavedcritics (accessed 30 August 2014).

Goode, Chris (2007) 'What's it all about, Albee?', 04 March, http://beescope. blogspot.co.uk/2007/03/whatsit-all-about-albee.html (accessed 5 September 2014).

Haydon, Andrew (2012a); 'Three Kingdoms – Lyric Hammersmith', http://postcardsgods.blogspot.co.uk/2012/05/three-kingdoms-lyric-hammersmith.html (accessed 31August 2014).

Haydon, Andrew (2012b) 'Three Kingdoms and Misogyny' http:// postcardsgods.blogspot.co.uk/2012/05/three-kingdoms-and-misogyny. html (accessed 31 August 2014).

Hytner, Nicholas (2007) 'What I really think about theatre critics', *Observer*, 3 June, http://www.theguardian.com/stage/theatreblog/2007/jun/03/ whatireallythinkaboutthea (accessed 31 August 2014).

Lathan, Peter (2014): 'How it all began', 26 July 2007/14, http://www. britishtheatreguide.info/features/how-it-all-began-102 (accessed 30 August 2014).

Paddock, Terri (2014) Unpublished interview with the author, recorded 28 July.

Radosavljević, Duška (2013) *Theatre-Making: Interplay Between Text and Performance in the 21st Century*, London: Palgrave (Routledge, 2013).

Shenton, Mark (2013) 'Another critical scalp, and this time it's mine!' *The Stage*, 05 December, http://www.thestage.co.uk/opinion/shenton/2013/12/ another-critical-scalp-time-mine/ (accessed 1 September 2014).

Shuttleworth, Ian (2005) 'Prompt Corner 05/2005 – Mercury Fur', http:// www.compulink.co.uk/~shutters/reviews/05141.htm (accessed 31 August 2014).

Shuttleworth, Ian (2007) 'Prompt Corner 10/2007 – A Matter Of Life And Death / the 'dead white males' brouhaha', http://www.cix.co.uk/shutters/ reviews/07123.htm (accessed 31 August 2014).

Shuttleworth, 'Who am I?', http://www.cix.co.uk/~shutters/welcome.htm (accessed 30 August 2014).

Singh, Anita (2014) 'Charles Spencer to retire as Daily Telegraph theatre critic', *Daily Telegraph*, 01 September, http://www.telegraph.co.uk/culture/ theatre/theatre-news/11066382/Charles-Spencer-to-retire-asDaily-Telegraph-theatre-critic.html (accessed 1 September 2014).

Tripney, Natasha (2007) 'Blogs and reviews should be best friends', *Guardian Theatre Blog*, 20 September, http://www.theguardian.com/stage/theatreblog/ 2007/sep/20/blogsandreviewsshouldbebe (accessed 30 August 2014).

Tripney, Natasha, Yates, Daniel B., Damian, Diana, Parry-Davies, Ella (2012) 'Hardcore critical girl-on-girl action', *Exeunt*, http://exeuntmagazine.com/ features/critical-girl-on-girl-action/ (accessed 31August 2014).

Trueman, Matt (2012) Review: Three Kingdoms, Lyric Hammersmith, http:// matttrueman.co.uk/2012/05/review-three-kingdoms-lyric-hammersmith. html (accessed 31 August 2014).

Vaughan, Megan (2012) 'An incitement to smash some fucking shit up', 17 May, http://synonymsforchurlish.tumblr.com/post/23221501522/an-incitement-to-smash-somefucking-shit-up (accessed 31 August 2014).

Vaughan, Megan (2015) 'The long tail of theatre criticism', *The Stage*, 30 April, https://www.thestage.co.uk/opinion/2015/megan-vaughan-long-tail-theatre-criticism/ (accessed 5 June 2015).

West End Whingers (2006) 'Resurrection Blues: well, it made us cross', 8 March, http://westendwhingers.wordpress.com/2006/03/08/resurrection-blues-well-it-made-us-cross/ (accessed 30 August 2014).

West End Whingers (2009) 'Death and the King's Horsemen', http://westendwhingers.wordpress.com/2009/04/08/review-death-and-the-kings-horsemannational-theatre/ (accessed 30 August 2014).

West End Whingers (2008) 'Fram at the National Theatre', http://westendwhingers.wordpress.com/2008/04/17/review-fram-at-the-national-theatre/ (accessed 30 August 2014).

West End Whingers (2010) 'Love Never Dies', https://westendwhingers.wordpress.com/2010/03/02/review-love-never-dies-adelphi-theatre/ (accessed 30 August 2014).

Wilkinson, Chris (2008) 'Reviewing audiences', *Guardian Theatre Blog*, 10/04/08, http://www.theguardian.com/stage/theatreblog/2008/apr/10/noisesoffreviewingaudiences (accessed 30 August 2014).

Blogs

Bye, Daniel: http://www.pessimismofintellectoptimismofwill.blogspot.co.uk/.
Damian, Diana: http://dianadamian.com/.
Ferguson, Alex: http://unknownpersonsunknown.blogspot.co.uk/.
Field, Andy: http://thearcadesproject.blogspot.co.uk/.
Perkovic, Jana: http://guerrillasemiotics.com/.
Purves, Libby: http://theatrecat.com/.
Trueman, Matt – Carousel of Fantasies now replaced by: http://matttrueman.co.uk/ (accessed 31 August 2014).

Websites

http://www.cix.co.uk/~shutters/welcome.htm (accessed 30 August 2014).
http://en.wikipedia.org/wiki/Sniffin'_Glue (accessed 19 June 2015).

PART II
CRITICS' VOICES

CHAPTER 9
DO THEY MEAN ME? A SURVEY OF FICTIONAL THEATRE CRITICS
Mark Fisher

One of the most memorable sequences in *Waiting for Godot* (1956) comes in act two as the two tramps Vladimir and Estragon are losing patience with each other. They trade a series of insults that escalate in intensity. Vladimir kicks off with 'Moron!' and Estragon counters with 'Vermin!' It proceeds in the same fashion until Estragon comes up with the insult to end all insults: 'Crritic!' (1979: 75). In performance, it always gets a laugh – and for two reasons. The first is simply that it is a well-crafted joke; the second is that it expresses solidarity with the actors. By laughing at their joke, we become complicit. Audience and actor bond against a common foe. When exposed by laughter in this way, the critic looks like the one sober guest at a drunken party, the boring person trying to be rational while everyone else lets their hair down.

But in other circumstances, audiences have little reason to be hostile to critics. On the contrary, many will have taken the advice of the critics in buying tickets in the first place. Newspapers and websites continue to carry reviews because readers continue to be interested in what they have to say. Yet the respect audiences have for critics is conditional and begrudging. Scan down the comments beneath pretty much any online newspaper article about criticism and you'll read considerable vitriol aimed at them. The assumption is that critics are fickle, weak-minded opportunists.

How pervasive is this view? The aim of this chapter is to answer that question by considering the way theatre critics have been represented in plays, films, novels, television and even video games. My sample is mainly from twentieth and twenty-first century Britain and North America, and it rests on the assumption that the thought processes behind the creation of a fictional character reflect attitudes in the culture at large. As a practising theatre critic, I am likely to be more than averagely sensitive to misrepresentation. Consequently, this is a subjective and partial survey, which makes no claim to academic rigour. It identifies some common characteristics and considers how close they are to my own experience and what they tell us about popular conceptions and misconceptions of the job.

My contention is that underscoring the majority of fictional representations, including some of the most sophisticated, is the erroneous belief that the critic's profession and the critic's personality are one and the same. The characteristics that people associate with a negative review are typically the characteristics of the fictional critic. High-handed, judgemental and humourless in print, the fictional critic has the same qualities in life, and is most likely friendless, malicious and psychologically damaged to boot. This is understandably the case when the critic is the butt of the joke (it's funny to see pomposity pricked), but less so when the same characterization appears in a more serious form. Whether presented as a Lothario or a drunk (two common tropes discussed in detail below), the critic is assumed to be at best emotionally flawed, at worst sociopathic. Their reviews are not seen as an honest attempt to engage in the theatrical event, as I believe them to be, but as an expression of a warped personality, a way of exacting revenge or yielding power. The image persists when, perhaps acting out some unconscious desire, the artist kills off the fictional critic. Only when fictional critics are shown to be theatre lovers, which in my real-life experience is most commonly the case, do they take on a personality that is not defined by their profession. Let's look at each of these categories in turn.

Critic by profession, critic by sensibility

In October 2014, Ben Brantley, lead theatre critic on *The New York Times*, had the tricky task of reviewing a show featuring multiple references to a character called Ben Brantley, lead theatre critic on *The*

New York Times. The updated revival of Terrence McNally's backstage comedy *It's Only a Play* had just opened on Broadway, its action pivoting on how the critics, including Brantley, would react to the first night of *The Golden Egg*, a play within a play. Brantley described his fictional incarnation as 'self-important' and 'vitriolic' (2014), attributes we will see repeatedly in this survey. He gamely played along by at first denying, then admitting to, the accuracy of the portrayal. More telling for our purposes was his subsequent observation that when the play was staged in 1986, the same character had gone by the name of his predecessor, Frank Rich. He speculated that a future revival would have to feature the name of his successor, whoever he or she may be. 'I still find it hard to take the references too personally,' wrote Brantley with justification. What this suggests is that people find the symbolic image of a theatre critic – one who, according to Brantley, was 'described in terms that are mostly unprintable here' (2014) – more potent than the truth about any individual journalist. In the public imagination, critics are interchangeable. They are regarded as the same, even though nobody could deny Rich and Brantley were different people.

The less sophisticated the portrayal, the more likely the critic is to have an intense dislike of the theatre and to carry their animus into real life. They will be proud, arrogant, callous and negatively critical of everything around them. When you reach level six of the videogame *Psychonauts (2005)*, you get to confront Jasper, the resident critic in Gloria's Theatre. Baring his many teeth, this purple-headed amphibian sitting in a theatre box promises to unleash 'the full destructive force of an angry critic' on the stage. He's a crude caricature, but he could be a descendent of John Hannigan, the theatre critic of the *San Francisco Dispatch* in *Mr Monk and the Critic* (2009), an episode of *Monk*, the light-hearted American TV detective series. In this one, Adrian Monk accompanies his assistant Natalie Teeger to the theatre where her teenage daughter is performing in a community show. As they take their seats, they spot Hannigan settling down in a box. Played by Dylan Baker, with a stately air and a patronizing drawl, this critic is high-handed, aloof and arrogant. Inevitably, he gives a damning review of Natalie's daughter ('had me begging for less') and when she confronts him at his desk in the newspaper office, he is rude and dismissive. Tellingly, his downfall is brought about by arrogance. Stung by such an inaccurate review, Natalie successfully proves Hannigan wasn't there. In truth, he had sneaked out of the theatre to murder his lover in a nearby hotel. The preposterous twist matches the comic tone of the show, but what persists is the idea of the critic-murderer, killing women and reputations with equal callousness.

Moving into more subtle territory, Addison DeWitt in *All About Eve* (1950) projects an image of the suave gentleman about town. He smokes a filter cigarette, invariably wears a suit and carries himself with an urbane confidence. On the surface, he is tolerated, even befriended, by the theatrical circles he mixes with, yet he is variously referred to as a 'venomous fishwife' and a 'professional manure slinger'. He is a man too powerful to shun and too slippery to trust. The best insight into his personality, however, is his own. Confronting the fraudulent Eve Harrington, an apparently meek actor who seems to have landed a lucky break, he says: 'You're an improbable person, Eve, and so am I; we have that in common – also a contempt for humanity, an inability to love and be loved, insatiable ambition and talent. We deserve each other.' DeWitt is a credible creation – you can imagine him writing witty, polished, even authoritative reviews – but once again, he is a sociopath, someone drawn to the job because of his inadequacy as a human being.

In that, he has much in common with Sheridan Whiteside in *The Man Who Came to Dinner* (1942). This 'first man of American letters' slips on the ice on his way to dinner and is compelled by his injury to spend Christmas in a family home in small-town Mesalia, Ohio. Annexing the first floor without waiting for permission, he is rude, patronizing, demanding, bossy, manipulative and elitist – charming to his cosmopolitan friends, arrogant towards everyone else. His secretary, played by Bette Davis, calls him a 'selfish, petty egomaniac'. Based on the 1939 play by Moss Hart and George S. Kaufman, the film was inspired by the critic and broadcaster Alexander Woollcott who had behaved in a similarly domineering manner on an unexpected visit to Hart's house. The foundation in real life makes Whiteside a horribly credible character, even if the portrayal reinforces the notion of the critic as pompous misfit, someone whose personality equates with their profession.

The critic as the butt of the joke

Such characterizations may be extreme, but real-life critics have their foibles too. In my experience, we tend to be self-reliant lone wolves, obsessive enthusiasts for the form, with a propensity to over-analyse (how else to explain this chapter?). We're a peculiar lot and certainly not beyond parody. That's the appeal of *The Regard of Flight* (1983), an Off-Broadway meta-theatrical comedy, in which clown Bill Irwin wakes up on stage and finds himself in a 'new theatre' performance. He is interrupted by a theatre critic played by Michael O'Connor, an earnest young man in a suit, bow tie and glasses. With notepad in hand, he leaps up from the audience to question Irwin's terminology with the air of a pedantic professor. From time to time, we see shots of him furiously taking notes, notepad held myopically close to his face, expression of serious intensity – one comically inappropriate for the chaotic scene on stage. The joke is that the critic is capable of pursuing only his own intellectual ends, imposing his own arid vision while missing the true nature of the show. He symbolizes dry intellect, the opposite of the spontaneity that the audience craves. For comic purposes, it's a caricature that works and, yes, it's funny.

It's not only critics who can't afford to be po-faced while watching Richard Brinsley Sheridan's *The Critic* (1779). Despite the play's title, few of the characters come out with any credit in this satire of an eighteenth-century theatrical profession beset with puffery, pomposity and opportunism. Such is the conceit of playwright Sir Fretful Plagiary and the ludicrousness of the tragedy presented in rehearsal by Mr Puff that, if anything, the two critics, Mr Dangle and Mr Sneer, end up the least scathed. Dangle is hypocritical in the opinions he shares and the friendships he keeps, but he thrives on the theatrical life and is at least genuine in that. You don't imagine Moon and Birdboot, the two critics in Tom Stoppard's *The Real Inspector Hound* (1968), having much of a life beyond the theatre either. One is forever fretting about his status as a second-string critic; the other socializes with pretty young actors and admits to vainly taking pictures of his own reviews pasted outside a theatre. Stoppard, who worked briefly as a critic for *Scene* magazine (1962–3), presents Moon and Birdboot as bumbling, self-absorbed and perhaps a little pathetic. He also gives a pretty accurate parody of critical purple prose, as Moon and Birdboot sing the praises of a shoddy whodunnit as if it were a life-changing experience.

In this, Stoppard counters the popular expectation for critics to be destructive by presenting the two men as gushingly over-the-top. Being too generous, I would argue, is just as common a flaw among real critics as the opposite. The rigours of doing the job mean the people who stick with it are those who are predisposed to liking theatre, which leads to a default position of positivity. As The *Guardian* critic Lyn Gardner told Kalina Stefanova (2000: 47): 'Another weakness is that we overpraise enormously. Sometimes we are cheer-leaders. You look at the *London Theatre Record* and you read things like "Brilliant!", "Marvellous!" when it actually was pretty average.' Moon and Birdboot are almost alone among fictional critics in that, for Stoppard's joke to work, we have to accept they are not critical enough.

The critic as Lothario

If gender imbalance is a problem among real theatre critics, it is doubly so among their fictional counterparts. Fictional theatre criticism is a male-dominated profession and, for some reason, the few female fictional critics that do exist tend to have a particularly improbable relationship with their job. Keira Cochrane in *The Reviewers* (2014), a musical by Elizabeth Charlesworth and Adam Holland Wells, is an ex-actor so damaged by a bad review that she sets herself up as a critic to inflict bad reviews on everyone else. Daisy Merrick in Laura Lee Guhrke's novel *With Seduction in Mind* (2009) writes her first and only review after she makes a speculative call on a newspaper proprietor on a day the regular critic happens to be ill. In *Birdman* (2014), the *New York Times* critic Tabitha Dickinson claims she's going to pan Riggan Thomson's play before she's even seen it simply because she regards him as a Hollywood outsider on a Broadway ego trip. Perhaps it's just coincidence that these unlikely scenarios all concern women. For the male fictional critic, however, it's a different story. Here, there is a recurring connection between professional power and sexual attractiveness.

For the male fictional critic, sex with actors is a big temptation. In the real world, this could be explained by socializing in the same space, but in the fictional world, it is also about an abuse of male power. In Fay Weldon's novel *Worst Fears* (1996), a widow gradually discovers the promiscuity of her newly deceased husband, Ned Ludd, a critic and Ibsen scholar. Most damning is the revelation that he pulled strings to get a girlfriend a part in a production of *A Doll's House* in which his wife was already starring. According to one character, women would lie down in front of him: 'Anything for a good review' (1996: 160). Although he adds that Ludd didn't necessarily give a good review in return, the image remains of a head-strong critic willing to abuse his position of power for his own carnal ends.

That's not a million miles from Oliver Latham, one of the cast of characters under suspicion in P. D. James's *Unnatural Causes* (1967), a murder mystery involving a mutilated corpse and a sleepy Suffolk community. Fitting into the mould of theatre critic as sociopath, he drives his Jaguar fast and antisocially, has a 'high arrogant voice' (2002: 205) and 'suffers from self-disgust' (2002: 86). Being 'wealthy, handsome [and] urbane,' (2002: 32) he fits the model of the mid twentieth-century London gentleman critic, dining at the Ivy and attending theatrical parties. It is presumably these qualities rather than his selfishness and envy that account for his success with the opposite sex: he was sleeping with an actor at the time of the murder.

Also willing to sacrifice his impartiality in return for sex was the late Virgile de la Pagerie, aka Delap, in the Dean Fuller novel *Death of a Critic* (1996). Writing for the weekly *La Revue Endimanché,* he was 'probably the most disliked as well as the most influential and widely read critic in Paris' (1996: 12) and being 'universally disliked' (1996: 121), provided many people with a motive for his murder. He is described as an 'intellectual bully' (1996: 40), a critic who would whimsically destroy popular shows and champion esoteric obscurities.

Like so many of our fictional critics, he suffered from the 'sin of hubris' (1996: 114) and managed to keep secret his need for an asthma inhaler, lest anyone would think him imperfect. Such was his conceit that he claimed the theatrical success of his former fiancée, Angélique Églantine, was due in part to the 'discerning eye of the critic' (1996: 139) and appears to have been unabashed about giving her rave reviews in print. As soon as they split up, he gave her a slating: 'Alas there is nothing there, after all ... She is no actress' (1996: 142).

Sex is also a driving force in Conor McPherson's play *St Nicholas* (1977), a monologue about a hard-drinking critic, full of self-hatred, who makes a rash decision to fly to London, leaving his family behind in Dublin, in the hope of running into Helen, an actor he has fallen for after seeing her in *Salome* at the Abbey Theatre. After drunkenly intruding on the director's digs (and failing to endear himself to Helen), the critic wanders the streets aimlessly and falls asleep in a park. When he awakes, he is recruited by a modern-day vampire and the play takes a supernatural turn. It sounds fanciful, but McPherson has a serious observation to make about the parallel between critic and vampire. He sees them as vain creatures who work at night, feed on the life of others, instil fear and instruct people about how to live their lives without having any conscience or scruples of their own.

In the afterword to *Conor McPherson Plays: One*, the playwright writes of his fears about creating a cartoon villain: 'Were we having a cheap jibe at an easy target, or were we exploring the nature of reason and responsibility?' (2011: 191). It's a remark that suggests he understood the risk of creating the kind of two-dimensional character so prevalent in the world of fictional criticism. A character who was a critic by sensibility as well as by profession would, indeed, be an 'easy target'. As it turned out, the real critics warmly accepted his fictional critic, as played by Brian Cox at The Bush in 1997. As Michael Billington observed in *The Guardian*: 'I don't know of any critic who has actually destroyed his life through his fixation with an actress; but it would be nice to think it could happen' (1997). Anecdotally, I've known more critics to strike up romantic relationships with admin staff (reader, I married the director's assistant) but, of course, sex with actors is well within the realms of possibility. Even so, I'd argue that the frequency with which it happens to fictional critics is actually an expression of the prejudice that they are corrupt, narcissistic and controlling.

The critic as drunk

St Nicholas demonstrates that, as well as sex, one of the fictional critic's great temptations is drink. Like everyone in show business, critics work anti-social hours in sociable places. In an atmosphere of post-show euphoria, the opportunities and inducements to drink are many. In *Citizen Kane* (1941), Joseph Cotten's Jedediah Leland falls into a drunken stupor on top of his typewriter before completing his over-night review, presumably because having to tell the truth about the dreadful performance of Susan, the young wife of his employer Charles Foster Kane, is too much of a strain. His sacking makes him a rare example of a fictional critic who suffers not for being too critical but for being too honest.

For the authentic word on hard-drinking theatre critics, you can do no better than Charles Spencer. This is the real life *Daily Telegraph* reviewer who, the day before the launch of his third novel, *Under the Influence* (2000), was discovered unconscious beneath a rhododendron in a neighbour's garden, the culmination of what he referred to as a 'three-day bender' (2001). In the list of educational establishments on his online biography, he included a well-known rehab clinic. Consequently, Will Benson, the fictional hero of Spencer's three crime thrillers, seems incapable of going more than a couple of hours' work at *Theatre World* without a drink. This critic is overweight, prone to intemperate outbursts and a little sleazy (in the second book, *Full Personal Service* (1996), he ends up writing pornographic stories for men's magazines). The alcohol doesn't stop him functioning, although, as with McPherson's critic, it does seem to be a symptom of some hidden self-loathing and need for psychological escape. Spencer has described Benson as 'an awful warning' to himself (2001). As with the temptation of sex with actors, the idea that fictional critics should drink a lot could be explained by opportunity (one I've never been known to turn down), but it also reinforces the prejudice that the typical critic suffers from some dark emotional damage that only alcohol can repress.

The critic as corpse

Perhaps it's my paranoia, but there does seem to be a death wish against fictional critics. Not every attack ends in death, but it's usually the intention. In Christopher Bram's *Lives of the Circus Animals* (2003), critic Kenneth Prager is lucky to survive when he is shot in the arm by the mother of an aggrieved playwright. By the end of *The Real Inspector Hound*, three critics have been shot. As we have seen, Ned Ludd is dead before the start of Weldon's *Worst Fears* and Virgile de la Pagerie is murdered in the stalls at the start of Fuller's *Death of a Critic*. Likewise, Jonathan McCarthy is found dead in his study clutching a copy of *Romeo and Juliet* in *The West End Horror* (1976), a Sherlock Holmes story written by Nicholas Meyer, and in Guhrke's *With Seduction in Mind*, nineteenth-century playwright Sebastian Grant fantasizes about 'the pleasurable notion of shooting critics' (2009: 31).

If artists do have a death-wish for critics, then the supreme example is *Theatre of Blood* (1973). This is the movie in which Edward Lionheart, an old-school Shakespearean actor, presumed dead, returns to enact revenge on the members of the Critics' Circle who passed him over at their annual awards. He murders each of them in turn in a manner inspired by the Shakespeare plays in his final season. The first dies from multiple stab wounds, à la *Julius Caesar*; the second has his head cut off, à la *Troilus and Cressida*; and so on. We get the critic as Lothario, lured away by the promise of sex and bumped off with a twist on *The Merchant of Venice*; and the critic as drunk, drowned in a vat of wine like Clarence in *Richard III*. In terms of characterization, they have something in common with Moon and Birdboot in *The Real Inspector Hound*: they have their foibles and their weaknesses, they're a tad eccentric and caught up in their own little world, but they are not defined by their jobs. Only the psychopathic Lionheart equates the critics' barbed comments in print with a personality flaw. All the same, his eagerness to see them dead seems to express a more general cultural anxiety.

The critic as theatre lover

The thriller plots of Spencer's trilogy may be fanciful but, as you'd expect from this writer, he makes sure the details of Will Benson's life are credible. Whereas other fictional critics are at best indifferent, at worst pleased by the misery their writing causes, Benson gives a more nuanced account of the push–pull emotions stirred up by having to file a negative review. Towards the start of *I Nearly Died* (1994), the first in the series, the critic reads over a piece he has written about a disastrous *Romeo and Juliet*. He admits to an 'ignoble feeling of excitement' at seeing the review in print, knowing he has done a 'demolition job' that he hopes will be entertaining. That's before he realizes how spiteful he comes across: 'Written in rage, but read in tranquillity, it was bad tempered rather than amusing, patronizing rather than wittily detached' (1994: 22). He does not change his opinion of the show, but he does become dissatisfied with his own response to it. Such self-doubts are what make him a rounded character – as is the life he leads beyond writing reviews.

Despite popular misconceptions, I have never met a theatre critic who did not like the theatre. This is something the most perceptive fictional representations appreciate. Take Yedidyah, the New York theatre critic in the fictional *Morning Post* in Elie Wiesel's *The Sonderberg Case* (2010). He loves the stage because, 'it's an experience that summons all the senses of the body and engages it completely: you look at a performance, you listen to it, you absorb it' (2010: 17). When his college professor suggests he should become a critic, he protests that he is not qualified, having never written a thing. 'You live and breathe theatre with all your heart and intellect. That's all that matters,' (2010: 51) comes the reply. It's a viewpoint that chimes with my own experience, but in fiction, it's relatively rare. You have to search hard for a character such as Mortimer Brewster in *Arsenic and Old Lace* (1944), whose personality is neither warped in some way nor defined by his profession as a critic. In Brewster's case, he is uncommonly well balanced and his job is just a job, not a psychological flaw.

The common factor uniting the characters in Bram's *Lives of the Circus Animals* is that they are obsessed with the theatre and continually let down by it. This is as true for the actor, the playwright and the PA as it is for Kenneth Prager, whose second-string position on the *New York Times* has earned him the soubriquet of the 'buzzard of Off-Broadway' (a play on the butcher-of-Broadway tag inherited by Frank Rich in the 1990s). It's not an accolade Prager warms to, as we discover in the novel's opening chapter in which this married father of one endures an uncomfortable second session with a psychiatrist. His relationship with his wife is strained, he seems to be depressed and his life has lost direction. Like Wiesel's Yedidyah and Spencer's Benson, Prager has not chosen his profession out of any predilection for cruelty, but out of genuine passion. 'I've always loved theatre,' he says. 'The immediacy of it. Real human presences' (2003: 3). He sees himself as an idealist agitating for better theatre. In psychological terms, the damage is in the opposite direction: the job has been taking its toll on him. He does not enjoy the power of being able to make or break a show, he feels uncomfortable competing for status with other critics and he avoids taking the subway for fear of bumping into aggrieved actors. His job is to criticize, but he hates to be hated. Like every critic-as-theatre-lover, he is one I more readily recognize than the destructive sociopaths elsewhere.

Critic by profession, critic by sensibility revisited

Although it is generally true that the least convincing portrayals of critics are those that confuse job description with personality, it is gloriously and defiantly not the case in Wilfrid Sheed's novel *The Critic* (1970) (first published in the USA as *Max Jamison*). Here is a vision of a writer whose compulsion to criticize dominates his private and professional lives in equal measure. For those of us doing the same job, it is a troublingly credible and wickedly astute portrait. Like Spencer and Stoppard, Sheed (1930–2011) wrote from experience. He worked as a reviewer and was familiar with the world of small-press publications and glamorous mass-circulation magazines that the fictional Max Jamison inhabits. Consequently, the details ring true of the critic's writing schedule, his relationships with editors, rivalries with colleagues and presence at New York first-night parties. Crucially, Sheed also knew how easy it is for critics to start applying the analytical tools of their trade to other aspects of their lives.

One of the jokes in this very funny and satirically stinging book is that Jamison never ceases to be a critic. He can't turn off his critical thinking even during his own stream-of-consciousness fantasies. No sooner has he drifted into a daydream than he finds himself picking it apart for implausible storylines and leaden dialogue. He repeatedly gives his own subconscious a stinker of a review. He subjects his wife, children, girlfriends and colleagues to the same level of scrutiny, alienating most of them in the process – or worse, turning them into mini-me critics themselves.

Sheed's vision stands out because he has a deeper understanding of what criticism involves in the first place. Jamison is not simply a parasitic vampire or a man with a grudge against humanity. He is not gratuitously destructive, although he can be witty in his expression and exacting in his judgements (his tragedy is that he becomes less so). He has high artistic standards and genuinely believes in them. In this, *The Critic* is one of the few works in this overview to take the idea of criticism seriously (even as it satirizes it) and allows for the possibility that a critic may be good or bad at their job, rather than just blindly malevolent.

As a human being, Jamison has many loathsome characteristics, narcissism, infidelity and vengefulness among them, but as a critic, he is formidably talented. Although arrogance is his undoing, it is partially justified. He does have a brilliant capacity for argument, it's just that, like any human quality taken to excess, it becomes overbearing. He finds himself estranged from his wife, distanced from his sons and bored by the students he seduces. Being a master of his trade cannot help him. As a result, his critical mind starts to short-circuit. In the end, he resolves his cognitive dissonance by settling into the sleepy life of an academic; his sanity saved but his talent neutered. Does he mean me? I really hope not.

Works cited

Beckett, Samuel (1979), *Waiting for Godot*, London: Faber and Faber.

Billington, Michael (1997), 'St. Nicholas', *The Guardian*, 25 February.

Bram, Christopher (2003), *Lives of the Circus Animals*, New York: HarperCollins.

Brantley, Ben (2014), 'Well, did what's-his-name like it?', *The New York Times*, 9 October, http://www.nytimes.com/2014/10/10/theater/matthew-broderick-nathan-lane-and-stockard-channing-in-its-only-a-play-on-broadway.html (accessed 24 October 2014).

Capra, Frank (1944), *Arsenic and Old Lace*, Warner Bros.

Charlesworth, Elizabeth and Holland Wells, Adam (2014), *The Reviewers*, unpublished, seen at Greenside Nicholson Square on the Edinburgh Festival Fringe.

Fuller, Dean (1996), *Death of a Critic*, New York: Little, Brown and Company.

Guhrke, Laura Lee (2009), *With Seduction in Mind*, New York: Avon Books.

Halvorson, Gary (1983), *The Regard of Flight*, PBS.

Hickox, Douglas (1973), *Theatre of Blood*, Harbor Productions.

Iñárritu, Alejandro González (2014), *Birdman*, Fox Searchlight.

James, P. D. (2002), *Unnatural Causes*, London: Faber and Faber.

Keighley, William (1942), *The Man Who Came to Dinner*, Warner Bros.

Levine, Jerry (2009), 'Mr Monk and the Critic' in *Monk*, Touchstone.

McNally, Terrence (1992), *It's Only a Play*, London: Penguin Books.

McPherson, Conor (2011), *Conor McPherson Plays: One*, London: Nick Hern Books.

Mankiewicz, Joseph L. (1950), *All About Eve*, Twentieth Century Fox.

Meyer, Nicholas (1976), *The West End Horror*, New York: E.P. Dutton & Co.

Schafer, Tim (2005), *Psychonauts*, THQ.

Sheed, Wilfrid (1973), *The Critic*, London: Weidenfeld & Nicholson.

Sheridan, Richard Brinsley (1779), *The Critic*.

Spencer, Charles (2001), 'I much prefer life now I'm sober, Charles Spencer', *Daily Telegraph*, 16 January.

Spencer, Charles (1994), *I Nearly Died*, London: Victor Gollancz.

Spencer, Charles (1996), *Full Personal Service*, London: Victor Gollancz.

Spencer, Charles (2002), *Under the Influence*, London: Allison and Busby.

Stefanova, Kalina (2000), *Who Keeps the Scores on the London Stages?*, Amsterdam: Harwood Academic Publishers.

Stoppard, Tom (1968), *The Real Inspector Hound*, London: Faber and Faber.

Weldon, Fay (1996), *Worst Fears*, London: HarperCollins.

Welles, Orson (1941), *Citizen Kane*, RKO Radio Pictures.

Wiesel, Elie (2010), *The Sonderberg Case*, trans. Catherine Temerson New York: Alfred A. Knopf. Published originally in France in 2008 as *Le Cas Sonderberg*, Editions Grasset & Fasquelle.

CHAPTER 10
BETWEEN JOURNALISM AND ART: THE LOCATION OF CRITICISM IN THE TWENTY-FIRST CENTURY
Mark Brown

'[I]t seems impossible to express what the practice of writing a commissioned piece to a deadline actually feels like', writes Tom Paulin, closing the introduction to his collection of criticism, *Writing to the Moment* (1996: xiv). He attempts to express it, nevertheless:

> The stress, the hurry, the excitement, the rapid research and background reading – if there's time – the hit-and-miss quality, furious checking, worry about mistakes – all that helterskelter wildness running with the sense of social connectedness and communication now – they're all part of the fun of this kind of writing. It begins with the search for an opening sentence, an invocation, a muttered *here goes*. Take a hazel rod, strip its bark and flex the lithe slippery sappiness – there you have the wand. Now wave it.

> Ibid

If there is a better description of the process of writing a short, critical review, I have not had the good fortune to read it. There is, in the breathlessness of its punctuation, an almost onomatopoeic evocation of the welter of thoughts and emotions that the critic must bring under control, and quickly, if she is to accomplish the task at hand. Some might say that there is, in Paulin's portrayal of the exhilarations and terrors of writing under pressure of time, a romanticization of the critic. Yet, at a time when the critic as craftsperson is being so widely dismissed,[1] it is both desirable and necessary to remind ourselves that, like any other artisan, the critic is, or at any rate *should* be, a person distinguished by her particular skill. Paulin's description of the process of writing a critical piece (be it journalistic or academic) to a deadline seems particularly appropriate to the work of arts and literary critics who write to short deadlines for newspapers, magazines, journals and professional online publications. Any serious critical writer should be happy to agree with Paulin's comparison of the author's pen (literal or metaphorical) with the magician's wand. To that I would only add that the critic's pen should also be 'a quill and a dagger'.[2] That is to say that if the critic must, like any writer, wield her pen as a wand, conjuring something from nothing and, she hopes, creating literary magic in the process, she also requires a quill, for style, nuance and high praise, and a dagger, for the sharp, incisive, carefully considered, yet boldly written expressions of disappointment, nausea and outrage that arts criticism should entail.

Criticism: chronicle of a death foretold

Rónán McDonald bemoans the seemingly inexorable decline of the professional arts reviewer in his 2008 book *The Death of the Critic*. As we will see below, he lays the blame for this at the feet of both academic and 'popular' criticism. However, to read people like Karen Fricker and Dan Rebellato,[3] both of whom contribute to both academic and 'popular' criticism, one might conclude the problem resides primarily in the attitudes of an older generation of critics in the printed press. In her article, entitled unambiguously '*The crisis in theatre criticism is critics saying there's a crisis*', Fricker points out, with considerable disdain, that leading critics in the London press, such as Mark Shenton of *The Stage* and Michael Billington of *The Guardian,* have gone public with opinions to the effect that there are 'currently "no jobs" for young critics' (Shenton) and that teaching theatre criticism in London universities has little purpose due to the diminishing number of jobs for critics in the print media (Billington). In Fricker's opinion, the problem here is a refusal to consider the quality theatre criticism that is being written away from the printed press, often in blogs, often by people who are unpaid; indeed, Fricker states boldly, 'I believe that quality criticism can happen for free' (2014). In an article, entitled simply 'Critical Thinking', Rebellato is equally irked by the likes of Shenton and Billington. He joins Fricker in acclaiming many of the online critics, writing that, 'the highest quality critical writing about theatre at the moment is on the blogs' (2014). Fricker also makes a plea for the historical and on-going importance of academic criticism. Rebellato asserts that the reduction in the space made available for individual theatre reviews in British newspapers over recent decades has reduced them almost to a position of inconsequentiality as compared with the longer reviews written by bloggers and academics. The newspapers and the press critics – or a number of the leading London figures, at least – stand accused.

Fricker and Rebellato are ·correct in the observation of the somewhat defeatist, even masochistic, opinions of certain leading theatre critics in the London press. However, raise one's eyes from the London theatrical village and take an international perspective, and one can see that the likes of Shenton and Billington are far from being the only people who are making the perceived diminution of the critical profession a regular topic of discussion. The International Association of Theatre Critics,[4] an organisation in which academic critics play an extremely prominent role,[5] holds regular symposia open to those engaged in both academic and 'popular' criticism. A major symposium held in Beijing in October 2014 was entitled 'A New World: The Profession of Criticism in the Internet Era'. The titles of a number of the papers presented at the symposium indicates that within the strongly academic IATC there is considerable anxiety about the role of online criticism. Titles included: 'Tweet this: We're not in charge anymore'; 'Can Anyone be a Critic in the Virtual World?'; and 'A Marginalization of Criticism in Consumer Society'.[6]

Looked at internationally, it seems clear that many established critics, both in academe and the popular press, are wallowing almost masochistically in such subjects as the remorseless rise of the internet, the decline of the printed page (particularly newspapers and magazines) and the much-vaunted 'death of the critic'. Many of us who are engaged in theatre criticism are bemused by the capacity of some of our colleagues to write about and discuss *ad nauseam* the potentially catastrophic impact of the internet on theatre criticism. Some of us are, thankfully, too much engaged in the practice of theatre criticism to spend so much time bewailing its supposed decline. The crisis of criticism in the traditional print media is undeniable. Those of us who write primarily for the popular press know the story; we live it every day. Every reduction in available column inches, every rejected review proposal, and every colleague who suddenly loses their position on a newspaper or magazine is a stark reminder that the press critic is an increasingly rare, insecurely employed and poorly remunerated creature. When would-be young critics ask us for career advice, we caution them to find another way of making their living. They must, we implore them, treat theatre criticism as a vocation, rather than a job, which they should pursue alongside properly remunerated employment. That is to say, by all means pursue criticism if you believe yourself to have a flare for and commitment to it, much as an artist pursues her art, but do not do so in the hope of wealth, or even a decent living. Pursue a reasonable and stable income elsewhere. In short, no intelligent theatre critic in the print media is blasé about the threats to the newspaper industry. However, contrary to the negativism of the likes of Shenton and Billington, this should not lead us to despair about the future of the critical profession.

Like Fricker and Rebellato, I am frustrated by the surfeit of discussion about the internet, the decline of print and the 'death of the critic'; albeit that my reasons are a little different from theirs. I do not, for example, share their apparently unqualified enthusiasm for bloggers; I am happy to champion a thoughtful online critic such as Andrew Haydon (who blogs for *The Guardian* among others), but I have concerns about the anti-professionalism and philistine pseudo-democracy contained within the idea that the internet's much-vaunted open access enables everyone to be a critic. I also do not share Fricker's seemingly blithe attitude to critics writing without payment. I may advise would-be young critics to try to make a living by other means, but I hope, on political and ethical grounds, for a future for professional criticism that is remunerative. The promotion of the idea of criticism as an unpaid 'hobby' is an open-door to hyper-exploitation on the part of unscrupulous publishers.

In fact, the primary reason for my frustration with the endless discussion of the 'death of criticism' is quite prosaic; namely, it is largely redundant. Journalists the world over feel themselves to be sailing on a river of ever faster flowing technological change. Some, exasperated by newspaper owners who have responded to the growth of the internet and falling newspaper sales, not by investing meaningfully in online strategies, but by cutting investment in journalists and journalism, have jumped ship and hauled themselves onto the banks. In my experience, theatre critics throughout the world, even some of those writing for prestigious titles, are among the most insecurely employed journalists. If my work in the IATC, particularly with young critics aged between 18 and 35, is indicative (and, given that IATC is the only truly representative body for theatre critics worldwide, I would suggest it probably is), it seems clear that many, probably most, critics working in the press worldwide do not make a living from criticism alone, are employed as critics on a freelance, often ad hoc, basis, and tend to draw their primary income from employment outside of criticism. Having worked with young critics from countries as diverse as South Korea, China, Iran, New Zealand, the United States, Canada, Georgia, Russia, Romania, Finland, Italy, Spain and the United Kingdom,[7] I have met very few who make a living from their earnings as critics. The primary sources of employment range from: working in the administration of a theatre company (a very common practice for young critics in the countries which belonged to the Warsaw Pact and the Soviet Union); to teaching in academe; commercial copy-writing; forms of journalism other than criticism; newspaper, magazine and book editing; online publishing; and, even, in two interesting cases, acting and professional singing.

With regard to their work in criticism in the press, critics are typically self-employed, isolated, barely represented by their trade unions (where they have them), and almost entirely lacking in influence or power over the direction of the publications for which they write. Consequently, while it might be interesting for academics to chart the forces and processes that have brought this situation about, it seems to me that an increasing number of critics, not least those still working primarily in journalistic criticism, consider the discussion to be circular and repetitive. The titles of the colloquia or articles may vary, but their subject – namely, the rise of the internet and the 'death of the critic' – remains the same. More importantly, this discussion seems to offer no solutions to the much-vaunted decline of criticism, but, rather, appears to continually reinforce the powerlessness of the newspaper critic. That is why I say that the endless speculation about theatre criticism in the age of a burgeoning internet is redundant. Not only do we critics have no power over the processes under discussion, but we, like everyone else, have no way of knowing how, if at all, the print will survive in any given society in 10, 20 or 30 years' time. Like everyone else, we have no way of knowing how publishers of newspapers and magazines will adapt and develop their various online strategies, and whether, be it via pay walls or, more likely, indirectly via advertising, readers will be persuaded to continue to pay for journalism. This being the case, there is little to be gained by the many hours presently being dedicated to speculation about the future of the press and, by logical extension, theatre criticism within it.

Those who enjoy such speculation will, no doubt, argue that the changes over the last decade or so in print and online theatre criticism (such as fewer, often shorter reviews in many newspapers, for example), the increase in unpaid criticism (usually by young writers), even on 'respected' titles, and the rise of 'citizen criticism'[8] (particularly on personal online blogs and websites given over to 'public reviews') have already altered the essential nature of theatre criticism. Consequently, one can almost hear their exhortations, we must examine and discuss the future changes to theatre criticism. However, the rise of the 'citizen critic', like the 'death of the [professional] critic', is much exaggerated. If twenty-first-century culture is characterized by the fragmentation of the audience (for example as a result of the massive diversification of broadcast and written media through the continuing growth of digital and internet technologies), those of us who are dedicated to a profound theatre (i.e. one which stands against populism and strives for an elevation of expression, be it in language and/or image) and intelligent criticism of it, should surely have more faith in our 'fragment' of the general readership than to accept the idea that it will happily desert the passionate, erudite and stylish professional critic for any Tom, Dick or Harriet with a laptop and an opinion. There is a world of difference between the notion of the fragmented audience, or readership, and the acceptance of the idea that the readership for professional theatre criticism is evaporating.

How do we define professional criticism in the twenty-first century? In an era when even some dedicated specialists pursue the craft without remuneration,[9] we can no longer define the professional critic as someone who is paid to write criticism. Rather, as alluded to above, professionalism in criticism today resides in a specialist dedication that marks the critic out as an artisan. If your neighbour was capable of fashioning a simple bird box out of wood, would you therefore assume that she was capable of crafting you a beautiful and robust dinner table? I suspect you would not. You would, rather, want a table built by one or more professionals. As I always say to students, when they ask that age-old question, 'isn't everyone a critic?': 'I can change a light bulb, but I do not assume that makes me a professional. If my home needs to be rewired, I call an electrician'. For the most part, the 'citizen critic' is an amateur, a mere dabbler, the critical equivalent of the person who can change a light bulb or fix a plug, but cannot and should not be considered a professional electrician.

The insistence upon professionalism in criticism is not merely self-interest on the part of established critics. It is put forward in the interests of the art of theatre and, therefore, of the general culture. Nor is it an insistence made only by critics themselves. Critics know from conversations with artists and audience members that many, if not most, of them believe strongly in the role of the professional critic. It is by better understanding the role of the critic and the nature of her craft, rather than speculating anxiously about the future of the printed page and the internet, that we best defend the cultural position of criticism. It is to such issues of practice, therefore, that I will turn in the remainder of this essay.

All change? The twenty-first-century critic

If, as I have suggested above, the rise of the 'citizen critic' (i.e. the amateur purveyor of online opinion) is exaggerated, is it not, nevertheless, true to say that structural changes within the mass media, driven mainly by the rise of the internet, have altered the nature of theatre criticism irrevocably? I would contend that it is not. The current period of change brings dangers to criticism (as outlined above) – that is undeniable. However, if I am correct in my faith that a discerning section of society continues to value professional criticism, and its role in, and often initiation of, a public conversation about works of theatre (just as a discerning section of the theatre-going public continues to value what one might term 'serious' theatre), then it follows that, despite the technological and structural developments, the critic's role actually changes very little. Indeed, talk of the technology-induced 'death of criticism' in the twenty-first century is comparable to the prophecies of the death of live theatre, as a consequence of the invention of the movie camera and the television, in the nineteenth and twentieth centuries. As Don Rubin, one of Canada's leading academic critics argues, technological changes do not rob our culture of its demand for professional criticism:

> Is [the internet and blogging] the future for theatre criticism? Certainly I don't know. What I can say with some certainty is that even if it is the future, I continue to have no doubt that there will always be a place – even there – for expertise, for experience and for people who have the ability to communicate effectively. These are the cornerstones of almost any field in contemporary knowledge-based societies.
>
> Rubin 2010

Of course, even if they agree on the continued importance of their profession, critics do not necessarily agree among themselves as to the nature of their role. In my set of aphorisms, 'Twenty-one Asides on Theatre Criticism', I try to sketch my own view of how a critic should consider and practice her or his craft. These aphorisms amount to a personal manifesto in which is embedded a hostility towards two closely related ideas. One is 'cultural relativism', the other is the notion of criticism as an 'art', rather than a literary craft.

Against cultural relativism: in defence of criticism

'Cultural relativism' in the so-called 'postmodern' era is a cultural theory which moves far beyond, and arguably greatly distorts, the important and legitimate concerns of the late-nineteenth/early-twentieth century anthropologist Franz Boas, whose 'relativism' sought to '[debunk] the prevailing beliefs that Western Civilization is superior to less complex societies' (Franz Boas staff page). Boas argued that the merits of non-Western cultures should be considered in relation to their own material and social development, rather than being measured against Western notions of 'progress'. By contrast, the postmodernists apply a 'principle', not of careful evaluation, but, effectively, of non-evaluation (in effect a belief that all manifestations of art, for example, are of relative and equivalent value), not *between* cultures, but *within* them. David Ashley summarizes the position of the postmodern cultural relativist well:

> [M]odern, overloaded individuals, desperately trying to maintain rootedness and integrity [...] are pushed to the point where there is little reason not to believe that all value-orientations are equally well-founded. Therefore, increasingly, choice becomes meaningless.
>
> quoted in Salberg et al.

Put crudely, cultural relativism, in its postmodern manifestation, leads to the conclusion that, as all 'value-orientations', including critical distinctions with regard to cultural importance and/or artistic quality, are now 'equally well-founded', i.e. redundant, the teaching of the soap opera *Coronation Street* on a university drama course is every bit as valid as the teaching of the plays of Shakespeare and Beckett.[10] In its disdain for evaluation, indeed for informed opinion, latter day cultural relativism impinges on theatre criticism, not only in terms of the argument, addressed above, that 'anyone can be a critic', but also in the faux radical, postmodern myth that there is something inherently 'democratic' in the idea that all art works and genres are of equal value. The denouncing as 'elitist' of anyone who dares to suggest, for example, that the plays of Caryl Churchill are inherently superior to those of John Godber, is an attack on the very role of the critic. It attempts to rob the critic of her right, indeed her *duty*, to compare, contrast, evaluate and *express an opinion*. The requirement to provide a well-informed and, crucially, stylishly written opinion is a key distinction between criticism, as a literary craft, and theatre, as an art form. A critic is obliged, by the very nature of her craft, to evaluate; criticism is, in that sense, functional. By contrast, any attempt to demand clearly expressed opinions in art runs contrary to the fundamental freedom of the artist. Art, unlike craft, should not be required to carry out a function. Criticism is, at its heart, an evaluative literary craft. Thus it is, or at least should be, distinguished from art.

Which is not to say that criticism in the twenty-first century always fulfils its evaluative function. In his provocatively entitled book *The Death of the Critic* (which is not, as the author rightly asserts, a work of celebratory 'grave dancing', 2008: vii), McDonald argues:

> [T]he public critic has been dismembered by two opposing forces: the tendency of academic criticism to become increasingly inward looking and non-evaluative, and the momentum for journalistic and popular criticism to become a much more democratic, dispersive affair, no longer left in the hands of the experts.
>
> 2008: ix

Unlike many, perhaps most, countries in eastern Europe (in which arts critics in the popular press are very often academics working in higher education institutions), Britain has a tradition of the exclusively journalistic arts critic.[11] One need only consider that the British Critics' Circle invites only critics in the popular media to be members; its exclusion of academic critics marks it out as unusual among the membership of the International Association of Theatre Critics, most of the national sections of which permit academics, and many of which are led by academic critics. In countries such as Romania and Russia, theatre criticism has, for many decades, been taught as a discipline within the same theatre academies where practitioners, such as directors, dramaturgs, actors and stage designers are trained. In such countries, criticism is, by very definition, an academic discipline. By contrast, in Britain, it is rarely, if ever, taught within conservatoires, such as the Royal Academy of Dramatic Art in London or the Royal Conservatoire of Scotland in Glasgow, where theatre practitioners are trained. It is rare that a critic writing in the British press has trained in criticism within a higher education institution; it is more likely that they read a major humanities subject, such as English Literature or History, at university. In Britain, an uncomfortable, some might say mutually suspicious, separation is maintained between journalistic and academic critics (even if some critics in the print media, such as myself, stray into academic teaching and publication). As if to prove the observation that dissatisfaction is inherent in the human condition, when I first voiced to my eastern European colleagues in IATC my jealousy of their having been trained in criticism in academies, they immediately responded that they were jealous of the professional independence of British critics, who, for the most part, were not educated alongside the practitioners whose work they review. Criticism in eastern Europe, they said, was often too tame on account of the familiarity between the critics and the practitioners.

McDonald is an Irish academic who studied and worked in English universities for many years. His writings on criticism are very much cognisant of the strong distinction, and yet the inevitable interrelationship, between journalistic and academic arts critics in Britain. His argument that there has, broadly, been a self-preserving retreat into non-evaluative specialization within academe seems virtually unarguable. For our purposes here, the more significant point is his contention that the evaluative role of the critic in the popular media has been all but overwhelmed by the cultural relativist, faux democratic notion that everyone and anyone is, or can be, a critic.

Despite, or perhaps because of, the fact that I am, primarily, an insecurely employed theatre critic in the print media (as opposed to McDonald, who currently holds a professorship at the University of New South Wales, Australia), I am less pessimistic on this question than McDonald. Critics may, as McDonald suggests, be 'sidelined', but many of us are far from 'slumbering' (2008: 149). As Michael Billington argues, there remains a discerning readership for professional theatre critics who resist both the cultural relativist attempt to devalue criticism (perhaps, even, to eradicate it) and the related efforts to package and sell works of art like any other product:

> [Kenneth] Tynan wrote beautifully. This is the bottom line of criticism, which never gets discussed. I don't mind if I disagree with a critic, or if it's inflammatory, as long as they can write [...]. To write with maximum volatility and make the arts sound exciting is the responsibility [...]. I'm not going to use the word expert – but there remains a definite hunger for someone who has more experience of a particular art form. People may dislike authority, but however much they regard critics as inadequate and parasitic, they still like an opinion to bounce off.
>
> Billington in Kirkwood 2009: 37

The notions of the critic as, firstly, an unusually experienced, knowledgeable and passionate specialist with a fine writing style and, secondly, an initiator of public discussion (rather than an all-powerful arbiter) express well the position of the critic in the early twenty-first century; although Billington concedes too much ground in seeming to accept that even assiduous readers of critics consider them (us) 'inadequate and parasitic'.

Tynan (who was, arguably, the finest English-language theatre critic of the twentieth century) was emphatic on the importance of style:

> What counts [about critics] is not their opinion, but the art with which it is expressed [...] The subtlest and best-informed of men will still be a bad critic if his style is bad. It is irrelevant whether his opinion is 'right' or 'wrong': I learn more from GBS

> [George Bernard Shaw] when he is wrong than from Clement
> Scott when he is right.
>
> 2007: 119

His brutally witty attack on Scott, by way of his appreciation of Shaw, notwithstanding, Tynan bends the stick a little too far in arguing that opinion is 'irrelevant'. In fact, Tynan did value opinion; his review of Harold Pinter's *The Caretaker* (in 1960) begins with an apologetic reassessment of his damning notice for Pinter's first staged work, *The Birthday Party* (1958) (2007: 203). This does nothing to detract from his argument about the pre-eminence of style, however; after all, it is style, first-and-foremost, that distinguishes the professional writer (including the professional critic) from the amateur. To read Tynan's splendid, metaphorical review of Beckett's *Waiting for Godot*, for example, is to agree with McDonald's contention that criticism is 'a craft and a literary form' (2008: 149) in its own right (one which, as I argue in my 'Twenty-one Asides', exists in 'the discrete space between journalism and art') and with his insistence that the discerning reader would choose a well-written critical essay (or, by logical extension, review) over 'a hundred bad poems or plays' (ibid).

In support of 'radical elitism'

Our culture has become so polluted by the pseudo-democratic shibboleths of cultural relativism that one can almost hear the cries of consternation, and accusations of 'elitism', as one draws a distinction between the 'professional' and the 'amateur'. Yet, now more than ever, we need 'radical elitism', the unashamedly evaluative stance proposed by Howard Barker (1997: 32–37), that insists upon the superiority of one art work over another. Its evaluations, like all aesthetic judgements, are subjective, of course, but they are based on no other criteria than the pursuit and elevation of quality. Cultural relativism, in its insistence upon the equal validity of all art works, is the undeclared friend of the hyper-marketization of culture.

Contemporary capitalism seeks to develop the perfectly targeted, eminently sellable artistic product for each niche market. Cultural relativism colludes in this by wildly distorting the perfectly reasonable challenges to the political biases involved in canon formation offered by Marxism and feminism, to take two examples, twisting them into a postmodern attack on all categories of excellence. It is by this process that a cultural equivalence is drawn between what Steven Berkoff memorably calls 'money-motivated *mulch for morons*' (2000) and great art.

By contrast, radical elitism, as conceived by Barker, is deeply hostile to notions of art as existing for the purpose of entertainment or, even, the fulfilment of a social function (whether it be educational or morally improving). Sometimes denigrated, wrongly, as proposing 'art for art's sake', it elevates the ambiguous[12] and the metaphorical (and, with them, myriad emotional, psychological, erotic, political and, in the broadest sense, spiritual possibilities) above the didactic and the expository. In other words, it prefers the timeless profundity of great art to the commercial imperatives of populist culture. In the face of the pressures to desist from evaluation, which McDonald identifies, criticism can only benefit from a strong dose of radical elitism.

Against miserablism: the future of criticism

Whatever technological, structural and cultural factors threaten print journalism and, with it, theatre criticism in newspapers and magazines (and I acknowledge the reality of those threats), it is rank cultural miserablism to concede 'the death of the critic'. As long as there exists an intelligent and sentient audience for a live theatre of quality and profundity (a live theatre which, as I argue above, has survived the technological threats many believed would destroy it in the twentieth century), there will also be a readership that seeks out serious, professional theatre criticism. The best way for critics to defend their craft in such circumstances is to practise it well.

Notes

1. As Rónán McDonald writes in the preface to his book *The Death of the Critic*: 'The age of the critic as the arbiter for public taste and cultural consumption seems to have passed', and the critic is perceived to have been replaced by 'blogs and discussion groups' (2007: vii).

2. As I do in my set of Howard Barker-inspired aphorisms, 'Twenty-one Asides on Theatre Criticism', first published in Spring 2010, in the second edition of the International Association of Theatre Critics' webjournal *Critical Stages*: http://archive.criticalstages.org/criticalstages2/entry/21-Asides-to-Theatre-Criticism?category=9 (accessed 16 March 2015), and subsequently republished in Rabey and Goldingay (2013: 1–1).

3. Rebellato is also a dramatist who remembers, in the above-mentioned essay, that he has received 'a couple of gloriously shitty reviews' from me. I apologize to him that my knowledge of my own work is not so encyclopaedic that I can recall the notices in question. However, I wish all the best to the unnamed playwright of his acquaintance who, he says, 'toyed with the idea of introducing an off-stage character in their next play who would only ever be referred to as "the cunt Mark Brown".'

4. IATC was founded, under UNESCO statute, in Paris in 1956. It is organized in national chapters throughout the world. Its website states that the organization's *principle aims* are: 'to foster theatre criticism as a discipline and to contribute to the development of its methodological bases; to protect the ethical and professional interests of theatre critics and to promote the common rights of all its members; and to contribute to reciprocal awareness and understanding between cultures by encouraging international meetings and exchanges in the field of theatre in general.' www.aict-iatc.org (accessed 5 June 2015). I have sat on the executive committee of IATC (representing Britain) since 2008, and have been its adjunct director of young critics' seminars since 2011.

5. Half of the current 14 members of the IATC executive are academics first and foremost; although, as noted above, the British chapter of IATC, the Drama Section of the Critics' Circle (which is based in London and holds all of its meetings there) does not allow academic critics to be members. Indeed, its membership is comprised entirely of critics working in the established print and broadcast media; a matter that is currently creating some debate.

6. A full list of the papers given can be seen at: www.aict-iatc.org/aict-5.html (accessed 5 June 2015).

7. This list is by no means exhaustive.

8. My term for the equivalent within theatre criticism of 'citizen journalism', which internet analyst Mark Glaser defines thus: 'The idea behind citizen journalism is that people without professional journalism training can use the tools of modern technology and the global distribution of the Internet to create, augment or fact-check media on their own or in collaboration with others' (Glaser 2006).

9. For example, the annual Critics' Awards for Theatre in Scotland, which were established in 2003 by professional newspaper journalists, have always included on the judging panel critics whose work is wholly for online publications and/or unremunerated. Indeed, the number of such critics has increased over the years. This contrasts with the Britain-wide organization, the Critics' Circle (the oldest professional body representing critics, established in 1914), which, at the time of writing, only invites into membership critics who are paid to review for established print, television and radio outlets.

10. During my time teaching the Drama, Theatre, Film undergraduate course at the University of Strathclyde in Glasgow (2007–2009), I found myself engaged in argument with a new course organizer who wanted to replace a classical text on the course with episodes of the British TV soap opera *Coronation Street*. In the end, the TV show was not put on the course.

11. Albeit that the tradition is breaking down, perhaps more in Scotland and 'provincial England' (i.e. everywhere outside of London), due to the near, if not outright, impossibility of the freelance writer making a living from criticism and arts journalism alone.

12. Barker argues in the 'Fortynine asides for a tragic theatre' that 'It is not to insult an audience to offer it ambiguity' (1997: 19).

Works cited

Barker, Howard (1997) *Arguments for a Theatre*, Manchester: Manchester University Press.

Berkoff, Steven (2000) 'All virgins welcome', *The Observer*, 13 August, London.

Fricker, Karen (2014) '*The crisis in theatre criticism is critics saying there's a crisis*', author's blog *The Mental Swoon*, 11 September, https://karenfricker. wordpress.com/2014/09/11/the crisis-in-theatre-criticism-is-critics-saying-theres-a-crisis (accessed 5 June 2015).

Glaser, Mark (2006) 'Your Guide to Citizen Journalism', *Mediashift*, 27 September, http://ec2-23-21-180-28.compute-1.amazonaws.com/mediashift/2006/09/ your-guide-to-citizen-journalism270 (accessed 16 March 2015).

Kirkwood, Elizabeth (2009) 'Boo, hiss, hurrah!', *New Statesman*, 10 August, London.

McDonald, Rónán (2008) *The Death of the Critic*, London: Continuum.

Paulin, T. (1996) *Writing to the Moment: Selected Critical Essays 1980–1996*, London: Faber and Faber.

Rabey, David Ian and Goldingay, Sarah (eds) (2013) *Howard Barker's Art of Theatre*, Manchester: Manchester University Press.

Rebellato, Dan (2014) 'Critical Thinking', author's blog, 17 September, http://www.danrebellato.co.uk/spilledink/2014/9/17/critical-thinking (accessed 5 June 2015).

Rubin, Don (2010) 'Too Important to be Left to Amateurs', *Critical Stages*, 2 (Spring), http://archive.criticalstages.org/criticalstages2/entry/Too-Important-To-Be-Left-to-Amateurs?category=9 (accessed 16 March 2015).

Salberg, Daniel, Stewart, Robert, Wesley, Karla, Weiss, Shannon (no date) 'Postmodernism and Its Critics': http://anthropology.ua.edu/cultures/cultures.php?culture=Postmodernism%20and%20Its%20Critics (accessed 17 March 2015).

Tynan, K. (2007) *Theatre Writings,* London: Nick Hern Books.

Franz Boas staff page, http://anthropology.columbia.edu/department-history/franz-boas (accessed 17 March 2015).

CHAPTER 11
CODE-SWITCHING AND CONSTELLATIONS: ON FEMINIST THEATRE CRITICISM
Jill Dolan

Over my years as an academic feminist theatre critic, I've proselytized for expanding our work from strictly academic venues into the largest public forums. Given the unequal representation of women artists and critics across disciplines – especially in theatre, film, and television, the arts about which I write – I've long believed that feminist critics need to speak into public debates as well as building knowledge through more academic research and scholarship. Our ability to be multi-lingual – or to 'code-switch' – enhances the political effects of our work and extends our contributions to social change. This essay, then, is an argument for feminist critics to produce rich historical and theatrical scholarship but also to ply our trade in the weeds of public discourse, where feminist voices are too often absent.

A range of issues confront American and global arts culture, from on-going gender inequity and racial disparities, to the ways in which theatre and other arts can be used for self-empowerment and economic development, to questions of access for large, socio-economically diverse audiences, and more. This persistent need for our commentary begs several questions about language and readership, labour and purpose. Who is the audience for feminist criticism? How might we attract wider and more varied readerships to the questions we find important? What language should we use to widely communicate our ideas? Why is it important for feminist critics to carve out our own spheres of influence by attending to the progress of theatre and popular culture and urging these fields in ever more progressive, socially just directions? How do we keep up our work, when so many of us have day jobs that leave only a few hours a week for writing that often feels more urgent than anything else? And finally, how do we maintain our poise in public forums that sometimes give readers permission to respond with ugly, vituperative criticism of their own?

Since I became a professor in 1987, the universities in which I've worked have structured how I deliver my ideas. They have rewarded me for good teaching, for publishing, and – rather solipsistically – for keeping them running with my committee work and my administrative labour. I've tried to be a feminist change-maker in those contexts, but working in higher education has organized my time and my outlook. As a university professor, I use the platform of my classrooms to teach students about women playwrights – and playwrights of colour and LGBT playwrights, identity categories and contents that often overlap in complex ways – and to offer them a critical perspective on their cultural consumption and their spectating habits. My scholarship calls attention to playwrights, directors, ensembles, and performers who might not otherwise receive public notice. In some cases, my writing has moved these artists onto the touring circuits of university and college theatre departments in the U.S. and around the world.

I established my blog, The Feminist Spectator, in 2005, to give myself a venue for public commentary alongside my academic career.[1] The convenient persona 'the feminist spectator' often facilitates my commitment to writing for public audiences. The Feminist Spectator is the title of my blog, but it's also my authorial voice; I sign each post with that 'handle'. This public identity, slightly detached from my real name, gives me permission to attend to the cultural prescriptions and resistances produced by live theatre, independent and popular film, and network, cable, and subscription television, which count among the proliferating forms of culture that many of us regularly consume. The feminist spectator persona also affords me a clear-cut public role, as it announces its political and ideological preoccupations up front and refuses to apologize for seeing from a particular standpoint. The 'blogosphere' has broadened its readers' appetites for alternative perspectives, and a number of websites openly trumpet feminist points of view. While much of this is 'niche' work, some popular

English-language websites take a broad perspective on politics and public debate. Feministing.com and Jezebel, for instance, are sites that consolidate and produce content about politics and culture from various feminist perspectives, while Indiewire.com, an internet blog host, provides content from Women and Hollywood, a site that tracks the status of women working in film.[2] Criticism for every taste is available somewhere on the internet; The Feminist Spectator carves out a place in which to make its contribution.

In fact, many people seem eager to think about their cultural consumption through a gendered perspective that takes racial justice, class inequities, and sexual difference into account. Some of my students might be hesitant to embrace the label 'feminist', but most of them – across their own proliferating gender, race, and sexual identity claims – find that the critical practices of feminism give them purchase on a worldview that helps them explain their lives, as well as their cultural tastes. Across my ten years of blogging, I've also heard from readers who never presumed to understand or align with a feminist perspective that they, too, have found new ways to think about what they see and how they organize their consumption and spectating practices from engaging the term in my posts. For other readers, my blog curates cultural experiences, as they decide to attend a performance or watch a television series based on The Feminist Spectator's recommendations. I take responsibility for taste-making seriously, but I also consider my criticism part of a larger conversation about what culture means and what it does in the global imaginary.

Demystifying criticism

My students and other readers are often curious about how my blog operates, as though they are eager to look under the hood of a process that's long been mysterious. They wonder how I decide what to write about and what considerations organize my critical view. How do I make the taste choices that organize my blog? Frankly, The Feminist Spectator engages what captures my attention. That said, I also set out ten years ago with the intention of practising what I call 'critical generosity', which entails writing only about theatre productions or films or television shows I 'like' (Dolan, 2013). My determination to be positive responded to common stereotypes of the critic as a person who advances mostly negative opinions about art. 'Critic' and 'criticism' both have a deleterious charge; I very much wanted The Feminist Spectator to dispel such presumptions. In addition, as my books *The Feminist Spectator as Critic* (1991/2013) and *The Feminist Spectator in Action* (2013) demonstrate, I am eager to join the notion of 'spectator' to the word 'critical'. As far as I'm concerned, being a spectator should in itself be a critical practice, in which 'critical' means engaging in a heightened, thoughtful, analytical way with the representations we consume. I teach a course called 'For Your Viewing Pleasure' that advances the surprisingly radical idea that you can be a feminist spectator and still enjoy your cultural consumption. That is, critical engagement and pleasure don't have to be mutually exclusive. Analysis can be a way to relish what we see on stage and screen.

I use the blog, then, to write about theatre productions and films and television series whose cultural, aesthetic, or political contributions I can discuss positively. When I describe work by women, lesbians, people of colour, and work that intersects these categories, I hope my writing will popularize examples that might not be more widely known. One of the most important historical gestures of academic U.S. feminist performance criticism and theory in the 1980s and 1990s, in fact, was to bring work by Split Britches, Holly Hughes, Carmelita Tropicana, and the Five Lesbian Brothers, among other feminist and lesbian performers, playwrights, and theatre artists, into public conversation and notice. Feminist theatre academics wrote about their work and invited them to our campuses, where they taught students how to be resistant artists, and how to consider gender, sexuality, and race in their performance practices while still having great fun.

I see the blog as another way to get the word out about performance that remains purposefully subcultural, as well as to address work by women that would rather not be so invisible in the mainstream. My first blog post was about the Five Lesbian Brothers' final ensemble production, *Oedipus at Palm Springs*, which they premiered at the

New York Theatre Workshop in the East Village of Manhattan in 2005 (see Dolan 2006). Although they were by that time more interested in larger audiences than the more sectarian, primarily lesbian crowd they began performing for at the WOW Café, many people outside New York didn't see the production. Writing about it became a way to let people know the new work existed as well as to describe its important formal innovations and the politics of its content. My blog continues to privilege performance work like this by women who don't get the serious critical attention they deserve elsewhere. I write about playwrights working Off Broadway or in regional theatres whose work is caught in a peculiarly gendered netherworld, writers like Madeleine George, Danai Gurira, Kristen Greenidge, Sarah Treem, Naomi Wallace, Bathsheba Doran, and many more. Their work should be more widely known and more frequently produced, and should garner the acclaim, income, and prestige of Broadway productions women rarely enjoy. I hope to bring these artists notice and deep critical engagement as they wait to be propelled to the next level of distinction.

I've never believed critics can be objective. We come to our ideas from a standpoint deeply imbued with beliefs about art and politics, culture and society. I've always been open about my feminist standpoint and how much I value racial, sexual, and economic equality. I try to articulate what I see as the intimate relationship between the arts and our aspirations as a culture. I believe that any theatre production speaks into an historical moment, responding to and shaping the cultural mores of its time and place. The flip side of my project, then, brings a feminist perspective to work that's too often let off the hook when it's judged by critics who hold themselves to old-fashioned standards of objectivity. Because Broadway is so visible, like it or not, as the apex of theatre production in North America and abroad, and because its plays are too often presumed as a yardstick of cultural value unblemished by gender, race, sexuality, or class in the canon of universality, all of its productions demand a rigorous feminist analysis.[3]

I curate my choices of what to see and write about based on intuition and expertise, as well as on my commitment to balancing attention to work by women and people of colour with a concern for the on-going project of theatre in America and the stories for which it makes space and time in the world. I'm sometimes inspired to write about things that are trendy but haven't been addressed from a feminist perspective, often musicals or splashy productions by white male playwrights that broadcast their cultural capital. But I choose what to see based mostly on hope: that a production will move me to feel or to think; that it will introduce me to a new idea, a new artist, or a new vision for theatre; or that it will be progressive in its politics and its aesthetics. When I choose wrong, I keep my pen still. When I choose right, and I'm thrilled or enthralled, I can't wait to start trying to communicate my excitement. The writing becomes a way to sort out the nexus between pleasure and politics and my professional perspective on what I believe theatre can do as a cultural force. Once I'm moved to write, I take pleasure from somehow using words to recreate, engage, and do justice to performance.

Modes of production and constellations of relationships

I also engage materialist feminist understandings of modes of production, and performance studies methods that help me understand how the details of a play or film's production situates it in a field of social meanings. I try to extend my critical purview beyond what I see on the stage or screen into production contexts that make certain forms and contents available to certain audiences and not others. Writing about lesbian feminist performances at the WOW Café in the early 1980s, for example, required taking into account the rent structures of lower Manhattan at the time, which made empty warehouse spaces and storefronts available to often renegade, multidisciplinary artists who could afford to live nearby. The relationship between art and real estate is a crucial part of how a feminist critic understands the politics of production. I'm also interested in audiences and how they're hailed and constituted by performances of all sorts across contexts. What happens off-stage – not just behind the scenes but in the audience and outside of the theatre – is another aspect of my feminist perspective. Performance studies methods first devised by scholar Richard Schechner (for example, 1988), among others, remind me that the journey to and from a performance, and what happens in the lobby, and what the programme looks like, has a lot to do with our reception and consumption practices. Taste, after all, is shaped in conversation with our own habits and the conventions of the culture through which we move. These relationships are always political.

As a feminist critic, I want to understand why some productions get financing and critical attention when others don't, and why some artists are constantly produced and others are ignored. But in addition to interrogating production contexts and decisions about which artists work in the most powerful – or most subaltern – theatre venues, feminist critics and spectators need to talk about the work itself, enumerating what it means, who it's for, and what ideological as well as aesthetic work it does in the world. Considering content and context helps me speculate about why so many talented women, for example, write for television as well as theatre, and helps me track the new constellation of artistic relationships that support work across venues.[4] Do women succeed in television because series writers' rooms are more collaborative, and the amount of product means less is at stake in each individual project? If so, we need to track women theatre artists who turn to other media to make their livings (Dargis 2014/15). As a feminist theatre critic, I write more and more about cable television and independent film, because so many writers who begin in theatre find more opportunities to get their work seen in other forms. In this new pattern of artistic labour, it's no longer considered 'selling out' to write for television. Writers can move from theatre to film to television and back to theatre, sometimes in the same season. This mobility effects cultural production in ways I find hopeful, as talented actors, directors, and writers blur the boundaries and taste presumptions among forms. The Feminist Spectator helps chart the cross-pollinations and influences and conversations staged among forms, contents, and contexts, and points out that the worlds of theatre, independent feature films, and cable television overlap in ways that might enhance not just opportunities for women artists, but for feminist social intervention and commentary. The revolution happens everywhere at once now.

Danger

Of course, the blogosphere is another site of public discourse where people sharpen their knives for feminism. Conservatives hope to defang its power and persuasiveness by publicly denigrating feminism. Self-proclaiming your politics, as I do on The Feminist Spectator, can make you a target for the shockingly violent and hateful comments that anonymous readers feel righteous about posting to school feminist bloggers into submission. In fact, I'm unsettled by people's willingness to publicly revile feminist ideas. Look what happened to Zoe Quinn, Brianna Wu, and Anita Sarkeesian in the August 2014 'Gamergate' controversy: they were incessantly harassed and threatened with rape and death because they criticized the misogyny of video games and the gender imbalances in the video gaming industry.[5] Taking a stand in a public forum, even about something that feels as inconsequential as a video game or a Hollywood movie, or as ephemeral as live theatre, can be hazardous. But the pay-off for advancing public dialogue about gender and social justice seems worth the risk that public writing sometimes entails.

My own experience with ideological violence comes from bringing feminist critical attention to Hollywood films that mainstream critics excuse by failing to mention their gender, sexuality, or race politics. For example, I excoriated director David Fincher's *The Social Network* (2010) for what I saw as its retrograde misogyny and racism. I criticized Darren Aronofsky's *The Black Swan* (2010), too, for how it depicted women artists as psychotic. And I abhorred Fincher's *Gone Girl* (2014) for its deep and virulent misogyny. I set aside my critical generosity ethos when it comes to criticizing Hollywood studio films, a scenario in which I'm only a David standing up to their Goliath. But when I write this sort of criticism, I often get attacked. The zealotry of feminist-bashers startles me. I can't imagine why feminist criticism on a small, politically partial blog would raise these people's ire. I'm also dismayed by the chastising, condescending tone strangers use in their public comments. For example, when I wrote positively about the film *Silver Linings Playbook* (2012) but remarked on things I found salient about gender in its narrative, my critique attracted this 2015 comment (three years after the original post):

It's called common sense people [...] Stop reading into it like this. There's no homophobic underlining. No political views. No sexism or feminism. It's just a movie that's a silly love story. Just like every other movie. That said, it's a well- acted well written screenplay. Oh and on a side note, the Eagles vs Seahawks game Pat Sr. said Eagles were winning 23–20 or something like that. I can't remember exactly. And then later Tiffany said the Eagles beat the Seahawks 14–7. I see all foul ups and that's the only significant flaw in this movie. Other than Tiffany being a needy controlling manipulating woman. Not a bad flick.[6]

This comment exemplifies the responses I often get when I post on Hollywood films: Get over yourself! It's just a movie! It's not political or sexist or feminist! The continuity trivia is more important! But the comment's writer feels justified to say with impunity that the lead, played by Jennifer Lawrence, is a 'needy controlling manipulating woman'. In his or her humble opinion. But that's not political or sexist, is it?

Representation remains a battleground. If it weren't, who would take the time to comment harshly or derisively on a blog called The Feminist Spectator? My posts critical of films with large budgets and visibility, which are often glowingly reviewed by mainstream writers, might bring me wrath. But perhaps this signals the important and productive on-going ambivalence and anxiety in public culture about gender, race, and sexuality. If these respondents weren't anxious about their masculinity (or their femininity, since my most brutal critics are sometimes women), or didn't feel they had to defend heterosexuality or whiteness, we'd be in a much less fearful place as a culture. I take my lumps as evidence that feminism is actually working, if it's making people defensive enough to strike out.

I'd prefer to think of feminist criticism as part of a more civil public discourse, a way of speaking into a forum that historically hasn't made room for minoritarian voices. I'd like to think that as a critic, I can listen carefully, respond thoughtfully, and still disagree with an interlocutor. I know the politics of civility often shut down those who are outside the norms of race, gender, sexuality, or class. Demonstrators from Selma, Alabama to Ferguson, Missouri, are too often accused of anger and unruliness. But in a discussion about culture, I'd rather really talk and listen than try to outshout my readers. I hope I can make a strong case for my feminist perspective and that my arguments will stand on their merits whether or not anyone agrees with them. I'm not in it for the mud-slinging. But because of my refusal to participate in the nasty aspects of public culture, and my avowed determination to practise critical generosity, I've been called 'an enthusiast' instead of a critic. One way to dismiss and disempower feminist criticism is to call it amateur.

Labour and code-switching

I've participated in several Public Voices workshops presented by The OpEd Project, a U.S.-based non-profit that agitates for more women and people of colour to be published on the opinion pages of major news and media outlets.[7] The organization crunches numbers that illustrate how those pages are dominated by white men who, as a result, control national public thought leadership. The OpEd Project workshop organizers encourage scholars to translate their academic specialties into public areas of expertise, and to position themselves as people who can be called on for opinions. The year I joined the Public Voices project at Princeton, our group of 20-odd women from across disciplines and university status productively translated our work to larger public forums.

As a feminist theatre critic, I found lots on which to comment in public discourse, though I was sometimes stymied by the need to find a 'hook', which required keying a think-piece to an upcoming or trending cultural event. I published an essay on the Tony Awards season on the Huffington Post, and another on actor Cynthia Nixon's comments about the malleability of sexuality on Alternet.com, both issues that were topical and relevant at the time (Dolan 2011, 2012). I persuaded even our sometimes dubious if supportive workshop leaders that cultural commentary was as important and newsworthy as opinions from my colleagues in sociology, the sciences, and the humanities pitched to editors. I left the workshop more determined than ever that my theatre criticism and writing about culture could resonate widely.

But as our OpEd Project leaders left to stage workshops on other campuses, my Princeton colleagues and I struggled to maintain our writing momentum. We were, after all, academics, not freelance journalists or people paid by think tanks. We had to teach; we had to produce scholarship, as well as public writing; and we had to serve the university in numerous ways with our labour. Our university admires public commentary enough to link this writing to its website, but not quite enough to reward it with salary merit increases, which are still weighted toward peer-reviewed research. How then might we continue finding the time to respond – quickly, as thought leadership requires – to current events? Public writers watch the clock and the calendar. If you miss your chance to comment, or if the wave of attention to an issue crests, the moment closes over and public attention moves to the next trending debate. You have to be nimble and quick to be a public intellectual, and often, the burdens of the academy slow us down. Feminist critics without the luxury of academic positions need to make their living in other ways, which might preclude paying speed and focus thought leadership demands. In other words, the economy in which we labour has important implications for our ability to truly and consistently engage public dialogue.

But the challenge is worth contemplating. As more and more theatre critics lose their paid positions at print newspapers, I can continue writing my blog because my salary is paid by a university and my primary preoccupation is teaching. And I see a lot of theatre without asking for press seats because my academic salary and research account let me· buy my own tickets. Because of that relative privilege, feminist theatre scholars hold a responsibility to public discourse, even as we continue to produce research vetted by juries of our peers. After all, scientists presume that once their colleagues certify their research, it will apply widely, to improve how we live in the world. Humanists, too, should be able to speak to multiple audiences and to presume the efficacy of our ideas. We should be adept at code-switching, not to water down our ideas or to pander to a low common denominator, but to popularize vital, transformative ways of seeing the world, which can and should extend well beyond our classrooms.

The arts perplex and enlighten us; frustrate and irritate us; enliven and exhilarate us; prompt us to think and to feel; and bring us an ongoing, ever-renewing sense of community and common cause. They invite us to contemplate the world as it was, as it is, and most importantly, as it might be. They urge us not just to observe, but to participate in creating and experiencing ever-new visions of human possibility. The arts introduce us to ideas and stories we might not otherwise experience. They provide platforms for narratives about who we are and who we might be to one another, not just in the future, but right now. Feminist critics participate in the project of democracy, and lend our insights to how we speak to one another and what we say. For me, The Feminist Spectator remains an activist project because writing about the arts and popular culture changes minds, prods conversation, and encourages pleasurable engagement with the most important issues of the day. As a tool for cultural as well as aesthetic commentary, feminist theatre and performance criticism intervenes in social meanings, and offers new perspectives on our common humanity.

Let me close by exhorting future generations of feminist critics and bloggers to continue writing; to write more; and to write with passion, precision, and persuasiveness. Code-switching allows us to increase our audience and readership, and to enlarge the conversation about the crucial effects of culture. Our ideas are too important to share only with one another or our academic peers. We need to multiply our voices in the public sphere, not to add to the cacophony, but to model the very best ways of engaging with cultural analysis devoted to the widest aims of social justice.

Notes

1. The Feminist Spectator can be accessed at www.feministspectator. princeton.edu.

2. See www.feministing.com, www.jezebel.com, and http://blogs.indiewire. com/womenandhollywood/ (all accessed 11 February 2015).

3. As an academic with a stable income, I can afford to buy myself tickets to Broadway productions, which represent the most expensive theatre in the U.S. I never ask for press tickets, as I don't want to be beholden to producers or to the artists who invite me to their shows. But I can pay for tickets because I have a day job.

4. For instance, these playwrights: Bathsheba Doran writes for the terrific Showtime series *Masters of Sex*; Sarah Treem for Showtime's Golden Globe-winning *The Affair*; Gina Gionfriddo and Laura Eason write for Netflix's *House of Cards*; and Diana Son and Julie Hébert for *American Crime* on ABC.

5. Sarkeesian cancelled a speaking appearance in 2014 at Utah State University after the school received several anonymous terrorist threats, at least one of which claimed affiliation with Gamergate. The threats included allusions to Montreal's École Polytechnique massacre, a 1989 mass shooting motivated by anti-feminism. Sarkeesian cancelled her appearance when the school could not assure her safety under gun laws in Utah. http://en.wikipedia.org/wiki/ Anita_Sarkeesian (accessed 11 February 2015).

6. Unsigned blog comment, submitted for approval January 24, 2015.

7. The OpEd Project, www.theopedproject.org.

Works cited

Dargis, Manohla (2014/2015) 'The Director Gap: Female Filmmakers and Their Fight for Equality' series in *The New York Times*, including:
—— 'Making History', http://www.nytimes.com/2014/12/07/movies/ ava-duvernay-makes-a-mark-with-selma.html (accessed 11 February 2015).
—— 'In Hollywood, It's a Men's, Men's, Men's World', http://www.nytimes. com/2014/12/28/movies/in-hollywood-its-a-mens-mens-mens-world. html (accessed 11 February 2015).
—— 'Lights, Camera, Taking Action', http://www.nytimes. com/2015/01/25/movies/on-many-fronts-women-are-fighting-for- better-opportunity-in-hollywood.html?_r=0 (accessed 11 February 2015).
Dolan, Jill (2013) 'Critical Generosity', in *Public*, http://public. imaginingamerica.org/blog/article/critical-generosity-2/ (accessed 11 February 2015).

Theatre Criticism

Dolan, Jill (1991/2013) *The Feminist Spectator as Critic*, Ann Arbor, MI: University of Michigan Press.

Dolan, Jill (2013) *The Feminist Spectator in Action: Feminist Criticism for Stage and Screen*, New York: Palgrave Macmillan.

Dolan, Jill (2006) 'Blogging on Queer Connections in the Arts and the Five Lesbian Brothers', *GLQ: A Journal of Lesbian and Gay Studies*, 12.3, pp. 491–506.

Dolan, Jill (2011) 'Tonys 2011: Where are the Women?' in http://www.huffingtonpost.com/jill-dolan/tonys-2011-where-are-the-_b_875065.html (accessed 11 February 2015).

Dolan, Jill (2012) 'Do We Need a More Nuanced View of Sexuality' in http://www.alternet.org/story/154053/do_we_need_a_more_nuanced_view_of_sexuality (accessed 11 February 2015).

Schechner, Richard (1988) *Performance Theory: Essays on Performance Theory 1970–1976*, New York: Routledge.

Websites

Center for the Study of Women in Television & Film, http://womenintvfilm.sdsu.edu/

Feministing, www.feministing.com

Jezebel, www.jezebel.com

The Feminist Spectator, http://feministspectator.princeton.edu/

The OpEd Project, www.theopedproject.org

'Women and Hollywood', *Indiewire*, http://blogs.indiewire.com/womenandhollywood/

Women's Media Center, www.womensmediacenter.com

CHAPTER 12
THE CRITIC AS INSIDER: SHIFTING UK CRITICAL PRACTICE TOWARDS 'EMBEDDED' RELATIONSHIPS AND THE ROUTES THIS OPENS UP TOWARDS DIALOGUE AND DRAMATURGY

Maddy Costa

It started with a hunch

In Spring 2011, Chris Goode, a maker[1] described by Lyn Gardner in *The Guardian* as 'one of the geniuses of British theatre' (Gardner 2014), was setting up a new company with producer Ric Watts, and thinking about sustainability. The companies that thrive, he wrote to me in an email, are those that tell their story best – to audiences, but also back to themselves. He had a hunch that the nascent Chris Goode & Company needed a 'narrator', someone who could be:

> A cross between a dramaturg, an archivist, a documentary artist, an outreach officer, a brand manager and Jiminy Cricket. Someone whose job it is to remind us what we do, to explain to others who we are, to have a long memory, to relate that memory to the present instant and to what seems likely to happen tomorrow.... Not just an outside eye (and ear) but also a memory, a conscience, a nagging voice. A heart.
>
> Goode 2011a

When he wrote this email, Chris knew I was a fan of his work. He knew that I was emerging from the relative isolation of early motherhood, and a lengthy period of disenchantment with theatre, triggered by the recurring sensation that the (fairly traditional, often fourth-wall) work I was seeing was inert, truthless, banal. He knew that I was ready to hear different stories in the performance space, and to write about theatre in a different way: not as a 'product' presented on press nights, but the process of making it in the rehearsal room then remaking it night after night with different audiences. What he didn't know was how it would feel to have anyone, let alone a practising critic whose main job at that time was with a national newspaper (*The Guardian*), observing his rehearsals, but he trusted that I would be conscientious. And neither of us had the slightest inkling that this tentative collaboration would soon be framed as a pioneering experiment in what has become known in the UK as 'embedded' criticism.

This term 'embedded criticism' was coined by British critic Andrew Haydon in April 2012, following a visit to Kurdistan with the Actors Touring Company: 'Being in Iraq and a journalist,' he noted on his blog *Postcards from the Gods*, 'jokes about my being "embedded" abounded' (Haydon 2012). The blog post, also entitled 'Embedded', went on to assess the ways in which the writing of criticism might be affected (for the better) if closer relationships were forged between people who make theatre and people who write about it.

For Haydon, critics entering the rehearsal room was one of many possibilities, a variation on a theme. My essay, however, focuses on that specific interpretation of 'embedded' criticism, using first-hand experience to build up an argument in favour of critics interacting with work in development. It is an argument that directors and critics have made before, and this historical perspective gives intellectual reasoning to what I otherwise do instinctively. I encountered 'embedded' criticism by accident, as I will demonstrate, and might not have pursued it to such a degree without Chris's support. At the time of writing (Spring 2015), the bulk of my work emerges from 'embedded' relationships, and since the most consuming and profound of these is with Chris Goode & Company (CG&Co), that is where I begin.

I use quotation marks around 'embedded' because I've never been comfortable with the militaristic connotations of the term, a feeling Chris shares. In 2013, when I became an official member of the company, we opted for the job title Critic-in-Residence, but this doesn't fit either, because it conveys a dictionary definition[2] we don't mean. The writing I do within CG&Co differs markedly from the reviews and articles I have written about theatre since 1997, for publications including *Time Out Magazine* and *The Guardian*. Journalism demands pithiness, and a semblance of objectivity, which I tried to achieve in this reflection on Chris's monologue *Hippo World Guest Book*, published in *The Guardian* in 2007:

> [T]he show – like so much of Goode's work – invites us to question what we expect from theatre. Polished writing? Detailed acting? That's what you get in most verbatim theatre; Goode, however, delivers neither, slyly hinting that to do so would be dishonest. At times you wish he [...] found more interesting ways to convey capital letters than simply shouting. But his performance is also a masterclass in self-effacement, not to mention deadpan comic timing, ensuring that the material, no matter how mundane, is also entertaining.
>
> Costa 2007a

My 'embedded' writing, by contrast, is more detailed, open to digression and personal in tone; the further it moves from journalism the more it inclines towards poetry. This extract, from a post published on my blog in August 2014, describes another solo show by Chris, *Men in the Cities*:

> As he shouts he clutches at the air, as if trying to prise answers from its atoms. Initially he leans into the microphone, then gradually pulls away, still ranting, but staggering now, flailing, stamping and swaying, bent over with the weight of anger and resentment and unbearable sorrow, drunk on the indignity of being human and alive. And the transcendent singing stops but the rant goes on, as steadfast and oppressive as the roar of machinery. My father and his father and his father. Misunderstood. Misunderstood. Misunderstood.
>
> Costa 2014c

Key to the difference between these two extracts is my approach to judgement. In *The Guardian* piece, I recognize my version of a prevailing critical practice concisely summarized by Irving Wardle in his 1992 volume *Theatre Criticism*: 'in brief, the critic aims to evaluate what the production is trying to do, whether it was successful, and whether it was worth doing' (1992: 1–1). The second example seeks less to evaluate, more to record, remember, respond. 'To give permanence to something impermanent' is another way of thinking about the work of the critic: one that Wardle ascribes to Kenneth Tynan, without quite concurring (1992: 13).

When Chris approached me about becoming 'a memory, a conscience, a nagging voice' for his new company, giving 'permanence to something impermanent' was certainly on his mind. But he was also in a process of transition as a theatre-maker, as described in a post on his blog, *Thompson's Bank of Communicable Desire*, in May 2011. Previously, he admitted, he had considered the rehearsal room a place of fiercely guarded privacy: 'I felt my duty of care to the actors and creative team meant they should be protected.' More recently, however, he had begun to ask: 'protected from what? And can't the necessary care be taken of whoever happens to come into the room?' (Goode 2011b). Inviting me in was a way to find out.

The following month, Chris wrote again about the rehearsal room, describing it as the place 'where theatre is most like itself: a liquid thing, restless, full of spontaneities and unexpected shifts'. It was here, he felt, that audiences could come closest to the 'important and transformative things theatre can do' (Goode 2011c). For Chris, those things are left-wing and anti-capitalist in ideology, dissident in nature, and community-building in spirit; they relate to how people work together and support each other.[3] By opening the doors to the rehearsal room, and increasingly working with participatory and verbatim practices,[4] CG&Co seek to dismantle social hierarchies, assumptions and accepted structures, and envisage alternatives.

What binds these thoughts together is a single idea, named by Chris, in another blog post from 2011, as 'polyvocality'. Here Chris emphasized his desire to 'keep remaking and rethinking theatre as a polyvocal space, a social space, a space that's scrupulously hospitable to difference but also in itself a place we can hold in common' (Goode 2011d). A space in which 'hearing other people's voices is absolutely central' (ibid). Putting a critic at the heart of his company, Chris ensured that at least one other voice would always be present.

I in turn honour this desire for polyvocality by making space for other voices in my writing. Sometimes my methods are journalistic: when writing about CG&Co's 9 (2012), a co-production with West Yorkshire Playhouse in Leeds, I interviewed producer Amy Letman and West Yorkshire Playhouse's chief executive, Sheena Wrigley, about the tensions that arise when an independent company works within an institution (after which Letman noted that her work had not previously been submitted to such scrutiny) (Costa 2012). Increasingly, though, I search for other forms. CG&Co's *GOD/HEAD* (2012) is essentially a monologue, but Chris performed it each night in the company of a guest,[5] who is simultaneously a companion, a foil and a representation of the not-knowing that characterizes human existence. At the heart of my writing about it is a fake group conversation with several of these guests, pieced together from interviews I conducted with them individually. Our words weave reflection and critique into a multifaceted, polyvocal response to the show (Costa 2014b).

Another idea central to Chris's work is that of the constellation. In a post published on his blog in October 2006, he recounted the experience of taking anti-depressants for the first time, then looking up at the night sky and having 'the strongest and most peculiar and compelling sensation that I could perceive – not see, exactly, but sense – connections, just simple linear connections, between the stars'. He went on: 'That sense of the connectedness of things [...] has underscored every piece of work I've done since' (Goode 2006). Like polyvocality, this idea of the constellation carries into my writing, which not only draws connections between CG&Co's own works but relates this to community-building, mapping the links between Chris and other theatre-makers and thinkers. A key to this map would identify recurrent themes: the damage wreaked by patriarchy and capitalism; fragile mental health; queer identity, sex, spirituality, otherness; inarticulacy, loneliness; fathers and mothers. The more work I see that shares these themes – by Andy Smith, Headlong, Peter

McMaster, the vacuum cleaner, Christopher Brett Bailey, Scottee, an ever-expanding galaxy – the more intricate the constellation grows.

I feel clear on the role I play in telling the story of CG&Co back to the company. I keep in mind the body of work while Chris and his producer focus on the limbs; while their impetus is to push the company forward, mine is to pull back, holding open a space for reflection amid the hurly-burly of touring, staging new work, and R&D. In reminding them what they have been, I (often unknowingly) illuminate paths towards new ways of becoming. Less clear is the role I play in forming a bridge between the company and a wider public. In theory, I open the door of the rehearsal room for all-comers to see inside, but how true is this in practice? I write this essay in another moment of transition: as CG&Co develop a new website, which will house all my writing about the company. Prior to this, it was all published on my personal blog,[6] amid an animated collage of reflections on theatre; references to books, films and exhibitions; YouTube videos, song lyrics and quotations from poetry; stories about my family and the occasional cake recipe. The accessibility and informal, conversational tone of this blog are undermined by the fact that most posts run from 3,000 to 10,000 words: only readers with stamina need apply.

I also worry that the writing appeals only to a theatre-making readership: people who aren't concerned when I write about a rehearsal process. Sometimes I might do so within a week or two of being in the room, but sometimes it takes me two months or two years. I take copious notes, but allow everything I write to register fallibilities of memory and fluctuations of mood, risking self-indulgence. Still, I aim to be rigorous – and that, combined with verbosity, tends to imply a 'final word' on everything CG&Co do, leaving little space for conversation with others.

But the collaboration with CG&Co is itself a work-in-progress. Increasingly, Chris and I are interested in the potential for creative documentation, in me beginning to write from the midst of rehearsals, and in curating other voices from within the process. We're intrigued by the idea of me writing more elliptically, or creating non-verbal (for instance, illustrated) responses. We're looking into the possibilities of print, creating fanzines to be distributed to audiences on tours. Compared with the days when I was confined to writing a 300-word review of Chris's work with a star rating, the possibilities feel limitless and invigorating.

It started with journalism

In December 2008 and January 2009 I spent several days at the National Theatre in London, watching a new production of Tom Stoppard's *Every Good Boy Deserves Favour* (*EGBDF*, my abbreviation) travel to the stage. At the time I was a regular contributor to *The Guardian*'s theatre pages, frequently interviewing directors, actors and playwrights, and developing an interest in visiting the rehearsal room. For one article, I spent a day with Michael Boyd's Royal Shakespeare Company Histories ensemble, mesmerized by the alchemical process by which actors transform text into performance (Costa 2006); for another, I witnessed Anthony Neilson's fraught method of writing a play by night and rehearsing by day (Costa 2007b). But the article that *The Guardian* arts desk commissioned me to write about *EGBDF* was different. I was to focus on the people behind the scenes: not the directors – Tom Morris and Felix Barrett – but those whose work often goes unnoticed (Costa 2009). I spoke not only to the stage, sound and lighting designers, but to the production manager, the woman who constructed the model box, the stage manager and her assistant. By the end of the month, I felt as though my eyes had been scoured: I saw theatre – and myself as a critic – completely differently.

I have scarcely any experience of making theatre: most of the stage design work I did at university was an excuse to lock myself away and paint. Watching *EGBDF* blossom, I boggled at my paltry understanding of what's required to put on a show. I saw creative ideas abandoned because the materials were too expensive, the concept breached health and safety regulations, the machinery couldn't execute them; I saw how staging problems might be solved by a producer's pragmatism or an actor's quick-thinking during a dress run. I began to recall with embarrassment the many reviews I had written pointing a finger at an individual director or designer or actor for some specific decision I assumed they had made; my ignorance of the true nature of collaboration, and that collective relationship with choice, convenience, time and money, made me blush.

A level of not-knowing can be useful to critics: it allows them to see the work clearly, without the distorting influence of the makers' perspective. So argued Wardle in *Theatre Criticism*, strenuously resisting the idea of critics being present during rehearsals because it: 'changes perception of the work'. The critic as observer, he wrote, becomes a friend to the company, and a source of sympathy: 'Having made the journey with them, you are only conscious of what they have achieved; and you want what they want – unconditional approval' (1992: 10).

Wardle's concern was echoed by critic Mark Fisher, in his comments below a work of 'embedded' criticism published by Karen Fricker on her blog in May 2014. Fisher's anxiety lies in the potential for mirrored indulgence: the critic 'can feel like they're running away with the circus', while the theatre-makers 'are encouraged to believe their every move is fascinating'. And while the relationship might be mutually beneficial to the two parties, he says, 'I have difficulty imagining the readership/audience who would want to be part of the conversation' (Fisher in Fricker 2014).

Wardle and Fisher agree that a critic's responsibilities lie in assessment and evaluation – and that the judgements of the 'embedded' critic are hard to trust. Haydon anticipated this objection in 2007, in a blog post entitled 'Critical Distance'. Close relationships between theatre-makers and critics, he agreed, can compromise the latter's ability to express negative opinions, short-changing readers, who: 'shouldn't have to second-guess how much any given critic's punches might have been pulled due to a misguided sense of "support" for a play' (Haydon 2007). But Haydon also questioned whether: ' "critical distance" is a deliberate space employed by a reviewer enabling them to score points and disparage' (ibid).

It's true: I feel little inclination to 'score points and disparage' within CG&Co. But this has been the case since August 2002, when I first encountered Chris at the Edinburgh Fringe Festival. His one-man show *Kiss of Life* began with an attempted suicide, detailed the fraught love between two troubled young men, and marvelled at how people are connected by the minute quantity of argon in the air we breathe. It was intricate, compelling and truthful, and it instantly made me a lifelong fan. As a fan, I wanted, in Wardle's phrase, 'unconditional approval' for and from Chris. The more rounded picture of how he makes theatre that I've since gained through access to his rehearsal room hasn't made this biased perspective more sympathetic but more exacting. I am scrupulously honest in declaring the moments watching his work when I feel bored, confused or disappointed: but I am also meticulous in taking the time to understand why I might be responding in this way.

I also argue that there are other roles possible for critics than that of judge: roles proposed by New York artist/producer/critic Andy Horwitz in his essay 'Re-framing the Critic for the 21st Century: Dramaturgy, Advocacy and Engagement', published on his website *Culturebot* in September 2012. The critic, he argues, fulfils those roles by working alongside theatre-makers to gather ideas, which can be shared 'with potential audience members to engender dialogue and promote conversations' (Horwitz 2012b).

Horwitz has been a considerable influence on my thinking about criticism. In an earlier essay, 'Culturebot and the New Criticism', he argued that: 'the traditional critical model proposes a "subject/object" relationship between writer and performance where the critic "objectively" judges the merits of a given performance'. Horwitz rejects this hierarchy, preferring instead a framework he dubbed 'critical horizontalism', in which: 'criticism is a creative practice unto itself and the writer exists in subjective relation to the work of the artist. The writer's response is the continuation of a dialogue initiated by the artist' (Horwitz 2012a).

Dialogue has become central to my conception of 'embedded' criticism[7], and the experience of watching *EGBDF* in rehearsal feels emblematic of the conversations such proximity to the creation of theatre makes possible. It's not just that I had new understanding of how theatre comes together to share with others; I also had new insights into the work: its shape, argument, politics and desires. On press night, *EGBDF* wasn't a single object but plural: I saw at once the production the company had attempted and the production they had actually made. That multiplicity invites debate.

The experience had another effect: it revealed to me how fascinated I am by theatre when it is mutable, before it becomes 'locked down' (a term I learned from *EGBDF*'s stage manager) on press night. I wanted to continue writing about theatre as a process, which led to me engaging more with work-in-progress performances, and with work that identifies as or overlaps with live- or performance-art. The hazards of such a path were illuminated in a column by Lyn Gardner. 'Furthering the dialogue between critics and artists,' she agreed, 'can only be good.' Yet she revealed that she was: 'increasingly wary about subjecting fledgling work to critical scrutiny. Although the show might change, the review remains set in stone – or at least in cyberspace' (Gardner 2012). I aim to refute this, by trying to make my writing feel as provisional and open as the work (-in-progress) I am documenting: sometimes vulnerable, sometimes faltering, always ready to rethink.

It starts with trust

The three words identified by Horwitz – dramaturgy, advocacy and engagement – have become the spine of my practice as a critic. Of these, it is dramaturgy that gives me most pause. In Chris's rehearsal rooms, I am present only to witness: not to contribute to the making of the work. Increasingly my response is sought in the moment, but by temperament I prefer to remain quiet and absorb.

And yet, with other theatre-makers I have begun to explore the crossover between 'embedded' criticism and dramaturgical practice. Already I have a negative experience that acts as a benchmark for how not to proceed. Late in 2013, I was invited by theatre-maker Andy Field to spend some time with him debating ideas for his new show, *Put Your Sweet Hand in Mine*. I had already read an early script and given feedback; this was the logical next step. However, my proximity to these initial ideas (which related to the ways in which romantic love stories are used to distract people from thinking about their ability to effect social change) proved detrimental weeks later, when I encountered the show Andy had ultimately created with his collaborators, which was more concerned with the tropes of romantic love stories. I wrote a blog post examining the differences in these ideas (Costa 2014a), confessing my discomfort at how I had watched the finished show: distracted throughout by the ghosts shivering in my peripheral vision of all the shows it had moved away from being. Effectively, I judged the show negatively, for not fulfilling my expectations.

Wardle offers a useful warning: 'An insight can open one door only to ensure that all other doors remain locked. It is valuable only as a provisional marker' (1992: 92). He recognized two things: the ways in which clinging to fixed ideas results in criticism that fails to see what a work is trying to do, so preoccupied is the critic with what they think the work should do; and the uncontrolled ego at the root of such writing.

In my relationship with poet and live artist Harry Giles, I keep that ego in check. Harry calls me his dramaturg, although since he lives in Edinburgh and I in London, we are almost never in the same room together. So we practice 'distance dramaturgy' – a term coined by maker Alexander Kelly and academic Deirdre Heddon (2010) when working together on Kelly's solo show *The Lad Lit Project* – using email to exchange ideas, questions, links to newspaper articles, discussion of twitter streams, and other rambling thoughts.[8] I see this work as a kind of feeding: nourishing Harry with material that enhances his own thinking, helping him craft the show that is within him to make. Since he leans heavily on improvisation, I experience a high level of surprise when seeing him perform. My dramaturgy is distanced in more ways than one.

It started decades ago

A few months after I joined CG&Co, Chris sent me a text message alerting me to a passage in Peter Brook's *The Empty Space*. The critic, Brook wrote, is 'a pathmaker', and as such shares a common aim with theatre-makers: of 'moving towards a less deadly, but, as yet, largely undefined theatre' (1968: 36). This interrelationship, Brook insisted, was imperative: 'like the fish in the ocean, we need one another's devouring talents to perpetuate the sea bed's existence'. He continued: 'It is for this reason that the more the critic becomes an insider, the better' (1968: 37).

The Empty Space was published in 1968. That same year, in *Plays and Players* magazine, journalist Helen Dawson wrote in exasperation: 'Plays have changed in construction and in subject matter, so has the intellectual awareness of performers and the education – and age – of the audience. Perhaps they haven't changed enough; but journalistic criticism has hardly altered' (Dawson quoted in Haydon 2014). Her solutions included the abandonment of press nights, on-the-night reviews, and standard review lengths; she also proposed a closer relationship between theatre-makers and critics, arguing that time spent in the rehearsal room could be: 'more worthwhile for critic, cast and director – and ultimately for the critic's readers – than 600 words on the revival of an ancient musical which would be equally well served by a picture and its caption' (ibid).

Underlying both of these texts is a recognition that theatre operates as an ecosystem – one that, as Horwitz wrote some 45 years later: 'supports the creative impulse in ourselves and in our communities. . . . [Theatre] is not entertainment and it is not commodity, it is a vital social function that supports civil society and human development' (Horwitz 2012b). This is the belief driving Horwitz's insistence that critics: 'shift our emphasis from trying to "sell a ticket to a show" to offering our communities a space to observe or participate in transformative experiences and engage with each other' (ibid).

Like Chris, Horwitz rejects the hierarchies inherent in class-based societies. This was the starting point for another British maker, Daniel Bye, who wrote a post for his blog in 2012 in support of 'embedded' criticism. What excited Bye was the potential for critics to 'illuminate' the politics of how theatre is made: the 'embedded assumptions about humanity' that charge a rehearsal room, and dictate how directors behave towards their actors, how makers collaborate, how work is created under pressure. Bye questioned whether all work that espouses 'collectivist left-wing politics' is made in genuinely collectivist ways, and looked forward to critical writing that 'could observe inconsistencies' and encourage artists to forge stronger relationships. His choice of verbs is crucial: 'observe' and 'illuminate'. He supports 'embedded' criticism not for what it might expose and judge, but what it might witness and invite others to see.

Despite these excellent arguments, past and modern, 'embedded' criticism remains a minority practice in the UK. I struggle to understand why. 'Embedded' practice has transformed criticism for me. It's no longer a lonely and frantic business of writing about a show seen once and quickly digested before moving on to the next. I no longer map constellations of star ratings, but build communities with constellations of people who make, watch and write about theatre. I've rejected the authority of the professional critic, in favour of dialogues in which my thoughts carry no more weight than any other audience-member's. My favourite dialogues take place at Theatre Clubs,[9] pop-up discussions that follow the format of book groups, which invite theatregoers to interpret a production for each other, not seek answers from the makers as they would in a traditional Q&A.

For the first two years of working with Chris Goode & Company, I rejected altogether the appellation 'critic', striving to avoid that connotation of judgement. I was reconciled to it in May 2013 by a blog post by poet/playwright/performer Hannah Silva, on the subject of labels such as critic, and the importance of, not rejecting them, but 'changing the associations/preconceptions around the word itself' (Silva 2013). She argued: 'To bring a label with a past into the present is to continue a journey' (ibid). I put quotation marks around the word 'embedded' because I don't think it's necessary. What I practice is criticism. And I practice it in a way that seeks constantly to discover new possibilities for how it can communicate, when, and with whom.

Notes

1. My use of maker or theatre-maker throughout this essay is partly influenced by Chris Goode, who calls himself a theatre-maker rather

than divide up his practice into writing, directing, performing, etc. I use it instinctively, and turn to Duška Radosavljević's book *Theatre-Making: Interplay Between Text and Performance in the 21st Century* for supporting academic argument.

2. In the 1993 edition of the *New Shorter Oxford English Dictionary*, the first definition of critic is: 'A person who pronounces judgement' (1993: 551).

3. On his blog in August 2010, Chris framed as a theatre manifesto a quote from *Crack Capitalism*, by socialist writer John Holloway: 'Stop making capitalism and do something else, something sensible, something beautiful and enjoyable. Stop making the system that is destroying it.' Quoted in Goode, C (2010).

4. Chris used verbatim practice in *Monkey Bars* (2012), which was performed by adults but used text spoken by children; and in *Stand* (2014), which retold the stories of everyday activists. *9* (2012) was a participatory show that invited people with no experience of professional theatre to portray themselves on stage.

5. Guests included other theatre-makers such as Chris Thorpe and Kieran Hurley, critics including myself and Honour Bayes, choreographers including Nicola Conibere and producers such as Ed Collier.

6. This writing is grouped within the category Chris Goode & Co: http://statesofdeliquescence.blogspot.co.uk/search/label/chris%20goode%20and%20co.

7. 'Dialogue' is so central to my critical work that in Spring 2012 I co-founded an organisation of that name, through which I curate a programme of conversations about theatre: some similar to book groups, providing an alternative to the post-show Q&A, others designed to question industry practice.

8. An edited transcript of our dramaturgical dialogue was published on the website *Something Other*. Costa, M and Giles, H (2015).

9. To date I have co-hosted Theatre Clubs as part of Dialogue with my co-founder Jake Orr; with Fuel as part of the New Theatre in Your Neighbourhood touring research project; and at the Young Vic with the Two Boroughs participation project.

Works cited

Brook, Peter (1968), *The Empty Space*, Republished 1972, London: Penguin.

Bye, Dan (2012), 'Embedded Criticism: Some Arguments, an Offer and a Dare', 24 April, http://www.danielbye.co.uk/blog/embedded-criticism-some-arguments-an-offer-and-a-dare (accessed on 29 April 2015).

Costa, Maddy (2006), 'We've Got Some Right Egomaniacs in This Company', 19 July, http://www.theguardian.com/stage/2006/jul/19/theatre.rsc (accessed on 29 April 2015).

Costa, Maddy (2007a), 'Hippo World Guest Book review', *The Guardian*, 13 August, http://www.theguardian.com/stage/2007/aug/13/theatre. edinburghfestival20074 (accessed on 29 April 2015).

Costa, Maddy (2007b), 'The More Pressure, the Better', *The Guardian*, 21 November, http://www.theguardian.com/stage/2007/nov/21/rsc.theatre (accessed on 29 April 2015).

Costa, Maddy (2009), 'Looks Great – But It'll Never Work', *The Guardian*, 4 February, http://www.theguardian.com/stage/2009/feb/04/every-good-boy-deserves-favour (accessed on 29 April 2015).

Costa, Maddy (2012), 'Chris Goode and Company's 9', http://statesofdeliquescence.blogspot.co.uk/p/chris-goode-and-companys-9.html (accessed on 29 April 2015).

Costa, Maddy (2014a), 'It Must Be Love, Love, Love', 21 February, http://statesofdeliquescence.blogspot.co.uk/2014/02/it-must-be-love-love-love.html (accessed on 29 April 2015).

Costa, Maddy (2014b), 'CG&Co's GOD/HEAD', http://statesofdeliquescence.blogspot.co.uk/p/cg-godhead.html (accessed on 29 April 2015).

Costa, Maddy (2014c), 'Each in Their Own Way Flailing', 18 August, http://statesofdeliquescence.blogspot.co.uk/2014/08/each-in-their-own-way-flailing.html (accessed on 29 April 2015).

Costa, Maddy and Giles, Harry (2015), 'Class Act', http://classact.somethingother.io/#/ (accessed on 29 April 2015).

Fricker, Karen (2014), 'Behind the scenes at Shaw', 15 May, https://karenfricker.wordpress.com/2014/05/15/behind-the-scenes-at-shaw/ (accessed on 29 April 2015).

Gardner, Lyn (2012), 'Critic's Notebook', *The Guardian*, 29 April, http://www.theguardian.com/culture/2012/apr/29/critics-notebook-lyn-gardner (accessed on 29 April 2015).

Gardner, Lyn (2014), 'This Week's New Theatre', *The Guardian*, 23 May, http://www.theguardian.com/stage/2014/may/23/this-weeks-new-theatre (accessed on 29 April 2015).

Goode, Chris (2006), 'Nostalgia Isn't What It Used To Be Thought It Was Going To Be in the Future', 6 October, http://beescope.blogspot.co.uk/2006/10/nostalgia-isnt-what-it-used-to-be.html (accessed on 29 April 2015).

Goode, Chris (2010), 'Stop Making Capitalism', 13 August, http://beescope. blogspot.co.uk/2010/08/stop-making-capitalism.html (accessed on 29 April 2015).

Goode, Chris (2011a), private correspondence with Maddy Costa, 3 May.

Goode, Chris (2011b), 'Tolstoy in the Rear View Mirror', 28 May, http:// beescope.blogspot.co.uk/2011/05/tolstoy-in-rear-view-mirror.html (accessed on 14 January 2015).

Goode, Chris (2011c), 'Opening the House', 11 June 2011, http://beescope. blogspot.co.uk/2011/06/opening-house.html (accessed on 29 April 2015).

Goode, Chris (2011d), 'Season's Greeblings; and Another Year Over', 30 December, http://beescope.blogspot.co.uk/2011/12/seasons-greeblings-and-another-year.html (accessed on 29 April 2015).

Haydon, Andrew (2007), 'Critical Distance', 2 September, http:// postcardsgods.blogspot.co.uk/2007/09/critical-distance.html (accessed on 29 April 2015).

Haydon, Andrew (2012), 'Embedded', 16 April, http://postcardsgods.blogspot. co.uk/2012/04/embedded.html (accessed on 14 January 2015).

Haydon, Andrew (2014) 'Shorts: plus ça change, plus c'est la même chose', 17 January, http://postcardsgods.blogspot.co.uk/2014/01/shorts-plus-ca-change-plus-cest-la-meme.html (accessed on 29 April 2015).

Heddon, Deirdre and Kelly, Alexander (2010), 'Distance Dramaturgy', http:// eprints.gla.ac.uk/39613/1/39613.pdf (accessed on 29 April 2015).

Horwitz, Andy (2012a), 'Culturebot and the New Criticism', 31 March, http:// www.culturebot.org/2012/03/12883/culturebot-and-the-new-criticism/ (accessed on 29 April 2015).

Horwitz, Andy (2012b), 'Re-framing the Critic for the 21st Century: Dramaturgy, Advocacy and Engagement', 5 September, http://www. culturebot.org/2012/09/13258/re-framing-the-critic-for-the-21st-century-dramaturgy-advocacy-and-engagement/ (accessed on 29 April 2015).

Silva, Hannah (2013), 'What It Says on the Tin', 22 May, http://hannahsilva. co.uk/what-it-says-on-the-tin/ (accessed on 29 April 2015).

Wardle, Irving (1992), *Theatre Criticism*, London: Routledge.

No author (1993) *New Shorter Oxford English Dictionary*, Oxford: Oxford University Press.

PART III
CHANGING FORMS AND FUNCTIONS OF CRITICISM

CHAPTER 13
CRITICISM AS A POLITICAL EVENT
Diana Damian Martin

As the lights dim, I become part of the fabric of this performance. I forget to take notes; perhaps occasionally, I am reminded of something else, creeping in from the edges of my memory, and this gives my encounter, in that moment, particular significance. This choreography of attention unfolds throughout my encounter, and later, as my eyelids start feeling heavy, as I rummage through my notes, as references and histories start pouring in, I begin to hack at this piece of criticism. Somewhere in that process, the performance starts to drift away; I move it back, and we dance together.

In *The Transformative Power of Performance* (2008), performance theorist Erika Fischer-Lichte makes a compelling argument for the ways in which a significant landscape of contemporary practices blur the boundaries between the perceiver and the perceived. We do not simply encounter performance, she proposes; our engagement with it is framed by an event. We produce meaning, Fischer-Lichte argues, through our perception, which in turn, returns to that which we are experiencing. She terms this an autopoietic feedback loop, marked by 'the perceptual shifts between the order of representation and the order of presence' (2002: 157). I am interested in the ways in which this shift allows for an opportunity for criticism.

The critic is an embodied presence in the performance encounter, navigating a landscape of meaning. Yet for the critic, this event does not end once she leaves the performance space; it carries through into the thought processes that begin to take shape during the performance and linger well beyond it. The shift between representation and presence gains a different iteration, extended beyond the initial encounter; we carry performance with us, enmesh it in a process of thinking and articulation that is contextualized by a cultural and political landscape.

I want to recuperate a politicized critical practice from this very vantage point. Amongst the scraps of notes, the memories, the detailed descriptions we want to render present in our critical texts, an opportunity emerges to consider a more complex relationship between performance and criticism. In this chapter, I return to the philosophical and political relationships that govern criticism in contemporary performance.

As critics, we are not alone in this series of movements that frame the critical event, which I mark as the process that begins with our encounter with performance and continues beyond the performance space, through to the point in which our thoughts are structured and delineated in the form of a critical text. At a time when governments are increasingly attempting to influence the position of the economic market in different aspects of everyday life, at institutional and individual levels, socially and culturally, we are confronted with a neoliberalisation of culture. In 'Enjoying Neoliberalism', political theorist Jodi Dean defines neoliberalism as 'a philosophy viewing market exchange as a guide for all human action [...], redefining social and ethical life in accordance with economic criteria' (Dean 2008: 47). In *The New Way of the World*, political theorists Dardot and Laval make an argument for neoliberalism as having a normative logic (2013: 2) that accounts for its distinctive character yet foregrounds it as a universal and strategic political and social problem. Challenging the delineation between economic policy and ideological manifestation, Dardot and Laval foreground neoliberalism as a normative rationality, in which generalized competition, an alignment of social norms with market models and a justification of social inequality become matters of day to day. The mechanisms that underpin criticism and its relationship to performance are being instrumentalized under the same political rationality that champions competition, individuality and marketization.

In this chapter, I think about the nature of this relationship between criticism and performance under neoliberalism, in order to foreground a politicized practice that might resist criticism's instrumentalization. In articulating the practical iterations of such political practice, one might consider criticism as a strategy for engaging with performance's appearance and discourse as well as its formal iterations. For example, one might account for this in relation to the increasing interest in collaboration across critical outlets. *Exeunt Magazine* have championed the collaboratively-written review, where several writers engage in a conversation surrounding a piece of work which foregrounds several topics and aspects at the same time, moving towards a plural debate. Another example is the development of curated critical projects, such as Quizoola LIVE, a project I curated in collaboration with Forced Entertainment for *Exeunt Magazine* that invited a number of writers to respond to the company's durational performance in real time, via a live-stream. And perhaps one can also look at embedded writing programmes that seek to engage orally and discursively with criticism, such as those hosted by Pacitti Company and Spill Festival of Performance or In Between Time Festival. The emphasis across these iterations of critical practice is on politicizing the encounter with performance, whilst foregrounding different strategies of engagement and analysis. In order to understand the increasing diversification and expansion of critical practice, a theoretical framework that foregrounds its intrinsic relationships is necessary. To that end, I am here concerned with delineating a theoretical perspective that locates the possibility of dissensus in criticism.

Towards a politicized critical practice

In my theorization of criticism as a political event I draw on the political philosophy of Jacques Rancière, who defines dissensus as pertaining to 'a conflict about who speaks and who does not speak, about what has to be heard as the voice of pain and what has to be heard as an argument on justice' (2001: 2). Rancière's political philosophy offers a way through which to think about those who participate in criticism, as well as foregrounding a model of understanding politics on the basis of process and an action of dissensus which it fuels.

I propose that we can understand the nature of criticism within contemporary culture as defined by Rancière to be one of dissensus, in which 'sense is matched with sense', that is, 'an accord is made between a sensory regime of the presentation of things and a mode of interpretation of their meaning' (2010: viii). This suggests the possibility of, and potential for, rethinking critical practice in terms of its capacity to engender productive dissent. That is, to consider it in Rancière's terms as a political event, that is, one marked by a dissensus which results in a series of shifts of position-takings between different participating agents.

I identify three aspects that are central to my own engagement with Rancière's politics. The first is the relationship between the political and the aesthetic that is foregrounded in the philosopher's elaboration of the distribution of the sensible and thus, sense experience. Although this has become a central tenet of performance scholarship's own engagement with Rancière's work, for criticism, this implication is different; it provides a method through which to consider the aesthetic dimensions of language and judgement as engaged with the referent itself.

The second is the role of dissensus in politics, which is made manifest through processes of visibility. This is central to my own politicization of criticism, because it implicates a highly disputed, but, productive, identification of dissensus within and in relation to criticism. Thirdly, the identification of a revolutionary event in Rancière's political philosophy, understood as the most productive process of a re-distribution of the sensible. How might we identify the revolutionary potential of criticism as a process, bringing back into the discussion a problematization of visibility as the central tenet of power within society.

Fundamental to Rancière's political philosophy is the articulation of politics as a form of emancipation through which a community is made visible, thus legitimized in the global social sphere. What marks this moment of confrontation is an engagement on behalf of its participants 'over the existence of a common stage' (2010: 26). This logic implies an essential process of disruption – equality is achieved when the sensible, that which marks out the common sphere of sense experience, has been re-distributed. Rancière thus differentiates between the process of politics, and the action of 'policing', which is attributed to be 'a system of distribution' (2010: 28).

In opposition to this process, policing is understood as a form of legislation; of maintaining what Rancière argues to be a form of consensus. In my own engagement with criticism, this is posited as a particularly relevant problematic. I introduce the potential of a form of differentiation between processes that might enable the visibility of a work's discourse, or those that might render it invisible.

In order to better understand the ways in which this differentiation might be productive for the study of criticism, I want to flesh out the role that aesthetics plays in this delineation of the political.

Rancière defines aesthetic practices as 'forms of visibility that disclose artistic practices, the place they occupy, what they "do" or "make" from the standpoint of what is common to the "community"' (ibid). Located around the properties of common spaces – politics requires a disruption of aesthetics that can erupt from within: disrupting partitions rather than replacing them.

We have already seen how the encounter with performance is shaped by an event in which the order of presence and representation are in constant motion; and I have discussed how this event extends, for criticism, beyond the encounter with performance. Here, the political is articulated through an aesthetic disruption. Performance itself offers a site in which the sensible can be re-distributed, that is, in which certain conflicts, ideas and sensibilities can be challenged and the terms of the conflict re-ordered. Criticism holds a responsibility towards the articulation of this re-distribution; in its relationship to a wider cultural and political context, criticism holds the ability to engage in a process of re-distribution of the sensible that operates discursively and aesthetically. Yet the only way in which this is possible is to begin, as Rancière does, from a position of equality.

Rancière defines politics as a moment that marks a shift in social space. The apparent antagonism towards the police serves to shift the system of legitimation, which is forced to acknowledge what the process has rendered visible. The logic of this operation is supported by the construction of the constant process of distributing the sensible, that which maintains divisions enforced by the police, but, more importantly, 'simultaneously discloses the existence of something in common and the delimitations that define the respective parts and positions within it' (2010: 12). Politics becomes, as Katharine Wolfe has argued, 'a possibility with the institution of common sense' (2011: 3).

For criticism, we might understand this confrontation as a potential mode of resistance; criticism is able, I propose, to shift the position of a performance in a certain social and cultural space, but also to address directly the discourses which are embedded within it.

By understanding what this conception of politics through dissensus can bring to the study of criticism, we are better equipped at deconstructing the mechanisms that underpin public discourse and knowledge under neoliberalism. Only then can we ask who distinguishes between, to reflect Rancière's distinction, those who are able to speak and those who are not, that which has a voice and that which does not – delineating between the right of gaining authority and inherent privilege. I offer a politicization of criticism that seeks to distinguish between processes of cultural legislation, and those concerned with discourse and visibility.

Criticism and the neoliberal: politics and aesthetics

Criticism is a practice concerned with the formation of public discourse[1] pertaining to and concerning performance. In this delineation, I draw together practices that emerge in a multiplicity of contexts, from the academic to the journalistic, the textual to the performative. I build on Roland Barthes' delineation of criticism in *Criticism as Truth* as engaged in processes of subjectivity:

> criticism is not at all a table of results or a body of judgments; it is essentially an activity, i.e. a series of intellectual acts profoundly committed to the historical and subjective existence of the man [or woman] who performs them.

> 1989: 12

Criticism is not solely an activity that re-iterates the constitution of the subject. Criticism always deals with and engages with a referent. In this manner, it pertains to the political, in its myriad of positions and relationships; to the aesthetic, in its gaze, its descriptive and analytical process; and to subjectivity, in its tense relationship with authorship. Criticism, then, is a matter of politics and aesthetics, and emblematic of a way in which judgement and discussion on art and its processes are enabled or censored in a different configuration of publics.

In his edited collection *After Criticism*, Gavin Butt outlines the tensions underpinning contemporary criticism. Citing art critic Benjamin Buchloh, Butt makes a compelling argument for a precarity of criticism.'For what of critical culture' he asks,'if it comes increasingly and narrowly to serve the interests of the market' (2005: 2). Butt argues for criticism that situates itself in relation to common doxa, freed from 'the protocols of institutionalized forms of thought' (2005: 5). This is informed by a displacement of authority on the basis of an acknowledgement of the critic's participation in the landscape of culture.

Butt foregrounds an increasing tension between criticism and the cultural fabric, pointing towards the ways in which critics have become 'enmeshed in the very, perhaps even "creative" production of the cultural fabric itself' (ibid). This is evidenced, he argues, by contestations brought to critical distance and the power of authority as privilege:

> Critical distance has come to look increasingly prone to collapse [...] as critics in their various professional guises have abandoned their claims to speak from any form of privileged or authoritative viewpoint.
>
> 1989: 3

Butt is advocating for a horizontal approach to criticism, one in which the critic acknowledges and works from her subjective relation to the work of art. Horizontalism is foregrounded elsewhere by US critic Andy Horwitz as 'a continuation of a dialogue initiated by the artist' (2012).

In the fields of art and architecture, Jane Rendell constitutes the term critical spatial practice to refer to writing that 'transgresses the limits of art architecture and engages with both the social and the aesthetic, the public and the private' (2006: 3). Rendell explores the spatial dimensions of the encounter between criticism and architecture; she focuses on the different spatial relationships that are at play in a critic's encounter with architecture, taking into account the context of that encounter as much as the identity of the building itself. She delineates a practice that works horizontally, in between the two realms.

Finally, literary theorist Mieke Bal also engages with horizontalism by way of a descriptive approach to criticism, where the work of art is rendered visible and present by way of the critic's subjective encounter with it. In *Louise Bourgeois's Spider*, Bal argues for the value of the close encounter. She adds that 'the closer the engagement with the work of art, the more adequate the result of the analysis will be' (2001: xxiii).

Horizontalism as an interdisciplinary movement in criticism has displaced certain fundamental concerns surrounding questions of authority and positioning, as I have evidenced in my overview of its different disciplinary articulations. What remains under-examined however is the direct encounter with performance that seeks to bring precarity to the process of critiquing work. I am interested in how dissensus with the performance and its event might be able to re-configure this relationship, emerging from the position of equality that horizontalism ensues for performance and criticism.

I am working from the same vantage point as Susan Sontag who, in *Against Interpretation*, cautions against a capturing of meaning, a re-inscription of the work. At the onset of the essay, Sontag cites artist Willem De Kooning, proposing that the content of a work of art is 'a glimpse of something, an encounter like a flash' (1966: 1). Barthes makes the same argument in *Criticism and Truth*:

> The critic cannot claim to 'translate' the work, and particularly not to make it clearer, for nothing is clearer than the work. What the critic can do is to 'engender' a certain meaning by deriving it from the form which is the work.
>
> 1987: 32

For performance however, the form is not the work, but the entire event of our encounter is what frames the experience from which we derive meaning. As a result, criticism concerns itself with an experienced performance event; this cannot be translated, but it can be unpeeled through the process of thought and, in most instances, writing. Lehmann and others argue that form is imbued with politics (2006: 40), yet the engagement and preponderance of that form are important in delineating any potential configurations. For criticism, this means that a political process might only be thought of in relation to *both* visibility and configuration. In light of this, politics and aesthetics are problems of criticism.

The fall as gesture of criticism

I want to mark what I term the gesture of criticism in between two photographic documents, in order to more clearly flesh out the relationship between position-takings, equality and dissent in

Image 1 (left) Yves Klein. *Saut dans le Vide (Leap into the Void): The Painter of Space Hurls Himself into the Void!*. 1960. Yves Klein, ADAGP, Paris; Photo: Shunk-Kender © Roy Lichtenstein Foundation.

Image 2 (right) Ciprian Mureşan. *Leap into the Void, after 3 seconds*. 2004. © Galeria Plan B.

criticism: Yves Klein's *Saut dans le Vide* (1960) and Ciprian Mureşan's *Leap into the Void, after 3 seconds* (2004). The visualization provides a matrix of associations that pertain to a configuration of political positions. These are occupied by the agents or performers of each respective image, and extend into a relationship with the viewer and with the other image. There is a parallel set of configurations that concern critical practice: the relationship between the subject of a piece of work and the critical text; the dynamic between the writer and the performance; and the dialogue with the reader and, sometimes, the spectator.

Yves Klein leaps from the window of a building in 1960s Paris; Mureşan has just fallen on a street in Bucharest in 2004. A leap occurs in one context, and is reflected in the immediate aftermath of a fall in another. My scope is to establish the fall as the gesture of dissensus residing between these two moments.

In both images, the artists position themselves in relation to a problem. In *Saut sans le Vide*, Yves Klein's apparent upward gaze suggests flight defiant of gravity; here the artist is attempting to elevate the everyday. In *Leap into the Void, after 3 seconds*, the artist has been defeated. He is no longer flying above the axis of the everyday, but has been consumed by it; the intervention is the mass of his body, rather than the void that shapes it in mid-flight. The conflict between gravity and defiance becomes that between the body and the site. The immateriality which Klein's image engages is flattened by Mureşan's body.

For Klein, the void had become both pictorial concern and formal engagement. Klein is making visible a doctrine of refusal, by which I mean, a positioning of the artist as a figure with potential. This is made explicit by the reflection of the possibility of the fall, relegated outside of the realm of this event. The leap is the fundamental operation of the image, on which the meaning hinges. It also operates in relation to the spatial arrangement of the photograph: the height, the implied observer passing by on his bicycle, the removal of the net which was to catch the leap in actuality. So what of this leap?

Art historian Andrea D Fitzpatrick speaks of Klein's image as a positioning of territories, arguing that what makes the leap so compelling both from an existential and representational point of view is its status as a pivotal gesture. She argues that this gesture is 'situated between artistic generations (modern and postmodern) and geographic traditions (European, American, and Asian)' (2007: 93). Klein's document presents both an artistic utopia and flippant commentary. On the one hand, the leap positions both the artist and the photograph as an artistic process referential to context; yet on the other, the photograph denies itself any level of seriousness, particularly in its overt representation of the upward gaze.

Mureşan's photograph exists in direct relationship to Klein's. The artist provides a critique of the position of the artist in post-1989 Romania that rests on the idealism of Klein's image, and its iconic status. Mureşan explains:

> forty years after Klein made his seminal image of the emancipation of the artistic impulse in Paris, our stone streets could be anywhere in Europe, even in Paris – but the difference between my world and the world Klein represents is embodied in those three seconds between the leap and the fall.
>
> Nathan 2012

In his re-staging of Yves Klein's leap, Mureşan's photograph is marked by the absence of a fall. The shift in time and place presents the moment after the event occurs – the landing. In this landing, Mureşan both politicizes the moment of the leap's staging and comments on the process of historical visibility and documentation. In the choice of setting, *Leap into the Void, after 3 seconds* provides a temporality and territoriality to the leap; it suggests a narrative in which the position of the artist has changed, but also clarifies the affordances Klein was able to perhaps make in 1960s Paris, when Romania was under dictatorial rule.

The image is a reminder of the fall's inevitable ending. It speaks of the uncertainty of the past, referencing the censorship of narratives and their illogical representation. *Leap into the Void, after 3 seconds* foregrounds the banality of this ending; much like the spectacular nature of the leap, the artist's fall bears no particular consequence. It is an event, like the leap, whose axis interrupts the flow of the everyday, the linearity of life on the street, yet the cyclist doesn't pause to encounter the event, merely to suggest its passing.

My interest lies between the moments made possible by the two photographs. Mureşan's is an explicit, critical response to Klein's work. By itself, it doesn't represent the fall – merely the moment after. The fall makes itself present in between the two images, in a nexus of two narratives of distinct historical moments. These are the development of performance and body art of the 1960s, confronting the nature of the everyday, immateriality and the position of the body in art practice on the one hand, and post-communist Romania, where artists are confronting the absence of historical narratives, the erasure of events and the denial of conflict, on the other. The fall emerges not only as that which links these two distinct moments; it also gains a material presence in between the two sites, and is constituted by our gaze as viewers.

The fall is the marker of the thought processes and critical operations deployed by the second photograph onto the first. The fall is the process that is present in neither image, yet imagined by the second onto the first. In this manner, it is a gesture of dissent in which the response to the initial referent re-configures the meaning of the first; the fall is the signal of this moment of dissensus. The fall is referenced by both images, and yet absent within their respective compositions. It is that which is withdrawn from visibility, yet made to appear by the second image. The fall is a productive conceptual movement that has an actuality in both photographs.

I associate the critical output – the review, for example – with the second image, and locate the critical process in its extension towards the referent – Klein's piece. I posit a consideration of critical process that doesn't assume the art might be *the original* discourse, and critique its secondary shadow. Locating the political in the critical process enables me to consider the two through the methodolcgical lens of a practice of equality that sees the two interrelated, dependent, in a productive tension.

I identify a triadic relationship between criticism, its referent and the site in which they both exist, on the proposition that this is neither singular nor fixed. In its productive absence, the fall is the gesture of dissensus, and this is key to my argumentation of criticism as a political event. The fall is a moment of dissensus, and makes visible the political and aesthetic dimension of the visualization.

The critic is enmeshed in the cultural fabric, in tension with the referent, that which criticism refers to. If we are to hark back to the visualization that marked this chapter, we notice the different positions at play: the authors of the photographs, the agents of the actions which they contain, the tension between the second and the first image and the suspension in which they are both kept as a result. The viewers are also gazing on the moment that has marked the landing – gazing on the absent fall, which keeps attempting to make itself visible. This visualization presents us with a political regime, in which agents take up positions in relation to each other.

Configurations of resistance: criticism as a political event

I argued that the critical act which the second image performs onto the first occurs in a shared site in-between the two. As such, the gesture of the fall constructs their differentiation as distinct works, whilst also re-iterating their explicit association. The gesture is a marker of the critical process enacted in between the two documents. Falling becomes, in this instance, a mode of thought as much as a marker of a dissensus within an enacted process of criticism.

I propose that understanding criticism as a political event allows us to explore the encounters that mark its relationship to performance. We can examine the critical process as comprised stages of dissensus, articulation and dialogue. In this configuration I want to move beyond a pragmatic reading of criticism that sees criticism's function solely as that of cultural evaluation. I open up the possibility of criticism doing and undoing in several processes at the same time, a multiplicity in which the referent is not a cultural commodity, economically quantifiable through normative interpretive models; on the contrary, I argue for multiplicity, not singularity.

We might call policing that which certain critical practices perform onto and against their referent. A policing critical practice is one that seeks to legislate the cultural landscape, maintaining forms of consensus rather than opening up productive conflict. Take for example, the increasing interest from mainstream media in short-form reviews that aim to capture the successes or failures of a performance, rather than engaging in interpretive processes that seek to maintain performance's own eventness. Consensus is crucial here because it confounds argumentation with cultural valuation; instead of a discussion on the particular problematics which a performance might be grappling with, we receive a diagnosis of value.

Rancière understands consensus as promoting a logic of heterogeneity, whereas dissensus is at the heart of politics as process. In *Philosopher and his Poor* (2004), Rancière explores the ways in which divisions of labour create situations of convenience and exclusion. He argues that conflict does not rely on any expression of disinterest or dissatisfaction; conflict and thus, dissensus, is that which enables 'what?' and shifts from a place of origin to one of destination.

I posit a question of identification here: what are consensus and dissensus, outside of operative tools of politics, if not the paradigms of criticism itself? Despite the association of such a paradigm with discourses of valuation, I am interested in placing this questioning in relation to the eventness of criticism as a process. I delineate criticism in this instance as both enmeshed in the fabric of culture, and inherently serving under the conditions imposed by the aesthetic regime.

If we return to the two images, we can understand the ways in which the re-configuration of the leap, and the inevitable fall, are political: they undo the distribution of the sensible that locates the first image within a particular regime, offering the possibility for Mureșan's image to stand alone. There is no politics without the process of re-configuration. In addition, the fall itself is understood as a form of dissensus; as a refusal to allow the leap itself to exist outside of its extrapolation.

Sense experience presents itself through what I call a problematization of the encounter between the referent and the critical output itself. This is where I identify the extension of criticism as a political event: in the moment between the two instances portrayed by the image, made visible by the reconfiguration offered by Mureșan, yet extended in a poetic gesture of dissensus. Poetic here is thought through in relation to the possibility of the leap, and the fall made inevitable by the circumstances portrayed. It is imperative to acknowledge that at the heart of any re-configuration also lies sensation, as presented by sense experience, and articulated and embodied within the critical process itself. The process of making visible is at play between Mureșan's image and Klein's leap, manifested as a disruption and within an encounter.

Aesthetics is what conditions that which presents itself as experience within the critical encounter. Moving from this, I identify a fundamental trait of criticism as a political event: any encounter between performance and criticism might not be seen to be dominated by linear operations, but by transactions of power. This affects the visibility of the work itself, and its associated discourse. More importantly, it invites a more considered analysis of the processes that are at play in operations of meaning-making, with the hopeful pursuit of a process of re-positioning of the work of art, of its re-appearance, but also of its internal architecture and complexity of manifestations. The politicization of the critical process as event occurs in relation to processes of meaning-making and the implication of the performance and its inner workings in a mechanism of appearance.

A final return

In my visualization, critical process resides within the extension of the leap into the landing, yet is isolated from the contextual discourse incited by the second referent. We can identify the event in this instance as that which breaks from the current moment, but also produces something new that is characterized by a lateral temporality and the construction of an adjacent truth. What the event offers up in this circumstance is the very identification of the process of criticism present in between the two images.

I call on a questioning of this captured critical process of actualization as a professional exercise of strategic imagination – when writing a piece of criticism, we might consider its process of enactment and development, outside of the formal remits of the page and text themselves.

This is also an invitation; it is a possibility to locate the wider breadth of critical processes operating in cultural discourse with a view towards resisting the legislation of the public sphere in which they might emerge.

Criticism as a political event always makes visible the space between the referent and the critic itself, in the same way in which Klein and Mureșan's photographs enact the process in their association. The site of this eruption is public; it makes manifest a conditioning of the perception and articulation of a referent for which there is a fight for shared experience and collectivity. Criticism presupposes an extended action that is by nature incomplete and uneven, filled with the possibility of the visible.

Note

1. Michel Foucault argues that discourse pertains to 'ways of constituting knowledge, together with the social practices, forms of subjectivity and power relations which inhere in such knowledges and relations between them. [...] They constitute the 'nature' of the body, unconscious and conscious mind and emotional life of the subjects they seek to govern (Weedon 1987: 108). I speak of discourse in this context as a system of communication and debate.

Works cited

Barthes, Roland (2007) *Criticism and Truth*, translated and edited by Katrine Pilcher Keuneman, London: Continuum

Butt, Gavin (ed.) (2005) *After criticism: New Responses to Art and Performance*, Malden, MA: Blackwell.

Dean, Jodi (2008) 'Enjoying Neoliberalism', *Cultural Politics: an International Journal*, 4(1), pp. 47–72.

Fischer-Lichte, Erika (2008) *The Transformative Power of Performance: A New Aesthetics*. London: Routledge.

Fitzpatrick, Andrea D. (2007) 'The Movement of Vulnerability: Images of Falling and September 11', *Art Journal*, 66(4), pp. 84–102.

Horwitz, Andy (2012) 'The New Criticism' for *Culturebot*, available at: http://www.culturebot.org/2012/03/12883/culturebot-and-the-new-criticism/ (accessed 25 January 2015).

Klein, Yves, Shunk, Harry and Kender János (Jean) (1960) *Leap Into the Void*, [Photograph], Roy Lichtenstein Foundation, *Metropolitan Museum of Art*.

Laval, Christian and Dardot, Pierre (2014) *The New Way of the World: On Neo-Liberal Society*, London: Verso.

Lehmann, Hans-Thies (2006) *Postdramatic Theatre*, translated by Karen Juers-Munby London: Routledge.

Mureşan, Ciprian (2004) *Leap into the Void, after 3 seconds*, Galeria Plan B, Berlin. *Artnet*.

Nathan, Emily (2011) *Strange Days: An Interview with Ciprian Mureşan*, *Artnet*. 20110720, available at: http://www.artnet.com/magazineus/ features/nathan/ciprian-muresan-7-20-11.asp (accessed 25 January 2015).

Rancière, Jacques (2010) *Dissensus: On Politics and Aesthetics*, translated by Stephen Corcoran, London: Contiunuum

Rancière, Jacques (2004) *The Philosopher and his Poor*, translated by John Dury, Corinne Oster, Andrew Parker, Durham and London: Duke University Press.

——. (2010) *Dissensus: On Politics and Aesthetics*. (Trans Stephen Corcoran.) London: Continuum.

Ross, Kristin (1991) 'Rancière and the Practice of Equality', *Social Text*, Volume 29, pp. 57–71.

Sontag, Susan (2001) *Against Interpretation: And Other Essays*, United States: St Martin's Press.

Wolfe, Katharine (2011) 'From Aesthetics to Politics: Rancière, Kant, Deleuze', *Contemporary Aesthetics*, http://www.contempaesthetics.org/newvolume/ pages/article.php?articleID=382 (accessed 25 January 2015).

CHAPTER 14
CONVERSATION AND CRITICISM: AUDIENCES AND UNFINISHED CRITICAL THINKING
Matthew Reason

The conversation takes place between eight of us; sitting in a circle in an upstairs room of the Tramway in Glasgow, just after watching Needcompany's *The Porcelain Project*. It is essentially an aftershow conversation, much like the many others that I imagine are taking place between audience members in the bar downstairs or on the train back to the city centre. These conversations take place between friends, family members, lovers. They are informal, often fragmented, slipping into other memories, other experiences, other topics entirely. These other conversations are unrecorded; I have no firm evidence that they have taken place at all, although it seems likely, based on personal experience and awareness of our natural proclivity to talk about the performances we have seen.

Other spectators leave the performance and also have something to say about what they have just seen, but do not communicate this something only to their companions. Instead, they disseminate it more widely. A few are professional critics but more are audience members who have something to say and say it online, via social media (on Twitter or Facebook), on a personal blog, or through commenting on a discussion thread.

For some this potential, that 'anyone with access to the internet can become a critic' (Newman cited in Lovink 2011: 65), throws the status of criticism itself into crisis. The resulting 'death of criticism' has become a meme – an idea that has spread with a rapidity that is almost viral – manifested in numerous articles and blogs. Witness Michael Kaiser's lament in the *Huffington Post* that 'arts criticism has become a participatory activity rather than a spectator sport' (Kaiser 2011); a *Guardian* hosted debate titled 'Is the age of the critic over?' (*The Guardian* 2011); or the declaration in Salon.com that 'in the age of blogging, great critics appear to be on life support' (Miller and Bayard 2008). As is the nature of a meme, the examples proliferate.

Chapters elsewhere in this collection will conceptualize this relationship between online comment and formal theatre criticism. This chapter, in contrast, will focus not on criticism but on *conversation* and on the possible conceptual relationships between newspaper criticism, online comment and audience conversations. Rather than the status of theatre criticism in an age of ubiquitous online comment, this chapter will explore the status and nature of audience conversation. While such conversations are not criticism per se, the manner by which they construct and seek to understand experiences of theatre enacts one of the functions of criticism. In particular I will propose that audience conversations are a performative process of 'unfinished thinking', speech acts that both recall experiences and bring them into being through a perpetual oscillation between knowing and not-yet-knowing.

Digital conversations

An early and influential assertion that the internet enables new kinds of conversations to take place is the Cluetrain Manifesto (1999), which responded to the impact of the internet on mass marketing. The manifesto declares that the internet enables a 'global conversation' to take place that will replace the one-directional and corporate communication of marketing and publication. The human-to-human nature of this conversation is central, characterized in a number of ways in a list of '95 Theses'. To select a few:

3. Conversations among human beings *sound* human. They are conducted in a human voice.

4. [. . .] the human voice is typically open, natural, uncontrived.

5. People recognize each other as such from the sound of this voice.

38. Human communities are based on discourse – on human speech about human concerns.

Here the human dimension of a conversation relates to both form and function – human speech (open, natural, uncontrived) about human concerns (of importance to the speaker). This is explicitly contrasted in the manifesto to corporate speech, which is 'hollow, flat, literally inhuman' and talks only about what the corporation is interested in letting the market know about. Following on from the Cluetrain Manifesto books have been published with titles like *Join the Conversation* (Jaffe 2007), encouraging businesses to engage with the 'authentic and meaningful conversations' that are taking place between consumers on social media. As a result, organizations and professions that previously had been in the business of one-directional communication – and here we can include newspapers and most specifically arts critics – have been increasingly driven to consider the potential of becoming part of a multi-directional conversation. This is the position taken by Lyn Gardner, critic for *The Guardian*, who declares that with the growth of below the line comment on newspaper websites 'the conversation begins with the review, it doesn't end with it, our word is no longer the last word' (Critics' Circle 2013). For Gardner the result is a rolling culture of debate, with criticism part of this digital *conversation*.

Art criticism as a digital conversation

This alignment between online comment and audience conversation is made both by commentators championing and fearful of the growth of virtual forums.

In the positive camp, Matt Trueman, himself a critic who first came to prominence online before starting to write for publications such as *The Guardian*, *Time Out* and *New Statesman*, takes the position that criticism is in crisis but that this is broadly a good thing. Among a range of benefits from the changing face of criticism – including the removal of restrictive word counts and lifting of a news agenda – he celebrates the conversational dynamic of online commentary, describing it as 'a reciprocal, conversational relationship with readers and other writers. Reviews that acknowledge and talk to and rely on each other. Criticism as a team sport' (Critics' Circle 2013).

A contrasting perspective is taken by Alisa Solomon, who also aligns online commentary with audience conversations but who describes this as something that 'blurs the lines between the blurt of opinion [. . .] and considered judgment' (Tompa 2014).

From both perspectives, online forums become metaphorically and/or literally aligned with audience conversations. The suggestion is that audiences are increasingly talking about theatre online, with one of the most prominent examples of this being theatres creating designated 'tweet seats' where spectators can comment on the production during the performance itself.

What is worth stressing here is how online commentary is related, simultaneously, to *both* art criticism *and* audience conversation. One interest in the following discussion is how these two activities, similar in being post-show discourses about theatre, are conceptually, experientially and functionally very different.

Before that, however, it is also important to point out the existence of skepticism about the depth and meaningfulness of the conversations that do take place via social media. Blogging about the legacy of Jaffe's book, Mitch Joel suggests that there are very few real conversations happening at all. Instead he observes the production of a series of linear comments that exhibit a tendency 'to chest-thump' with Twitter especially 'more like everyone screaming a thought at once than a conversation that can be followed and engaged with' (Joel 2010).

Another sometimes skeptical voice about the idealized potential of social media is Geert Lovink in *Networks Without a Cause*. Here internet commentary is once again aligned with oral rather than textual culture: 'commentary is seen as oral, informal, fast and fluid' writes Lovink (2011: 55). However, while Lovink describes how participation has become commonplace – 'Participation has moved from something that had to be fought for to something entirely normal, expected, and, indeed, encouraged' (2011: 51) – he also acknowledges the limitations of this participation – 'Rarely do we see respondents talking to each other' (2011: 52). More politically, Lovink stresses that the internet manifests unequal power dynamics: while everybody can be a participant, not everybody gets to be heard. Debate instead clusters around a few voices and a few sites in a manner that produces a 'new-internet-specific-hierarchy' of texts (Szilágyi-Gál 2014). The result is what Davenport and Beck (2002), among others, describe as a shift from an information economy to an attention economy.

One conclusion might be that for all the idealization of the conversational potential of the new medium, the internet has become little more than an alternative form of publication. Conversation at best becomes a metaphorical – or even aspirational – designator rather than a literal description.

Amongst all this, however, what remains missing is the actual conversation. What does it mean for an audience to talk about a performance; what is the grammar and goal of a conversation; in what way is it human exchange about human concerns? Here I want to return to that upstairs room at the Tramway and listen in to not just what spectators said about the performance but also how they said it.

Audience conversations

First to acknowledge that there were some structural and social differences between the exchanges I'm going to interrogate here and the naturally occurring post-show conversations that I imagine were taking place in the bar downstairs.

Unlike those organic and unrecorded conversations, the one taking place in the upstairs room is a little more artificial for this is a group of spectators that I have brought together to form a 'dance group', organized as part of a wider AHRC-funded research project titled Watching Dance (www.watchingdance.org). The participants have been selected from respondents to a questionnaire circulated via dance companies and venues in Glasgow (such as Scottish Ballet and the Tramways). All have been identified as 'experienced dance spectators', defined as attending at least five dance performances a year, but without having had any dance training since childhood. The participants include two men and five women, aged between late twenties and early sixties. A little like a book group, together we have seen a series of dance performances and talked about them afterwards. The performances have been largely selected pragmatically, responding to what is on in Glasgow at the time, including contemporary dance (Phoenix Dance), ballet (Scottish Ballet) and dance-theatre (Needcompany). In return for the free tickets their conversation is recorded, but otherwise the evening fits into what the participants might naturally do with friends or family. This chapter focuses on the conversations surrounding the Needcompany performance alone, partially to enable clarity in the analysis but also because as a provocative performance it elicited some interesting conversations.

Methodologically, this research sits within a tradition of qualitative audience research, which typically engages participants in wide-ranging, reflective conversation (Barker 1998). The epistemological underpinning for this chapter is that of participatory enquiry into the phenomenological experience of watching dance. Creswell describes the participatory worldview as one that sees meaning as 'constructed by human beings as they engage with the world they are interpreting' (2009: 9). There is also an alignment between my approach here and what Willmar Sauter describes as 'Theatre Talks', a research method that aims not to be 'too different from what theatregoers normally would do' (2000: 176). Whether naturally occurring, or slightly artificially, crucially such aftershow discussions are oral/aural and dynamic/dialogic in character, and it is this status as human conversation about theatre that is of interest here.

In that upstairs room of the Tramway, having seen *The Porcelain Project*, I open the discussion:

> **Matthew**   Starting is always difficult but if anybody wants to start just by saying what their immediate responses were to Porcelain Project ...
>
> **Alison**   I'd just like to make the point that they were scaring me.

Alison's response is immediately subjective (starting with 'I'), experiential (about affect), and lacks critical reflection. It is these kinds of qualities – immediate, hesitant, affective, always becoming – that are readily apparent in human conversation.

Written criticism

In some ways, however, the character of audience conversation becomes clearer by looking first at what it is not, which is written criticism, and by considering the language of some of the reviews written by critics about *The Porcelain Project*. This discussion draws from six different reviews, published in newspapers and magazines, from productions presented in Glasgow, London and Belgium.

As a starting point, Kelly Apter's review in *The Scotsman*, which, in contrast to Alison's 'I'd just like to make the point they were scaring me', begins:

> It all started so beautifully, the wide space of Tramway One covered in porcelain object d'art; some hanging by a string, others placed strategically across the stage. The pure white pottery had us captivated long before the performers came into view – in some ways, it might have been better if it had stayed that way.
>
> 2008

Two carefully crafted sentences from an established critic. As Michael Coveney asserts, in whatever form it is published – whether in print or online – the ability to write is a central but sometimes overlooked component of criticism (Critics' Circle 2013). These two sentences have clear rhetorical features: the very first words ('it all started so beautifully') have a welcoming familiarity of being if not a direct quotation then something that feels like one; they have an elegiac quality and a sense of foreboding. Lady Bird Johnson, wife of the then vice President Lyndon Johnson, began her diary of the day Kennedy was assassinated with the phrase 'It all began so beautifully'. Already we know it isn't going to end so well and, like the opening line of a good novel, it has us hooked. Something confirmed by the delicious reversal of the second line: what praise is given with one hand ('had us captivated long before the performers came into view') is taken away with the other ('it might have been better if it had stayed that way').

This isn't Solomon's 'blurt of opinion' but a crafted piece of writing. It has a certain style and a sense of carefully using language to construct its meaning and impact. This is present again later in the review, in a description that communicates the affective experience of the performance, describing the 'laboured interactions where dancers clung to each other in displays of vulnerability or dragged themselves in anguished torment along the floor'. This is engaging writing, crisply and succinctly bringing to the reader's imagination something of the experience of being there in the theatre. Here, if not in the evaluative judgements, it comes close to fulfilling Sontag's demand for the critic to produce 'accurate, sharp [and] loving description' (1967: 12).

This status of written criticism as something crafted – where meaning, impact and sense of purpose is located in the very deliberate choice of words – is found across the range of written critical responses to *The Porcelain Project*. These include other evocative openings:

> Cups and saucers, white and gleaming, hang everywhere, as if in waiting for some Mad Hatter's tea-party.
>
> Brennan 2008

where there is definite poetic rhythm to the structure – short short long, short short long – followed by an evocative comparison.

Or:

> In *The Porcelain Project*, Grace Ellen Barkey serves up a heap of utter nonsense. And gets away with it too!
>
> de Regt 2007

here there is a writerly pleasure in the rhetorical reversal – this utter nonsense is good! – that echoes Apter's review.

Or:

> After sitting through one and a half hours of *The Porcelain Project* at the Barbican Theatre last night I doubt if I will ever look at a porcelain – or, in this case, a bone china vase – in the same way again.
>
> Cooper 2009

which wryly evidences a clear understanding of the specific interests of *The Ceramic Review*'s readership.

It is not that my participating audience members were especially inarticulate, although there are few moments in our conversation that have the quotability of the newspaper reviews. Rather, the broad point is that the language used in written criticism is literary, structured, edited and drives towards closure.

In its best instances such writing can be engaging and fun to read. At the same time, however, it can be viewed as a result of the form and function of a review, which is often characterized by the requirement to be snappy (all the reviews here are of between 206 to 403 words long), produced quickly (in order to be topical and timely) and to be both entertaining and evaluative. Various commentators have complained about the impact this has on writing style, Gordon Rogoff declaring it can lead to 'a punching bag style' and quick resort to 'easy-come adjectives' (1985: 133) while Patrice Pavis remarks that reviews 'often conclude with a paradox, an expression of regret, a metaphor of witty punch line' (1982: 104).

The reviews, in short, become performances in their own right – they are their own acts of presentational theatre, their own little *shows*. However, if this is the case then they are 'performic' (Hall 2013: 156), not performative. I'll return to this distinction later.

This is because as well as being crafted – as well as being consciously made as a thing to be read – the written review is also final. This finality resides both in the context of its publication and in the nature of its language.

In terms of publication the review is fixed by the platform of its dissemination. While historically this finality might have been articulated in terms of the absolute nature of the printed word, in many ways online dissemination only adds ubiquity and power.

Whether in print and/or online, the review endures. It is archived, it is recoverable, it has a permanence that conversation does not. The opinions, feelings, memories or perspectives articulated within them may have been fleeting, but the sentiments present in their written articulation are permanent. Criticism functions here as canonization.

In terms of language the review is fixed by its very constructedness. The self-aware crafting of the language – 'In his speeches, megalomania transforms into meaningless lunacy' (de Regt 2007) – is presented as a conclusion. It has the property of a statement: this is how it is.

As performic utterances, written criticism is assertive. Like this sentence itself, it is declarative. Like this chapter, like this writing now, it presents itself as finished thinking.

Unfinished thinking

In contrast the audience conversations are often very much unfinished, sometimes even to the point of saying nothing:

> **Matthew**   Nathalie, what's your immediate response to that?
> **Nathalie**   I don't know what my immediate response was. I'm not quite sure what to make of it.

In other moments it is evident that what is being said is being negotiated in the moment of saying it:

> **Alison**   I don't know, because it is quite difficult to put into words I think, and as I say a few of the bits, the middle bit, it just suddenly seemed they're all dancing, and there was other bits where they were also moving and I really enjoyed watching the slower bits as well. I don't know what to think, I don't know if I was trying to think, well, what are they doing, I just liked watching the movement I think. I don't know how ... I just enjoyed watching the people dance, really.

That oral language full of hesitations and qualifications is something we know – 'I'm not sure that I didn't' – and typically such things get written out of written language. This is obvious and commonplace. However, the impact of this writing out is significant, marking a shift from the performative (a doing that brings into being) to the performic (a declarative showing).

For what the transcribed conversations demonstrate more than anything else is a *struggle for comprehension* that occurs in parallel to the *struggle for articulation*. Here it is worth drawing on understandings of the relationship between language and intention in the cognitive sciences, where it is argued that 'the intent to speak lacks form and gains it only through the emergence of language' (Lutterbie 2013: 107).

[In parenthesis I want to reflect upon and acknowledge the fact that this is also the process of writing, which begins for the author as a performative doing, and enacts its own struggle for comprehension. This is certainly the process of my writing of this very text, where as I write I discover what it is I think. E. M. Forster's dictum seems very apt here for the manner in which writing is enquiry, 'how can I know what I think till I see what I say'. In the moment in which it is happening, writing is very much a doing, which brings about its own comprehension. The same is true for written theatre criticism. However, while speech is produced in a perpetual now of becoming, writing arguably settles into a declarative state of determinacy. It is possible to try to maintain elements of this sense of process and temporality, perhaps through self-referential techniques such as this digression, by notions of performance writing that draws attention to its own materiality, or by writing under what Derrida terms erasure. Such strategies, however, compete against what is almost the ontological nature of writing, if we weren't always already so fearful of ontologies, which is its concreteness. Here we might remember Hans Keller's condemnation of 'black magic of the print word, which lends authority where there is no authority, interest where there is no interest, power where there is no force' (1987: 191).

In the aftershow conversation the struggle for comprehension is one that occurs both at the level of the individual – beginning during the moment of watching – and in a dynamic social process of negotiation and disagreement. That is, in the back and forth of human interaction. In contrast to the written language of the reviews, which have the appearance and status of declarative finished thinking, the utterances of spectators is that of unfinished thinking. Here ideas, positions, responses are actively coming into being in the moment of speaking.

The phrase 'unfinished thinking' is borrowed from Henk Borgdorff and his discussion of the kinds of knowledge produced through practice-based research in the arts. Borgdorff writes that 'Artistic research is the deliberate articulation of such unfinished thinking', continuing that it is

> directed at a not-knowing, or a not-yet-knowing. It creates room for that which is unthought, that which is unexpected – the idea that all things could be different. Especially pertinent to artistic research is the realization that we do not yet know what we don't know. [...] Artistic research is the deliberate articulation of these contingent perspectives.
>
> 2010: 61

Borgdorff is primarily writing about the artist's processes of contingent not-knowing. However, the position also works for me to articulate the forms of knowledge (or understanding; or experience) that audiences can gain *through* art. This is knowledge that is often unthought, and which often resides as a contingent process of knowing and not-knowing. Crucially, unlike the written review, the aftershow conversation is never finished; neither structurally nor temporally does it have fixed boundaries, but always bleeds ever outwards.

The struggle for articulation that is evidenced in the audience conversation can also be considered in terms of its relationship to memory – that is memory both of the performance (which while recent is already absent) and other associations and memorial connotations that are produced through the act of recalling. E. J. Lowe makes the distinction between the capacity to remember something – which is an unenacted potential – and actually recalling it. As Lowe points out, recalling something is commonly phrased as 'a "reliving" of a past experience' and, while inevitably not as vivid, nonetheless is a mental act that impacts on the present experience (2000: 278).

For Jerome Feldman the act of speaking 'gives rise to memories of experiences, previous linguistic expressions, and associations that serve as frames or boundary conditions for the emerging expression'. In this dialectical relationship between intention, memory and present situation the appearance of 'mixed metaphors and incomplete sentences in conversation' may reveal the cracks or failings of emergent and unfinished process (Feldman's work is cited in Lutterbie 2013: 107–9).

In considering the spectators' discussions of *The Porcelain Project* it is therefore interesting to look for those moments that enact and embody the processes of not-knowing and not-yet-knowing. These are moments where the breaking and failing of language reveals the dialectic between intention, memory and language. In the audience conversation, these moments often seem to reach their most apparent when participants seek to articulate their affective, embodied experience of the physicality of the performance.

Remember that first, hesitant response 'I'd just like to make the point that they were scaring me'. A recurring theme in the conversation was the spectators' individual and collective attempts to make sense of the different kinds of discomfort produced by the performance. This discomfort was something produced by the imposition or requirement of the audience to *look*:

Jenny   Yes, I mean. I'm not sure that I didn't ... yeah, I suppose I didn't want to see it. It was just not very comfortable viewing.

And by a feeling of being *looked at*:

Barbara   But the man who came on first with the big pointy nose, the hairy man. He looked at the audience. There was something in that, and I found that ... I thought, God, I hope he doesn't look at me. I found that wasn't a comfortable thing to have him look, because I really didn't like him.

In these descriptions, *looking* and being *looked at* has a coercive, forceful power, produced through the sense of the mutuality of live co-presence. This was articulated elsewhere as a form of voyeurism or of an involuntary contribution to the action on stage. Note also in both these examples the process whereby the unfinished and disjointed sentences indicate an active recall that brings a previous memory into the present moment.

In this extended passage of speech – and there are very few blocks of transcribed text any longer than this – it is possible to see Jenny working through some of these questions of looking and not-looking, of responsibility, of reliving memory and of struggling for articulation.

> **Jenny** Well, just all this sexual stuff was quite uncomfortable to watch, I thought. Erm … I may be someone that wouldn't go and see a film if it was an 18. So, not to say … it was very well … done, because it must have been, because it made me want to look away. It was … it was … And the violence in it as well, in it erm … I just saw, I suppose, like a different world. Like you were saying, it was like walking into a different world, and I think you were saying, that everything was kind of going on, and also that you weren't part of it. It was like watching a different thing, and I think the humour kind made you … kind of took you off guard a little bit, because it made you almost expect, like, a children's story or something. You know when the guy came in with the pointy nose, and it was twinkling, the broken ceramics and the cups and saucers and things, and he was almost like a character from a children's fantasy fairy tale thing, I suppose.

This articulation is hesitant. It is a recalling that is partly a reliving. It is coming into being in the moment of its utterance. It represents a struggle for comprehension that in its fluid contingency seems much closer to the particular kind of knowledge or experience of the performance, than the resolved, edited and finished articulations present in the formal written reviews.

Some conclusions and a table

Through the operation of language, audience conversations and written criticism hold very different relationships to the performance event. One is performic, a matter of resolved statements that assert their knowingness through both the style and substance of the language. The other is performative, where not-yet-knowing is manifest through contingent, unfinished thinking.

In his discussion of social media, Lovink bemoans 'there is no end to comment' (2011: 55). For him this is something to regret, for he sees value in the critical codification – the coming to a conclusion – that traditional criticism enables. 'Print reviews,' writes Lovink, 'no matter how short and shoddy, are an oasis of content in comparison with social media's crude and invasive short messaging' (2011: 72). In contrast to art criticism what distinguishes online comment is its 'unfinished nature'. While compared to both, the digital exchange is therefore neither wholly criticism nor conversation. It resides in neither the one-directional and performic sphere of written criticism, nor the multi-directional and performative realm of the conversation. Instead the online exchange has a liminal position that is both between and inclusive of both.

Table 1 presents this position in a manner that is inevitably both partial and contentious. Please feel free to disagree with it.

Table 1

	Newspaper Criticism	Online Exchange	Audience Conversation
Archive	Longevity ensured	Longevity uncertain	Ephemeral
Authority	'Expert discourse' (Melrose 1994: 77)	'Democratization of taste' (Lovink 2011)	Authenticity of experience
Authorship	Named expert	Anonymous or pseudonymous	Mutual (rhizomatic)
Community/ Communication	Mass communication	Dispersed community	Face-to-face
Economy	Information economy	Attention economy	Social economy

Epistemology	Conclusive	'No end to comment' (Lovink)	'Unfinished thinking' (Borgdorff)
Exchange	Singular monologue	'Reciprocal, conversational' (Trueman in Critics' Circle 2013) OR 'everyone screaming a thought at once' (Joel 2010)	Conversation
Form	Written	Written (with qualities of oral)	Oral/Aural
Hierarchy	Hierarchy of publications	'Fragmented presence of ideas' (Szilágyi-Gál 2014)	Hierarchy of social relationships
Production to reception	Binary: consumers and producers	Fluid: users as producers	Neither users or consumers
Style	'Elegant argumentation' (Solomon in Tampa 2014)	'Blurt of opinion' (Solomon in Tampa 2014)	Struggle for articulation
Temporality	Singular	Asynchronous	Synchronous

Through mapping parallels and differences in areas from its status within the archive, to authorship, to temporality, this table indicates how online exchange about theatre operates in an area at once between and within both criticism and conversation. The online exchange is participatory, community-based, fluid; but it is also written, authored and distributed.

The excitement over new and innovative ways of engaging with audiences virtually – through tweet-seats, embedded criticism or simply by embracing the explosion of blog-based criticism – of course does not have to be at the expense of recognizing the distinct characteristic of face-to-face conversations between spectators. Perhaps the discussion here might prompt consideration of how online exchanges might more actively cultivate a sense of the conversational, how they might become more performative and collaborative and less performic and declarative. Theatres and cultural institutions need to consider how they can actively cultivate the genuinely conversational exchange, as well as the critical articulation of expertise and the virtual expression of democracy. Examples here might include projects such as Respond (www.yorkshiredance.com/respond) or Dialogue (*welcometodialogue.com*), which in their different ways seek to facilitate audiences in conversations about performance. Other examples include those imagined conversations taking place in the bar downstairs or on the train back into town, which although undocumented and unfacilitated are in many ways the enduring resonance of the performance. For it is in the *conversations* of their audiences, as oral/aural human-to-human encounters, that we can embrace the contingent and unfinished nature of the theatrical experience.

Works cited

Apter, Kelly (2008) 'Dance Review: The Porcelain Project', *The Scotsman*, 7 October, www.scotsman.com/news/dance-review-the-porcelain-project-1-1135928 (accessed 31 July 2014).

Barker, Martin (1998) *Knowing Audiences*, Luton: University of Luton Press.

Borgdorff, Henk (2010) 'The Production of Knowledge in Artistic Research' in M. Biggs and H. Karlsson (eds), *The Routledge Companion to Research in the Arts*, Routledge: London, 44–63.

Brennan, Mary (2008) '*The Porcelain Project*', *The Herald*, 6 October, www.heraldscotland.com/the-porcelain-project-tramway-glasgow-1.891230.

Cluetrain Manifesto, The (1999), 'The Cluetrain Manifesto: 95 Theses', www.cluetrain.com (accessed 31 July 2014).

Cooper, Emmanuel (2009), 'The Porcelain Project', *Ceramic Review*, 15 April, ceramicreview.blogspot.co.uk/2009/04/porcelain-project.html (accessed 31 July 2014).

Creswell, J. W. (2009) *Research design: Qualitative, quantitative and mixed methods approaches*, Thousand Oaks: Sage.

Critics' Circle (2013), The Critics' Circle Centenary Conference: The Future of Criticism, 28 September, www.theatrevoice.com/10311/the-critics-circle-centenary-conference-the-future-of-criticism/#.U3YbJcdtKPV (accessed 31 July 2014).

Hall, John (2013) *On Performance Writing: with pedagogical sketches*, Shearsman: Bristol.

Joel, Mitch (2010) 'The End of Conversation in Social Media' *Twistedimage. com*, 23 August, www.twistimage.com/blog/archives/the-end-of-conversation-in-social-media/ (accessed 31 July 2014).

Kaiser, Michael (2011) 'The Death of Criticism, or Everybody is a Critic', *Huffington Post*, 14 November, www.huffingtonpost.com/michael-kaiser/the-death-of-criticism-or_b_1092125.html (accessed 31 July 2014).

Keller, Hans (1987) *Criticism*, edited by J. Hogg, Faber and Faber: London.

Lovink, Geert (2011) *Networks Without a Cause: A Critique of Social Media*, Polity: Cambridge.

Lowe, E. J. (2000) *An Introduction to the Philosophy of Mind*, Cambridge University Press: Cambridge.

Lutterbie, John (2013) 'Wayfaring in Everyday Life: The Unravelling of Intricacy' in *Affective Performance and Cognitive Science*, N. Shaughnessy (ed.) Bloomsbury: London. 103–15.

Melrose, Susan (1994) 'Please, Please Me: "Empathy" and "Sympathy" in Critical Metapraxis', *Contemporary Theatre Review*, 2:2. 73–83.

Miller, Laura and Bayard, Louis (2008) 'Who killed the literary critic', *Salon. com*. 22 May, www.salon.com/2008/05/22/critics_2/.

Pavis, Patrice (1982) *Languages of the Stage: Essays in the Semiology of Theatre*, Performing Arts Journal Publications, New York.

Regt, Danielle de (2007) 'Needcompany with *The Porcelain Project*: Nonsense Squared' *De Standaard*, 12 October, www.needcompany.org/EN/review/1033 (accessed 31 July 2014).

Rogoff, Gordon (1985) 'Theatre Criticism: The Elusive Object, the Fading Craft', *Performing Arts Journal*, 26/27, 133–41.

Sauter, Willmar (2000) *The Theatrical Event: Dynamics of Performance and Perception*, University of Iowa Press: Iowa City.

Sontag, Susan (1967) *Against Interpretation*, Eyre and Spottiswoode: London.

Szilágyi-Gál, Mihály (2014) 'Criticising the End of Criticism: The Critical Genre and the Internet'. *Critical Stages*. Issue 9 Feb 2014. www.criticalstages.org/ (accessed 31 July 2014).

Tompa, Andrea (2014) An interview with Alisa Solomon. 'Mere Opinion and Considered Judgment: Amateur and Professional Criticism Today', *Critical Stages*, Issue 9, Feb, www.criticalstages.org/ (accessed 31 July 2014).

Various (2011) 'Is the age of the critic over?' *The Guardian*, 30 January, www.theguardian.com/culture/2011/jan/30/is-the-age-of-the-critic-over (accessed 31 July 2014).

Vile, Gareth K. (2008) 'Unneeded: *The Porcelain Project*', *The Skinny*, 4 October, www.theskinny.co.uk/theatre/reviews/43966-unneeded_porcelain_project (accessed 31 July 2014).

CHAPTER 15
CROWDSOURCING THE
REVIEW AND THE RECORD:
A COLLABORATIVE APPROACH
TO THEATRE CRITICISM AND
ARCHIVING IN THE DIGITAL AGE
Michelle MacArthur

On 7 July 2008 at 1:49pm, Canadian theatre critic J. Kelly Nestruck posted a round-up of reviews of the Shaw Festival's production of *A Little Night Music* on his *Globe and Mail* blog. Included amongst the notices was one written by the show's star Thom Allison, who, on his personal blog, recounted that the audience 'jumped to their feet' at the end, a perspective which Nestruck suggested might be 'slightly slanted' (2008). Nestruck, however, did not have the last word on the matter. At 7:27pm, the production's director, Morris Panych, was the first to respond in the online comments section: 'Excuse me, dude, that was hardly a slanted perspective. They did jump to their feet; en masse [...]. A slanted perspective I would think is when somebody blatantly fails to report an event that occurred, or downplays that event to make their point' (2008). Others quickly joined in, expanding the conversation from the politics of standing ovations to the functions and purpose of theatre criticism. By the time the *Globe* closed the comment section, the heated debate had grown over several days to involve artists, audience members, and critics from as close to the Shaw Festival as Toronto to as far away as London, England; and, at over 3,700 words, the commentary ran more than six times the length of Nestruck's original post.

The case of the contested curtain call is illustrative of several urgent issues related to the changing state of theatre criticism, in Canada and beyond. From online reviews, to live tweeting during a performance, to 'liking' a production on Facebook, the blogosphere is transforming how we engage with, talk about, and archive theatre. As Linda Hutcheon points out, the explosion of reviewing websites and the concurrent slow death of print publications has led to a 'major shift in reviewing practices around the world' (2010: 157). No longer the exclusive terrain of professional reviewers, in the digital era theatre criticism can be practised by anyone with internet access. This also has implications for the geographical and temporal boundaries of theatre and criticism: participants across borders can engage in conversation about a performance before and after it occurs, often without ever seeing it. Pundits like Panych can respond to critics with increased immediacy, having their say in the blogosphere sometimes within seconds of reading a review. However, online critical discourse, like performance itself, is ephemeral and can disappear just as quickly as it can appear, as was ultimately the case with *A Little Night Music*. After a *Globe and Mail* website upgrade in 2013, the review round-up and commentary vanished, only to resurface months later on an obscure *Globe* portal. Other reader commentaries from Nestruck's blog remain what Jodi Dean calls 'digital zombies': posts copied, pasted, and circulating somewhere in the virtual ether, unable to be fully contained once released (2010: 47).

Indeed, the current shift in reviewing practices has yet to be followed by a corresponding shift in archival practices, meaning that we have not yet found a comprehensive way to preserve the vital conversation about theatre happening online. Archiving is particularly challenging when it comes to 'crowdsourced theatre criticism', the collaborative critical dialogue created in response to single-authored theatre reviews online (Hatton 2014: 105). Comment sections following reviews can be closed or may disappear when a publication reformats or upgrades its website, while discussions occurring on social media platforms such as Facebook or Twitter may not be open to the public and, especially in the case of the latter, can expire unless captured using an app such as Storify.

In this chapter I consider the role of crowdsourcing in theatre criticism and the extent to which it is challenging traditional approaches to reviewing and recording theatre history. Through an analysis of examples of crowdsourced theatre criticism, I will define the genre and suggest its uses and limitations for audiences and scholars. After establishing the importance of this bourgeoning branch of criticism, I will outline some key questions for historians wishing to preserve this genre of writing. I argue that while crowdsourced theatre criticism is not immune to the pitfalls of traditional theatre criticism, namely its exclusivity and privileging of hegemonic voices, its ability to foster a more collaborative, extensive, and richer conversation about theatre should not be ignored by researchers. Theatre researchers must consider this genre of writing in their historiographic practices and seek ways to archive it. By continuing to ignore crowdsourced criticism, we reify hegemonic critical voices and collude in the disappearance of valuable archival material about individual performances and the artistic, cultural, and sociopolitical contexts in which they are embedded.

Crowdsourced theatre criticism

I borrow the term 'crowdsourced theatre criticism' from Oona Hatton, who, in her article "'Hey, asshole: you had your say": The Performance of Theatre Criticism' examines playwright Neil LaBute's intervention into the comment thread of a 2010 *Time Out Chicago* online review of his adaptation of *The Taming of the Shrew*. Calling the review 'a sorry excuse for theatrical criticism' (Hatton 2014: 103), user 'neil labute' unleashed a heated exchange, which, like *The Globe and Mail* comments thread described above, moved between a discussion of the production itself and a debate of broader issues, in this case LaBute's oeuvre and the role of the critic.[1] Also like the *Globe* exchange, this one incorporated multiple voices, totalling nearly sixty comments from approximately twenty-five contributors (2014: 103). Measuring the comments thread against the American Theatre Critics' Association's (ATCA) membership criteria,[2] Hatton argues:

> Taken as a whole, I suggest that the comments thread is another legitimate, albeit nontraditional example of theatre criticism.

> While it may not meet ATCA's guidelines regarding the professionalism of the contributors or the regularity of their engagement with this topic (and this would be difficult to establish), the conversation is generally conducted with sincerity and an interest in issues related to theatre and performance, with personal experience as the principal source of evidence. Overall, [*Time Out Chicago*] commenters are eager to defend the critic's right to work, as well as their own right to contribute to the conversation.
>
> 2014: 107

Indeed, the conversation made such an impact that Hatton ultimately decided to adapt it into a play. *The Time Out/Neil Labute Radio Play* is a word-for-word performance of *The Taming of the Shrew* review and the ensuing comments, recorded by local Chicago actors and dramaturged by Hatton. The play not only draws attention to the inherent drama of the comments thread, but also acts as an archive, creating 'a (relatively) enduring object that could be accessed repeatedly at any time and virtually any location' (2014: 107) – a point I will return to later in this chapter.

Experience as evidence

Hatton's defence of the comments thread as a legitimate form of theatre criticism begins to outline some distinguishing features of the genre of crowdsourced theatre criticism which I would like to expand on here. Hatton notes that in the comments thread, personal experience acts as the principal source of evidence (2014: 107), a key feature that characterizes criticism on the blogosphere more generally. Indeed, as Linda Hutcheon points out, in the digital age experience has replaced expertise as the prime criterion for critical authority. Hutcheon examines this shift and its implications in her 2009 article 'Reviewing reviewing today':

> In the great democratization of reviewing that we are witnessing, anybody and everybody can become a reviewer, or what some

would call an 'empowered consumer'. Buy a book and you can review it on Amazon.com. In fact, you might be able to do so without even reading the book. Who would check? You do not have to be an expert, or a professional, or even honest. And this applies not only to books, of course, but to anything that can be evaluated, from Toronto restaurants to Paris hotels, from DVDs to video games.

2009: 6

It also applies to theatre, where, following Hutcheon's reasoning, 'experience' does not necessarily entail direct contact with the performance under discussion – one need not see a show to participate in online discussion about it.

This is certainly the case in the comments thread, where experience with the art form more generally facilitates entry into the conversation. In the comments following Kelly Nestruck's review round-up, for example, only Nestruck himself and Morris Panych claim a direct connection to *A Little Night Music*. The majority of the other commenters establish their credibility through explicit or implicit references to their broader theatrical experience, whether as audience members, artists, or both. MK Piatkowski, who contributes three times to the conversation, twice asserts his/her credibility as a regular theatregoer. His/her initial comment simply responds to Nestruck's lede, which asks his readers for Fringe Festival recommendations: 'Seen three shows, all winners. Barbeque King, Totem Figures, Take It Back' (MK Piatkowski 2008). His/her second comment, weighing in on the standing ovations debate, reinforces his/her extensive experience as a seasoned audience member: 'I see a lot of theatre and too many times I feel railroaded into standing Os'. Saxon Conrad joins the conversation shortly thereafter, starting his lengthy comment about standing ovations with the following allusion to his career as an artist: 'Hmmm. Alas (because I feel like I'm betraying my kind), I must agree with the critic on this issue. First of all, my career in the theatre has not been as long, as storied, or as high-profile as Mr. Panych's, but I've certainly experienced more than 30 or 40 standing ovations [. . .]' (2008). MK Piatkowski and Saxon Conrad's responses are representative of the general structure of the comments in the thread, where, aside from Nestruck and Panych themselves and the three users whose engagement is limited to simply promoting their Fringe shows, each of the other seven participants frames their comments with reference to their experience, legitimating their opinions and their participation in the conversation in the first place. This is particularly important in the comment thread of a public review (versus in the comment thread on an ostensibly private platform like Facebook, which I will discuss in my next example) because users are less likely to know each other and can be anonymous or pseudonymous.

The broad spectrum of experience claimed by the review round-up commenters should also be noted. While the majority of the experience evidenced is theatre-related, two of the commenters make note of their intellectual engagement with criticism more generally. Michael Lista, who posts one lengthy comment chastising Panych for defending the standing ovation of his own show, cites his experience as a reader as he addresses the director: 'I get the same shame-faced sensation of butt-tingles when I read poets contesting the handling of their Pulitzer shoe-ins in the pages of the TLS, or historians fact-correcting their detractors in the NYRB' (2014). [P]hilippa lloyd chambers, writing from London, begins her comment by referencing the fact that she has been 'following this dialogue, if that is an accurate description (or perhaps not)' (2014) and develops her argument about the critic's role with references to Northrop Frye and *Toronto Star* critic Richard Ouzounian. In both cases, these demonstrations of users' active engagement with critical discourse are enough to qualify them for the conversation, which is and is not about *A Little Night Music* – while on one level, the 'debatable' dialogue is about the merits of the production and whether or not it actually received and/or deserved a standing ovation on the night Nestruck attended, on another it is also about the politics of the relationship between artists, critics, and audiences. Only participation in first level of the conversation requires a ticket stub to validate one's opinion; the baseline level of experience required to participate in the latter is having read the review. But, as the contributors above demonstrate, some degree of evidence of investment in the arts and arts criticism compensates for missing the show – this is what Hatton refers to as 'sincerity and an interest in issues related to theatre performance' (2014: 107).

In Hutcheon's discussion of online reviewing, honesty is also at stake, especially in the case of Amazon-type reviews, where publishers and friends of the author pose as 'empowered consumers' to bolster book sales, perhaps never having read the book in the first place (2009: 7). In the case of crowdsourced theatre criticism, I would argue, there is no need to hide one's inexperience. In fact, in the example above, multiple contributors outright admit to never having seen *A Little Night Music*. Guy Yedwab, writing from the United States, draws on his general experience as an audience member and actor to compensate for not seeing the show – unfeasible given his geographic location – providing a caveat in the middle of his discussion of the artist–critic relationship: 'I can't judge how fair [the review] was without having seen the performance myself (I'm not even in Canada) but to a certain extent, a work of art does not come across the same as a critique, which is a log of the critic's impressions of a production' (2008). While each contributor in any kind of critical conversation has his/her own motivations and biases, in crowdsourced theatre criticism there is no obvious reason to lie because of the concurrent levels of conversation. Moreover, while mainstream reviews such as those featured in *The Globe and Mail* are sometimes accused of primarily serving the function of consumer reporting, crowdsourced theatre criticism's focus on debating the broader issues surrounding a performance distinguishes its goals.

A collaborative conversation

And so, in addition to its privileging of experience over expertise, crowdsourced theatre criticism is characterized by multiple strands of conversation. Though comment threads often begin with a focus on the performance at the centre of the review, they quickly expand to debate other issues of theatre production and reception. These strands tend to intersect at different points along the thread, one informing the other, ideally resulting in a rich critical discussion that situates a given performance in wider artistic, social, and political contexts. To illustrate this aspect of crowdsourced theatre criticism I turn to an example from Facebook, which is increasingly providing a platform for such discourse.

On 10 April 2014, Western University theatre professor Kim Solga posted a review of *A View from the Bridge* at London's Young Vic Theatre on her blog, *The Activist Classroom*, where she writes about diverse issues including pedagogy, theatre, research, and of course, activism. In her review, Solga examines the production's representation of race, class, and sexuality and questions the implications of staging Arthur Miller's 1956 social realist play about working-class Italian immigrants in Brooklyn in the present-day UK. Challenging the play's overwhelmingly positive critical reception, she argues,

> Where we need to be pressing against the dangerous anti-immigrant, anti-underclass rhetoric that has gripped this country since 2008, [director Ivo] van Hove's production makes that rhetoric pretty, epic, 'universal'. From my perspective, the choice to do so is a fundamentally irresponsible one.

2014

On the same day that Solga published her review, Brock University theatre professor and professional critic Karen Fricker shared it on her Facebook page, framing it as 'another smart, interesting piece of against-the-grain theatre commentary by another London-based Canadian theatre scholar' (2014b). Fricker's share of the post elicited a total of twenty-five comments from eight participants plus Fricker herself.

Like the example from *The Globe and Mail* above, the Facebook comment thread in response to Solga's review features two main intersecting lines of conversation, one about the play and another about issues stemming from it, in this case identity politics, the critical reception of British plays by 'foreign' critics (a term used contentiously by one of the contributors), and the representation of American plays on British stages. Not only do the commenters share their differing opinions and debate one another, but they also add resources to the discussion: a total of five links are shared in addition to the initial link to Solga's blog, consisting of two other reviews of the same production, and two articles and one review addressing the various other issues at stake in the conversation. Through their agreements and arguments, the commenters collaborate to develop the conversation, pulling at the various threads to unravel new questions and directions. At the same time the conversation is notably cohesive, with users responding to one another by tagging names in their posts and logically building upon previous comments.

This act of collaboration is reflective of the key qualities of crowdsourcing more generally, a term coined in 2006 by *Wired* contributor Jeff Howe and initially applied to web-based business models. Elaborating on Howe's definition in their article 'Maximizing Benefits from Crowdsourced Data', Barbier et al. write:

> The term crowdsourcing describes a new web-based business model that harnesses the creative solutions of a distributed network of individuals through what amounts to an open call for proposals (Howe 2006). According to Howe (2006), crowdsourcing entails the work previously performed by employees and outsourcing it to an undefined (and generally large) network of people in the form of an open call by a company or institution. [...] Crowdsourcing is often used to obtain solutions to a problem that are cheaper and superior in quality and quantity to those that are obtained from traditional professionals in the same industry.
>
> 2012: 258

This lengthy definition merits examination here because it illuminates some important points about crowdsourced theatre criticism, as demonstrated in the Facebook example. First, crowdsourcing begins with an open call, which Fricker issues by sharing Solga's blog post. Second, the open call outsources the critical discourse to an 'undefined (and generally large) network of people' – Fricker's Facebook friends, as well as friends of friends invited into the conversation as they are tagged by commenters – rather than limiting it to 'employees', i.e. professional theatre critics. Indeed, while a business perspective would argue this second quality is beneficial because outsourcing produces cheap labour, another benefit in the context of theatre criticism is that the open call increases participation in critical discourse and diversifies the voices that typically dominate it, namely white, male, and heterosexual.[3] I have previously written about this benefit as it relates to theatre blogging more generally (2013), and will return to it shortly here. Third, these solutions are 'superior in quality and quantity', a point which the authors repeat at the end of their definition, simply stating '[T]he solutions provided by crowdsourcing are better than the solutions provided by traditional problem-solving methods' (Barbier et al. 2012: 258). While the quality of crowdsourced theatre criticism varies, at its best it extends the critical conversation about a performance beyond the limits of static, single-authored theatre criticism. In the example of *A View from the Bridge*, the Facebook-generated crowdsourced theatre criticism developed Solga's original review exponentially, enhancing its scope and adding multiple perspectives.

An open archive

The interwoven threads of conversation produced by crowdsourced theatre criticism also hold the potential to enrich the historical archive, not only by holding clues to a specific production or performance in the past, but also by documenting valuable information about the wider artistic, social, and political landscape in which it exists. Writing about theatre criticism in a special issue of the journal *Shakespeare*, Peter Holland argues that by creating 'a community of knowledgeable participants in a culture of theatre, eager to add opinions and correct others' errors' (2010: 302), blog threads can provide significant evidence to scholars hoping to develop a clearer picture of 'the cultures of reception both of reviewing and of what is reviewed' (2010: 303). Holland suggests that Shakespearians' current ignorance of audiences means that their impressive efforts at 'uncovering and piecing together of the culture of early modern theatre' are unmatched by their knowledge of 'the culture of Shakespeare playgoing now' (2010: 303). This critique is not limited to Shakespeare studies but could be applied to the field of theatre history more broadly, where it is only in the last five to ten years that scholars have started to consider the blogosphere and the critical discourse occurring therein more seriously.[4] Eleanor Collins, in her contribution to the same special issue of *Shakespeare* as Holland, makes a similar argument in support of the value of blog and blog threads for the theatre historian. Seeing blogging as an 'alternative to the traditional single-authored review, [which] enables a plurality of voices to comment on performances throughout the run of the production' (2010: 334), Collins suggests that blogs and blog threads could become archives in and of themselves, amassing perspectives across geographical and temporal boundaries. She writes:

[W]hy shouldn't productions continue to generate views and ideas even after the moment of performance has passed? They should be allowed an afterlife of generations that is not dependent on the three hours' experience of a few privileged critics. This already occurs in memory, and is a valuable cultural process. The blog would then become a live archive, and constantly evolving: it can offer new conclusions to literary scholars, historians, directors and the interested public at different stages of its life and, through its dialogic nature, become more than merely a collection of isolated, freestanding responses to a performance.

2010: 334

Collins' notion of the blog as an open-access archive is a very promising one – indeed, the case studies discussed here reflect the potential of online platforms to facilitate critical discourse that is evolving, dialogic, and collaborative. However, Collins' assumptions about access and privilege require further interrogation. Is crowdsourced theatre criticism democratic? Does it provide a genuine challenge to the 'few privileged critics'?

Accessibility and its limits

While there is no doubt that the blogosphere has opened up critical discourse about theatre, this discourse is not necessarily easily accessible. The Facebook conversation surrounding *A View from the*

Bridge illustrates both the possibilities and limitations of crowdsourced theatre criticism. To be sure, Fricker's 'open call' solicited responses from critics, scholars, and audience members in Canada and Europe and extended the conversation over a few days – likely until it became buried in her active newsfeed. In this way it illustrates how Collins' 'live archive' would use the review as a starting point to inspire continual critical discourse long after the moment of performance. However, because the conversation took place on Facebook, it is only accessible to those directly connected to Fricker on the social media site. As one of her Facebook friends, I was able to 'like' it, screen capture it, and use it as a central example in this chapter, but to future researchers, practitioners, and interested audience members, this valuable instance of crowdsourced theatre criticism may be completely inaccessible. Kim Solga's blog, *The Activist Classroom*, which *is* publically accessible and open to comments, only solicited a response from one reader, even after she encouraged people to do so on Facebook. ['I beg to differ though, and couldn't agree less,' posted Peter M. Boenisch (2014), to which Solga responded, 'So go to the comments and say why, Peter!' (2014).] Further, the reader who did respond on Solga's blog was also part of the Facebook conversation, which alerted her to the blog post initially.

Facebook has obvious appeal as a platform for crowdsourced theatre criticism, with its emphasis on sharing, liking, and commenting. As a social networking site, its ability to facilitate connections between acquaintances, friends, and colleagues who share similar interests also means that there is a built-in audience for posts, a crowd eager to answer Facebook's repeated invitation to 'Write a comment . . .'. For theatre enthusiasts like myself who are connected to many like-minded 'friends', Facebook acts as an aggregator of arts news and criticism, making it more convenient than visiting multiple sites or consulting print publications – one-stop shopping for the Information Age. Moreover, because Facebook eliminates the possibility for anonymity that exists on news sites and online publications, users' credibility is pre-established in their profiles. Whereas commenters in *The Globe and Mail* case study discussed at the beginning of this chapter implicitly or explicitly made reference to their level of experience in their posts in order to legitimize their participation in the conversation, this was not necessary for the participants in Karen Fricker's Facebook feed, because they were either already connected to each other or could check out one another's profiles. The visibility of their identities has another implication as well: it promotes an environment of 'self-policing', wherein, as Hille and Bakker suggest in their comparative study of news and Facebook commenters, 'loss of anonymity ensures that Facebook commenters become more hesitant about posting abusive and offensive comments' (2014: 565). This, of course, does not mean that users never post abusive or offensive comments – this is always a risk, particularly in Facebook forums attached to groups or news pages, where users do not necessarily have any connection to one other. However, when users are 'friends' or friends of friends, they may feel a heightened sense of accountability and decorum as they engage in critical discourse with one another.

While Facebook and online publications requiring users to login before posting might decrease the number of trolls in comment sections, they do not protect against more nuanced manipulations of power. As research conducted on the blogosphere has shown, though the web opens up the critical conversation to a greater diversity of voices, these voices are not necessarily exercised and/or validated equally.[5] Tracy L.M. Kennedy summarizes the reasons for this in an article on feminist blogging, noting the persistence of gendered communication patterns online as well as the dearth of women listed in top blog lists (commonly referred to as 'A-list blogs'), which tend to be dominated by 'white, right-wing, heterosexual men' (2007: 3). In her research with Robinson, Kennedy found that 'women tend to be more expressive and inclusive of others in their comments, while men's comments are generally assertive and competitive' (2007: 3), leading her to conclude: 'We need to keep in mind the implications of such gendered interaction patterns within blogs, as women's opinions may not be heard, validated, or taken seriously by other readers' (2007: 3). This applies to other marginalized identities as well, as social inequities are reproduced online and influence access to discursive power. Canadian theatre artist David Yee, in his article 'On Moderation in Social Networks', points out several examples of racist and colonialist remarks in online arts-related commentary – or what he calls, 'a deluge of libel, bigotry, and outright idiocy'– underlining the need for moderation (2012: 76). Hatton's article about the response to Neil LaBute's *The Taming of the Shrew* also draws attention to the power dynamics underlying crowdsourced theatre criticism, as LaBute takes several shots at the reviewer of his play that, in addition to critiquing her writing skills, disparage her financial status and sexual orientation (2014: 105). When faced with others' suggestions that he cannot handle criticism of his work, LaBute once again asserts his dominance by 'mock[ing] commenters for working low-level jobs and jeer[ing] at their presumed lack of success' (Hatton 2014: 106). LaBute's attempt to control the conversation by drawing on his class privilege is made very explicit here; in other instances, power dynamics operate more surreptitiously. Though it is beyond the scope of this paper to undertake an empirical study of power, language, and identity in crowdsourced theatre criticism, these issues are in urgent need of further study so that we, as scholars, can avoid reifying dominant voices as we employ this material to reconstruct performances and write theatre histories.

Crowdsourcing the archive

Indeed, limitations related to access and power should not deter theatre researchers from taking crowdsourced theatre criticism seriously. As illustrated by the case studies discussed here, the critical discourse occurring in comment threads provides a nuanced, diverse, and rich record of a performance, its reception, and its publics; it also provides evidence of the broader material conditions in which each of these is embedded. Seeking ways to preserve this ephemeral and hidden discourse, researchers might take a page from crowdsourcing itself and adopt a collaborative approach. This was ultimately what Hatton chose to do, gathering local actors to create a performance with 'archival value' (2014: 108). While Hatton acknowledges that preserving the crowdsourced criticism in a radio play does not leave it open for revision, a key element of Collins' vision of the live archive, she argues, 'the multiple layers of voices, beginning with [the reviewer] and ending with the actors reading the comments, challenges the image of the monolithic record' (2014: 109).

Collaboration is also the principle behind the AusStage database, a free digital archive of Australian live performance that, as of 6 February 2015, boasted 73,488 event records and 109,356 contributors (AusStage c2015a). This impressive scope is possible because the database is administered by multiple stakeholders, including universities, government agencies, and arts organizations (AusStage c2015a). AusStage is also open sourced, meaning that anyone can become a contributor: by registering with the site, users can take an hour-long training session in person or via Skype to become familiar with 'data entry protocols and procedures to learn how to create, edit and copy records' (AusStage c2015b). This collaborative approach might be adapted in similar contexts: for example, participants in a Facebook comments thread could capture the conversation using existing technology and upload it to an open-access archival site. As researchers and archivists explore possibilities like this one, we will also have to closely examine the underlying ethics related to privacy, sharing, and permission, and create policies and procedures accordingly.

Developing new approaches to archiving and widening the scope of what we consider legitimate archival materials in the first place introduce a host of research questions, debates, and technological challenges that can best be explored through collaboration on several levels: between researchers in the field of Theatre and Performance Studies; with colleagues from other disciplines, such as Information Studies and Computer Science; and with the theatre community and theatre audiences more broadly. Returning to the definition of crowdsourcing cited earlier in this chapter, by using a collaborative model to shape our historiographic practices, we can ultimately create an archive that is 'superior in quality and quantity' (Barbier et al. 2012: 258) to existing databases. In other words, as we start to take crowdsourced theatre criticism more seriously, our archival strategies might start by mimicking the practice itself.

Notes

1. Hatton asserts that while the identity of 'neil labute' cannot be verified, 'Based on [his] (alleged) history of responding to critics, as well as the content of these posts, I believe that the poster is, in fact, LaBute' (2014: 120).

Theatre Criticism

2. Hatton refers to the American Theatre Critics Association's membership criteria posted on their website, which states that, 'Membership is open to all who review theatre professionally, regularly and with substance for print, electronic or digital media' (2010).

3. While an examination of the outsourcing of cheap labour is beyond the scope of this chapter, it is a matter that requires further investigation in the context of theatre criticism, as the decline of print criticism and the rise of the blogosphere have created a pool of talented and insightful writers who review theatre online but are not compensated for their work. This is a point that emerged in our discussions during the seminar Blogging in/ and Performance at the 2014 Canadian Association of Theatre Research conference; it is briefly touched on in Karen Fricker's position paper from the session, 'The Liminal Space of the Blogosphere' (2014a).

4. Recent studies have examined how blogging can be adapted in other contexts, including performance analysis (Holland, 2007), historiography (Holland, 2010), and archiving (Collins, 2010). Others have examined how the practice is redefining arts criticism (Dolan (2006, 2013), Fricker (2014a, 2015), Hatton (2014), Hutcheon (2007, 2010)). Harvey, Grehan, and Tompkins' (2010) research on Australian theatre blogging is the only study that attempts to survey the landscape of this virtual territory and provide an initial taxonomy; their groundbreaking work on the AusStage database (2009) will be briefly discussed in the conclusion of this chapter.

5. See, for example, Harp and Tremayne (2006), Harp et al. (2014), and Pacea (2014).

Works cited

American Theatre Critics Association. (2010), 'Apply for Membership', *American Theatre Critics Association*, http://americantheatrecritics.org/apply-for-membership/ (accessed 12 March 2015).

AusStage (c2015a), 'About AusStage', *AusStage*, https://www.ausstage.edu.au/pages/learn/about/ (accessed 21 January 2015).

AusStage (c2015b), 'Contribute', *AusStage*, https://www.ausstage.edu.au/pages/learn/about/ (accessed 21 January 2015).

Barbier, Geoffrey, Zafarani, Reza, Gao, Huiji, Fung, Gabriel, and Liu, Huan (2012), 'Maximizing benefits from crowdsourced data', *Computational and Mathematical Organization Theory*, 18, 257–79.

Boenisch, Peter (2014), Karen Fricker Profile Page, [Facebook], 18 April 2014. (accessed 23 January 2015).

Collins, Eleanor (2010), 'Theatre reviewing in post-consensus society: Performance, print and the blogosphere', *Shakespeare*, 6(3), 330–36.

Conrad, Saxon (2008), 'Re: Review round-up: A Little Night Music at the Shaw Festival', *The Globe and Mail*, 7 July, http://v1.theglobeandmail.com/servlet/story/RTGAM.20080707.WBTheatre20080707134933/BStory/WBTheatre (accessed 2 September 2014).

Dean, Jodi (2010), *Blog Theory: Feedback and Capture in the Circuits of Drive*, Cambridge: Polity.

Dolan, Jill (2006), 'Blogging on queer connections in the arts and the Five Lesbian Brothers', *GLQ: A Journal of Lesbian and Gay Studies*, 12(3), 491–506.

Dolan, Jill (2013), *The Feminist Spectator in Action. Feminist Criticism for the Stage and Screen*. New York: Palgrave Macmillan.

Fricker, K. (2015), 'Blogging', *Contemporary Theatre Review*, 25(1), 39–45.

Fricker, Karen (2014a), 'The liminal space of the blogosphere', *Blogging in/ and Performance*, [Blog], https://catrblogging.wordpress.com/papers/the-liminal-space-of-the-blogosphere/ (accessed 23 January 2015).

Fricker, Karen (2014b), Profile Page, [Facebook], 18 April 2014 (accessed 23 January 2015).

Harp, Dustin, Loke, Jaime and Bachmann, Ingrid (2014), 'Spaces for feminist (re)articulations: The blogosphere and the sexual attack on journalist Lara Logan', *Feminist Media Studies*, 14(1), 5–21.

Harp, Dustin and Tremayne, Mark (2006), 'The gendered blogosphere: Examining inequality using network and feminist theory', *Journalism and Mass Communication Quarterly*, 83 (2), 247–64.

Harvey, Neal, Grehan, Helena and Tompkins, Joanne (2009), 'AusStage: From database of performing arts to a performing database of the arts', in K. Bode and R. Dixon (eds), *Resourceful Reading. The New Empiricism, eResearch, and Australian Literary Culture*, Sydney: Sydney University Press, pp. 325–33.

Harvey, Neal, Grehan, Helena and Tompkins, Joanne (2010), '"Be thou familiar, but by no means vulgar": Australian theatre blogging practice', *Contemporary Theatre Review*, 20(1), 109–119.

Hatton, Oona (2014), '"Hey, asshole: you had your say." The performance of theatre criticism', *Theatre Topics*, 24(2), 103–124.

Hille, Sanne and Bakker, Piet (2014), 'Engaging the social news user. Comments on news sites and Facebook', *Journalism Practice*, 8(5), 253–72.

Holland, Peter (2010), 'Critics and their audiences: The rhetoric of reviewing', *Shakespeare*, 6(3), 292–304.

Holland, Peter (2007), '"It's all about me. Deal with it"', *Shakespeare Bulletin*, 25(3), 27–39.

Hutcheon, Linda (2010) 'Reviewing in Canada as the "civil exchange of ideas"', *Canadian Literature*, 204, 157–59.

Hutcheon, Linda (2009) 'Reviewing reviewing today', *Literary Review of Canada*, 6–8.

Kennedy, Tracy, L.M. (2007) 'The personal is political: Feminist blogging and virtual consciousness-raising', *The Scholar and Feminist Online*, 5(2), 1–4.

Lista, Michael (2008) 'Re: Review round-up: A Little Night Music at the Shaw Festival', *The Globe and Mail*, 7 July, http://v1.theglobeandmail.com/servlet/story/RTGAM.20080707.WBTheatre0080707134933/BStory/WBTheatre (accessed 2 September 2014).

lloyd chambers, philippa (2008) 'Re: Review round-up: A Little Night Music at the Shaw Festival', *The Globe and Mail*. 7 July, http://v1.theglobeandmail.com/servlet/story/RTGAM.20080707.WBTheatre20080707134933/BStory/WBTheatre (accessed 2 September 2014).

MacArthur, Michelle (2013) 'The feminist spectator as blogger: Creating critical dialogue about feminist theatre on the web', *Theatre Research in Canada*, 34(2), 162–86.

Nestruck, J. Kelly (2008) 'Review round-up: A Little Night Music at the Shaw Festival', *The Globe and Mail*, 7 July, http://v1.theglobeandmail.com/servlet/story/RTGAM.20080707.WBTheatre20080707134933/BStory/WBTheatre (accessed 2 September 2014).

Pacea, Otilia (2014) 'Are we really wor(l)ds apart? On gender, genre and language use in blogs', *Journal of Research in Gender Studies*, 4(1), 670–86.

Panych, Morris (2008) 'Re: Review round-up: A Little Night Music at the Shaw Festival', *The Globe and Mail*, 7 July, http://v1.theglobeandmail.com/servlet/story/RTGAM.20080707.WBTheatre20080707134933/BStory/WBTheatre (accessed 2 September 2014).

Piatkowski, M.K. (2008) 'Re: Review round-up: A Little Night Music at the Shaw Festival', *The Globe and Mail*, 7 July, http://v1.theglobeandmail.com/servlet/story/RTGAM.20080707.WBTheatre0080707134933/BStory/WBTheatre (accessed 2 September 2014).

Solga, Kim (2014) Karen Fricker Profile Page, [Facebook], 18 April 2014 (accessed 23 January 2015).

Solga, Kim (2014) 'On "A View From The Bridge" at London's Young Vic', *The Activist Classroom*, [Blog], 18 April 2014. https://theactivistclassroom.wordpress.com/2014/04/18/on-a-view-from-the-bridge-at-londons-young-vic/ (accessed 23 January 2015).

Yedwab, Guy. (2008) 'Re: Review round-up: A Little Night Music at the Shaw Festival', *The Globe and Mail*, 7 July, http://v1.theglobeandmail.com/servlet/story/RTGAM.20080707.WBTheatre20080707134933/BStory/WBTheatre (accessed 2 September 2014).

Yee, David (2012) 'On moderation in social networks', *Canadian Theatre Review*, (150), 76–79.

CHAPTER 16
ARTICISM (ART + CRITICISM) AND THE LIVE BIRDS OF PASSIONATE RESPONSE

Nataša Govedić

I

Criticism is a form of *agon*. It deals with the interpretative dissent of the performance observers, as well as with the social dissent built into the performance by its makers. In my case, it is also a durational performance. For nineteen years now, I have written criticism in various media formats (daily papers, specialist theatre journals and academic press). And the act of interpretation is persistently regarded as the most ar(t) rogant move in the entire art-making business. When people hear the word 'critic', they immediately think of somebody who plays a Homeric demigod, half-blind from constantly misreading her/his contemporaries. In popular imagination, the critic is a colossally-opinionated creature. Harold Bloom comes to mind: 'My concern is only with strong poets, major figures with the persistence to wrestle with their strong precursors, even to death. Weaker talents idealize; figures of capable imagination appropriate for themselves' (Bloom 1997: 5).

'To wrestle', 'to persist', 'to be capable', 'to appropriate', 'to face death'. Is this the vocabulary of a critic or a military strategist?

Like the endeavour of criticism itself, Bloom is famous for exclusive interpretative decisions that are both canon-making (see Bloom 1999) and full of stubborn hierarchies.[1] Furthermore, he is guilty of being evaluative and interpretative to the point of deciding what is, and what is not worthy of our literary attention.[2]

Is this competitive posture in performing criticism really necessary? Is it *persuasive*?

Does all criticism amount to similar evaluative over-inflation? Is it possible to avoid or change it? Is it possible to express critical thoughts without imposing them on anyone?

II

Frankly, one's style might be truly humble, but decisions about art will nevertheless be perceived as dangerously exclusive. And critics are certainly not alone in their prison of opinions. During and after the rehearsals, artists themselves make the same exclusive, sometimes fatal, distinctly provocative decisions as their critics (and change their minds just as often, especially if you continue to watch their performances and discuss them after each viewing). Much like the critics, the artists also choose their vocabularies and passionately stick to a selected action. Some performances are even written in a form of the strict directive, like FYEO – FOR YOUR EARS ONLY (2012). I quote NOID (aka Arnold Haberl), the choreographer:

Ear fountain

// lie down on your side

// ask a trusty person
to take a mouthful of
sparkling water, keep it in
the mouth for the moment
to warm it up
and then gently release it
into your eardrum

// listen and relax

Heun et al. 2012: 63

If I do so, I fail to see the difference between artist-listener and critic-listener. In both cases, you misbehave. You stop being a conventionally operating unit and become a horizontal water-listener. You accept the precise task and exercise it. There is nothing arbitrary about it. The task even requires certain performative discipline. And, of course, *post hoc* thinking about the procedure. Perhaps even the chain of repetitions.

WORKING PROPOSITION no. 1: *Neither art nor criticism are free from the disturbingly daring endeavour of decision-making and constant re/construction of criteria.*

When a critic or an artist avoids the slippery ground of proposing outrageous things, the result is mediocre, in art and criticism alike. Or, as writer and theatre director Tim Etchells says:

> Investment links to passion, politics and rage. It slips out in laughter, numbness, silence. Investment happens when we're hitting new ground, when we don't quite know, where we can't quite say, where we feel compromised, complicit, bound up, without recourse to an easy position.
>
> 2003: 49

And that is my first point: artists and critics invest themselves in establishing a certain … carefully constructed misbehaviour. Or, to quote another provocative artist *and* critic, the first one to link two sides of the aesthetic coin, Oscar Wilde:

> To be good, according to the vulgar standard of goodness, is obviously quite easy. It merely requires a certain amount of sordid terror, a certain lack of imaginative thought, and a certain low passion for middle-class respectability.
>
> 1891: 128

But to be *bad*, well, this requires high passion for both social and stylistic challenges. As Arthur C. Danto stated in 'Stopping Making Art',[3] one never ends up being 'only a critic' or 'only an artist'.

WORKING PROPOSITION no. 2: *One might practice art and/or criticism in order to explore them both, since the two domains mirror each other endlessly, within both methodologies of production.*

Making is closely connected with unmaking, just as a search for self-expression is linked to a constant self-questioning, self-editing and, last but not least, thorough self-criticizing. If one looks at the writings of Mark Rothko or at Joseph Beuys' interviews, to name a couple of prominent and very different artists who have constantly reflected on their own work, one immediately notices that acclaimed artists are not only capable, but fluent in expressing their critical views on art making. They are not *stuck* in the process; they understand that the value of making is not only emotional, but socially reflected. Mark Rothko:

> Art is not only a form of action, it is a form of *social*[4] action. For art is a type of communication, and it enters the environment. It produces its effects just as any other form of action does.
>
> 2004: 10

Rothko, who calls for '[t]he necessity of an empirical inquiry instead of vague enthusiasms' (2006: 12), also insists that one cannot understand art without understanding and performing idealism:

> Because these people, by the very act of their idealism, are really fulfilling a need as great as that of the physical needs. Idealism here forms a kind of action which takes its place side by side with other self-expressive forms of action without which man cannot continue in good health. Art is such an action.
>
> 2004: 10

And the critical knowledge, besides being strategic misbehaviour, is also an act of (social) idealism. It is an attempt at Socratic stinging.[5] The critic addresses the community members directly and demands/displays public criteria, sometimes even *without being asked*. From Plato's *Apology*:

Socrates   For I go around and do nothing but persuade you,
both young and older, not to care for bodies and money before, not
as vehemently as, how your soul will be the best possible.

1984: 81

What philosophy, art and criticism inherit from the Socratic
performative practice is the relentless, layered, tense, unresolved
listening and questioning procedure. The critic trusts and listens to the
artist's own demarcation of the field, just as much as the artist trusts
and listens to the critic's description, demand or feedback. The trial
turns into a dialogue which turns into a polemic which turns into a
reworking of the whole set of reflective proposals. Even if the artist
and the critic perform parallel or angry monologues, without the
possibility of making an open dialogue, both instances are more than
public singularities. Their performances are never indifferent or
separate from each other. The audience always regards and listens to
them parallelly. This joint, yet conflicting, voicing probably prevents
both art and criticism from being engaged merely to 'illustrate' general
agendas of social critique, as Boris Groys noted (2008: 111–121).

Articism (art + criticism) is therefore not an attempt to 'appropriate'
art by means of the critical theory; it is an experiment with languages
of perception, expression and reflection. The style of it is decisive. And
the polyphony necessarily permeates both sides of the coin, regardless
of which came first, the performative or the interpretative gesture.

WORKING PROPOSITION no. 3: *Both the artist and the critic
claim similar expressive and reflective autonomy and similarly refuse to
be reduced to totalitarian, chorus-line commentary.*

It is also important to notice that *no one can end* the process of reflection
once it begins. Think about the Shakespearean criticism as a vast
interpretative and performance-making field or about the growing
trends in education and performance alike, where 'Practice as Research
through Performance' is recognized as open surface for exploring
movement *as* idea and idea *as* movement (compare Kershaw 2009).

Practice is a key term for both performance artists and the critics, since interpretative practice provides the foundation of extended, deepened sensuality of any expressive endeavour. Articism as practice therefore includes the skills of composition, declaring or deliberate hiding of interpretative intentions, phrasing, design of evocative space, the control of perceptive time, the choices of energy levels, the rhythmic instances of authorial performance, personal style of expression and the relationship of an author to a broader social group we are addressing. All of these features are fundamental concerns of both criticism and art.

Maybe we can approach articism by declaring its difference from the militaristic dramaturgy of the chess game. Artist and critic refuse to play by the rules. They deliberately 'misrecognize' assigned roles and social positions. For instance, we can read Sanjoy Roy's description of Rosemary Butcher's dance piece *Episodes of Light* (2008) as a choreographer's refusal to follow the geometrical, fixed, chess-like spatial and social hierarchies:

> Framing the stage are two screens on which strange architectural drawings (designed by Matthew Butcher and Melissa Appleton) are projected: a simple grid, a schematic diagram, a spatial plane dotted with geometric flyovers. Cathy Lane provides a reverberating soundscape, first of steamy hisses and deep-sea rumblings, and later with distant voices and city noises. Solo dancer Elena Giannotti is floor-bound throughout. In slow, crab-like scuttles, painfully hesitant walks and laborious shunts she moves around the perimeter. That is about it: 45 minutes later, the piece ends.
>
> Roy 2008

The chess as a war game pretends that the social territory has only two classes: the 'royals' and 'proletarians', serving the colonial desire to win the opponent's space and governed by the unshakeable rules of movement. But whoever participates in the field of articism makes a *risotto* out of social hierarchies (this is just a feminist homage to Brecht's notion of *culinary criticism*).[6] In articism, the notions of both social victory and social defeat are dismantled and our chief strategy in both instances is *to stop* faking the status quo, which in itself creates new realms of action. For instance, within the frame of militaristic culture, which is especially relevant to Croatian context, we can choose *not* to fight. Instead of accepting the war zone, we can choose to stage provocative 'still life' of Manet's *Le Déjeuner sur l'herbe*, served on the battlefield. Or we can undress and ride the white horse through the centre of the town, as Croatian performer Vlasta Delimar did in the guise of *Lady Godiva* (2001). I agree with Viktor Misiano's assertion (2011) that throughout the history of Russian art various artists insisted on 'paralyzing' the conventional system of value distribution. With one notable difference. Sometimes the artist becomes a valuable and repressive museum piece or even a chess queen diva (like Marina Abramović), but only rarely does a critic lose the capacity to frustrate the establishment.

BORROWED SKEPTICISM no. 1: 'One might easily have supposed that after the critic has crossed over to the side of the artist, he would have won the artist's gratitude and become his confidante. But it doesn't work that way. The critic's text – so most artists believe – seems less to protect the work from detractors than to isolate it from its potential admirers. Rigorous theoretical definition is bad for business. Thus, many artists protect themselves against theoretical commentary in the hope that a naked work of art will be more seductive than one dressed in a text.'

Groys 2008: 116

And yet, is it really possible for an artwork to remain 'naked' or free from interpretation (even if nobody writes about it)? I don't think so. (*Exit Susan Sontag*).[7] Just as the artist hates to be assimilated within the ruling interpretative economy, so the critic disdains the hypocrisy of art community regarding the artist's desire to miraculously step-outside-the-history or to 'outsmart' the whole idea of the given context. It is therefore very useful to go back to Walter Benjamin's attitude towards criticism, expressed in his dissertation 'On the Concept of Criticism in Early German Romanticism' (Benjamin 2004: 152), where criticism is not just an interpretative business aiming to produce far-reaching attitudes, opportunistic legitimations and valuations, but also a disturbing, highly unconventional authorial gesture, capable of radical hesitation, refusal of reductive evaluations, as well as an effort in destabilization of the existing interpretative field. There is no art and no criticism, claims Benjamin, where we encounter propagandistic politicization of art or the decorative aesthetization of military procedures. We make art and we produce criticism, insists Kenneth Burke (1931) in his *Counter-Statement*, where a special kind of refutation goes on. Refutation of the commonplace.

SMALL CHOREOGRAPHIC HYPOTHESIS: Critical gesture and artistic gesture are not of a combative ('And the winner is . . .'), but of a contemplative kind (all my most valuable discoveries arose from defeats).

To nourish a difference of opinion, to endorse refutation as everyday praxis, in both art and criticism, is a way to resist the linearity of thinking. Abundance of reflective possibilities and an eloquence in expression require high intensity of argumentation, both in terms of formal and stylistic elements (our language technique and the type of experience we create), and in terms of political focus (type of disobedience we choose to perform).

III

Criticism is also a kind of rhetorical art. It persuades. In this respect, I want to repeat the very useful Terry Barrett's principles of criticism (1994). These same principles are important for considering various works of art, in formats such as live performance or more static media of expression. According to Barrett, artworks have 'aboutness' and demand interpretation and interpretations are primarily persuasive arguments. Valuable interpretations of art say more about the artwork than they say about the critic, and there can be different, competing, and contradictory interpretations of the same artwork. All interpretations are based on a critic's worldview which can be judged by coherence, correspondence, and inclusiveness. An artwork is not necessarily about what the artist wanted it to be about. Good interpretations invite us to see for ourselves and to continue on our own.

It seems to me that being a critic is a job of relentless public commitment. The community holds me responsible for a certain system of description,[8] although my response to artworks constantly changes, depending on the very performances I attend and on the theoretical grid that interests me the most at a given moment. There is no 'system', only the constant research and faithfulness to the (remembered, reflected upon, experienced) art-event. But it is funny how the critic is forced to 'play a role' of a critic and how the critical role is not a very popular one, regardless of historical context. In his book *The Function of Criticism* (1984), Terry Eagleton wrote about the critic as a public educator, *flâneur,* romantic prophet, modernist *bricoleur,* judge, censor, the mirror of the public sphere, the mediator, inventor of trends, even the natural knight of distinguished taste.

But what about the critic who is simply a student of art?

What about the critic who likes to change and challenge established analytical procedures? What about the critic who is a rhetorical joker, in a prolonged exile of deliberate interpretative belonging? What about the critic who joins the art community in order to show solidarity with the performers and who wishes to step outside the projective, false, controlling distance between art-making and art-reflecting? Let me introduce you to a critical voice which escaped Eagleton's qualifications.

GUEST OF HONOUR: *'Criticism is worldly and in the world so long as it opposes monocentrism, a concept I understood as working in conjuncture with ethnocentrism, which licenses a culture to cloak itself in the particular authority of certain values over others'*

Edward Said 1991: 53

I will give example of Croatian artists Selma Banich and Maja Drobac, who travelled to Nepal and afterwards performed the dance piece about the Croatia-Nepal-Croatia round trip called *Walk with Her* (2013), not because they wanted to exhibit nice souvenirs from a distant country, but because they needed to renounce the idea of any kind of state belonging. In an empty room, they put on display their own walking shoes, used T-shirts, maps, ropes, the Croatian favourite KiKi taffy, audio recordings of conversations with other travellers, an audio recording of a conversation about political tortures in Croatia, private letters, facts and figures about the women's movement in Nepal, poems, herbs picked during their journey. The visitors, being the real dancers of this journey, were invited to pick up the displayed pieces, to bend over them and smell them, to crouch down and touch the sleeping bag, to stretch in order to reach for more distant objects, to sit on the floor in order to listen to the audio tape, to hold something that is hanging above their heads or to unwrap an object placed in front of them. Another level of thinking the space through the performative body of the visitors was the discreet invitation to decide which *line* divides the Croatian from the Nepalese zone of reminiscence (it was impossible to decide) and which percussive sound belongs to which country. The native instruments of Nepal reminded many people in the audience of crickets in Croatia (or vice versa). Banich and Drobac didn't leave the event entirely; they were accessible to the audience outside the main room, where they talked with visitors about the sheer freedom of the walking experience, about the body desiring to move through spaces unrestricted by political violence (present in both Nepal and Croatia) and about the impossibility of 'ending' the journey. They stated that wandering has always been a disturbing praxis, very close to homelessness, but also akin to freedom. They were the 'missing bodies' in both Croatian and Nepalese staged landscape, sharing with the audience intimate reluctance to 'admit' any kind of territorial belonging. The walking itself is stateless.

IV

Of course, writing about theatre (or any live event for that matter) is even more difficult than writing about literature or painting, since a theatre event has something that John Cage, in his text *2 Pages, 122 Words on Music in Dance* manages to capture in quite an unusual way.

Cage writes something that resists classification and is usually considered a poem, while to me it seems as a perfect example of theatre performance and theatre criticism at the same time. In the left column, Cage writes:

> To obtain the value
> of a sound, a movement,
> measure from zero. (Pay
> attention to what it is,
> just as it is).

In the right column, he writes:

> A bird flies.

The middle column:

> Slavery is abolished.

Cage in Lepecki 2012: 28

The writing goes on and it becomes more and more preoccupied with politics of time and incongruence of perception, but it is amazing that Cage creates, at least for me, a very complex theatre scene in the form of short, written discourse. I think he accomplishes this because he plays with attention sequencing (expressed with accumulation of several short, but conceptually rich sentences) and then he introduces a sudden trace of unexpected action. This *live bird* of the actual event is the most disturbing and the most productive part of thinking and/ or doing theatre works. And it really does abolish our conceptual and emotional slavery.

Because, somehow, we cannot represent it.

We are able to pay attention to sound, to movement, to bodies, to words, staging, acting, choreography, corpography, directing, to compositional principles of performance and the dramaturgy of the whole piece, but what surprised us and therefore affected us and changed our perceptive habits remains difficult to grasp.

Maybe it wasn't so sudden and romantically feathered as Cage writes, perhaps it lasted for several hours instead of a second, but we always know that it happened when we have difficulties representing it. It is later, in our prolonged time of reaction, that we remember (or misremember, imagine, invent) the experienced abolition of slavery and then *the line of flight* slowly becomes an abstract entity, something to build an interpretation on. Or our reaction becomes a line for musical notation. Or it becomes a new theatre piece. Or it becomes a poem. Or it becomes a PhD thesis and a book on the subject. Or it becomes performative praxis.

FATA MORGANA: That is why criticism is a deeply imaginative endeavour: our task is not to repeat 'the official truth' nor to produce a thick description of an artwork, but to offer another interpretative score for its viewing, and maybe even for its performing.

What is also true is that our attention is not always at its best. As critics, we become tired, inattentive, blind to certain aspects of the performance, receptively lazy or overloaded. The bird flies, but we fail to notice. Therefore I developed a habit of watching the performances and theatre pieces that failed to resonate with me more than once. I undertook another viewing experiment in cooperation with several actors, directors and performers; we assembled a collective called 'Special Purposes Audience' (2008), and watched the same theatre piece repeatedly, in order to observe what changes on stage and off stage on the next viewing.[9] For six months, we behaved as passionate bird watchers, deliberately returning to the scene of (possible) flight.

The articism is also a vocation that is not realized at the time of the actual presentation of the written or performed work. We carry the multiple traces of the performance and its semantic richness/poverty or the political lucidity/conformity with us for a very long time. The job is always unfinished, rethought in several other performative instances, burdened by many layers of new questions and thoughts. There are performances that become our constant 'tenants', like *Croatian National Surrender* (2010) by Selma Banich (an artist standing with both hands in the air, on the street, for four hours, in front of the Zagreb City Hall/Office for Culture, in an act of surrender to the corrupt office while receiving strange and unpredictable gestures of support from accidental passers-by), or the deeply sardonic, metatheatrical *Semi-interpretations or How to Explain Contemporary Dance to an Undead Hare* (2011) by the director Goran Sergej Pristaš and the choreographically very eloquent dancer/choreographer Nikolina Pristaš (here reading and reflecting on Beuys' performance), or the careful tiptoeing of actor Vilim Matula around the field of the dead in Oliver Frljić's *The Bacchae* (2008). All these performances continue to work with our attention long after they ended in real time. The productive part of art is therefore never in its result, but always in the (almost invisible) Return of the Agon.

DISCLAIMER: In the twenty-first century the artist is forced to sell the process, sell the workshops, sell the artist's books. The market acts as if now the art is finally 'under control': we witness the gradual becoming of the final product, we pay for the revealed sequences of its making. But we still do not own it. Process escapes fetishization. The artist, however, suffers from working in a constant fishbowl.

The invisible part of articism is also similar to editorial work. We work carefully on the details. We re-write, re-shape, re-observe, re-create, re-read, re-perform, re-invent, re-work, re-member and re-nounce our work. And then we start anew, from the very beginning, the first movement, the first word. What kind of time do we establish by doing this?

V

Now we enter a very interesting ethical and philosophical field that I would like to call 'the Re/Action' (much more complex and sometimes involuntary then the notion of a deliberate response). Myriam Van Imschoot quotes choreographer Mark Tompkins: 'Score is a determination of one or more parameters for decision-making in action'

(2005: 2). I have never encountered a better definition of 'constructive criticism'. What's the point of doing art if we cannot accept the implementation of criticism we receive? What's the point of doing criticism if we cannot accept the criticism we receive? Observe any musician or dancer rehearsing a piece and you will notice that the main element of building an interpretation is her/his openness to self-correction. And then, during and after the performance, openness to social response. Re/Action is the very material from which art, as well as criticism, are constructed. And re/action that wants to be more than 'spontaneous' self-indulgence or self-defence must constantly work with various levels of criticism-taking. It is true: taking criticism is the hardest thing. It is also a way of respecting the community we are facing.

As a critic, I need to work in a medium that has nothing to do with articles printed in daily papers, nothing to do with reviews printed in the books published by mainstream publishers or with the self-published reviews on the net, nothing to do with analyses done for specialist magazines, and nothing to do with condensed impressions that we find in e-magazines and on new digital platforms.

The medium that I, as a critic, work in is called real life collectives.

Regardless of the place where people can read my reviews or talk to me, they will accept the dialogue or refuse it based on the premises of how I deal with ideologically and emotionally highly charged issues. For me, this is the demanding aspect of being a critic. Because in many (if not all) circumstances, the gaze of the critic is too reductive to sustain the original encounter between the process of art-making and the process of art-reflecting or remaking. The passion of the critic herself or himself can stand in the way of understanding and hearing artists' propositions. As history shows, critics are frequently oblivious when faced with novelty. Or, to go back to Bloom, it is too easy to write only about yourself, the critic, and not about the disturbingly alien content of an artwork. The imperialist gaze of the critic presumes that difference between art and criticism is so absolute that the critic must colonize, tame and discipline the wildness of an artwork. At the same time, the imperialist gaze of the artist presumes that the difference between art and criticism is so absolute that the artist must ignore the chains of critical reflection in order to remain authentic. I passionately disagree with both perspectives. And I call for another witness, Philippe Lacoue-Labarthe:

> Yet thought supposes what I am calling, of course for lack of a better term, intimacy or the intimate difference. It supposes, or more precisely, it originates an intimacy as the possibility of *relating to* in general. It is in this sense that the poem thinks or is a dialogue. The dialogue is a speaking and a naming (. . .). But speaking and naming are, in turn, a 'letting speak'. To speak to the other being or thing – to address him or it, is to let what speaks in him to occur and accept this word in the very heart of the poem (in its 'immediacy and proximity') as the gift of the other. It is to prepare, ecstatically, for the 'presence' of the other within oneself; to let intimacy open up.
>
> 1999: 64

In this praxis of *relating to*, the critic is just as vulnerable as the artist. That is the rewarding part of writing about art. When I started being a critic, vulnerability of the relation that is established between my viewing and the performance scared me. The small Croatian theatre scene I faced demonstrated 'familiarity' that censored any kind of confrontational thinking. What I felt was the need to enhance this distance between my perspective and the artists' perspective, in order not to be involved in artists' immediate spheres of aesthetic and/or political interest. For many years, I refused to talk to theatre makers or to participate in any reflective procedure before officially seeing the actual theatre piece. But this ideology of sustained participation blocked many possibilities of responsible and innovative configuring of performing materials. What helped me, in the beginning, to establish independence from theatre cliques, started to become after a while too rigid a shield of avoiding various intellectually nourishing aspects of communality. With time, I started to accept a more open attitude and to challenge my own fear of social accessibility and emotional vulnerability. Now I think that artists and critics work best when they deliberately and consciously develop their dialogue. And I cannot imagine either an artist or a critic who are 'happily divorced' from the desire to overstep the bounds (otherwise called art-making) or the desire to rethink the rules and principles of expression (otherwise called criticism). And just as the artist will gain the most from performative praxis if s/he endures or accepts the constant demand of critical self-correction and careful self-examination, so the critic must work in another direction. The critic needs to embrace radical uncertainties of artistic re/search; the anxiety of being there without quoted influence. I have difficulties trusting critics who refuse to collapse discursive control into some kind of free play. 'The mind that is not baffled is not employed', says poet Wendell Berry (in Nachmanovitch 1990: 84).

Today, after many years of favouring theoretical tools in approaching art, when I think about teaching criticism, I primarily choose to think along and converse with artists (visual artists, sound artists, performers, writers etc), not theatre theorists, as models for reflection and sources for analytic vocabulary. Because theory, as Adorno noticed a long time ago, can easily become just another 'compulsory order' (2003/1964: 29). Very useful (and unavoidable), for sure. But at the same time, cleverly restrictive. I need both art and criticism as methods to practice freedom. Finally, I would like to mention pleasurologist Roland Barthes, a figure constantly oscillating between art and criticism. Barthes: 'The pleasure can be spoken: whence criticism' (1973: 51). And one page further: 'The text (should be) that uninhabited person who shows his behind to the *Political Father*'. The respect for disorder we meet in this order of sentences is certainly close to John Cage's live birds, mentioned earlier. Or, to go back to Cage's original instructions:

Are eyes open?
Where the bird flies, fly.

Cage in Lepecki 2012: 28

Notes

1. In review of Bloom's book *Genius*, critic Frank Kermode writes: 'Bloom cannot help thinking in terms of competition – no doubt his Oedipal

obsession is a version of this habit, though it sometimes seems more appropriate to sport. He cares indefatigably about who is greater than whom, who can be called "the greatest" and why another poet does not make it onto his all-time team.' (Kermode 2002)

2. 'Time which decays and then destroys us is even more merciless in obliterating weak novels, poems, dramas, and stories, however virtuous these may be. Wander into library and regard the masterpieces of thirty years ago: a handful of forgotten book have value, but the iniquity of oblivion has rendered most bestsellers instances of time's revenge.' (Bloom 2005: x)

3. Talk presented at the University of Illinois on 23 September 2009.

4. All emphases within quotes are original, unless otherwise stated.

5. I refer the reader to Socrates in Plato's *Apology* (1984: 82), where Socrates compares himself to the gadfly which stings and upsets the inert horse of Athenian politics.

6. 'Culinary theatre' and thereby 'culinary criticism' are Brecht's terms for undemanding, propagandistic, easily digested theatre pieces. They are elaborated in Brecht's text 'Modern theatre is the epic theatre' (1930).

7. Or at least her work *Against Interpretation*.

8. For instance, when I published my first novel for children (*Mrežir*, Zagreb: Algoritam, 2012), the review of it was published in the most commercial daily *Jutarnji list* (12. 3. 2013) under the title 'The Terror of the Theatre Community Reveals a Gentler Side'.

9. Actors hated it; the acting community thought we were doing something offensive and inappropriate, because theatre performance is a 'one-off viewing experience'. The experiment, however, had many interesting outcomes in the sense of establishing a public demand for the deliberately reflected process of acting.

Works cited

Adorno, Theodor (2003/1964). *The Jargon of Authenticity*, London: Routledge.

Barrett, Terry (1994). *Criticizing Art: Understanding the Contemporary*, Mountain View, California: Mayfield Publishing Company.

Barthes, Roland (1973). *The Pleasure of the Text*, New York: Hill and Wang.

Benjamin, Walter (2004). *Selected Writings*, Vol. 1. Ed. Marcus Bullock, Cambridge: Harvard University Press.

Bloom, Harold (1997) *The Anxiety of Influence*, Oxford: Oxford University Press.

Bloom, Harold (1999) *Shakespeare: The Invention of the Human*, London: Fourth Estate.

Bloom, Harold (2005) *Dramatists and Dramas*, Chelsea House Publishers.

Burke, Kenneth (1931) *Counter-Statement*, Berkeley: University of California Press.

Flusser, Vilim (2002) *Writings*, Minneapolis: University of Minnesota Press.

Groys, Boris (2008) *Art Power*, Cambridge MA: The MIT Press.

Heun, Walter; Kruschokova, Krassimira; Mehanović, Lejla and Noeth, Sandra (eds) (2012) *Scores No. 2: What Escapes*, Wien: Tanzquartier Wien.

Kermode, Frank (2002) 'Hip Gnosis', *The Guardian,* 12 October, http://www.theguardian.com/books/2002/oct/12/featuresreviews.guardianreview14 (accessed 20 April 2015).

Kershaw, Baz (2009) 'Practice as Research through Performance' in Smith, Hazel and Dean, Roger T., eds, *Practice-led Research, Research-led Practice in Creative Arts*, Edinburgh: Edinburgh University Press.

Lacoue-Labarthe, Philippe (1999) *Poetry as Experience*, Stanford: Meridian Books.

Lepecki, Andre (ed.) (2012) *Dance. Documents in Contemporary Art*, Cambridge MA: The MIT Press.

Misiano, Viktor (2011) 'On Critique Declared but Not Realized or, Realized but Not Declared (Or, On the Love of Power)', http://monumenttotransformation.org/atlas-of-transformation/html/i/impossibility-of-criticism/on-critique-declared-but-not-realized-or-realized-but-not-declared-or-on-the-love-of-power-viktor-misiano.html (accessed 20 April 2015)

Nachmanovitch, Stephen (1990) *Free Play*, New York: Penguin.

Plato's 'Apology of Socrates' in *Four Texts on Socrates* (1984), edited and translated by Thomas G. West and Grace Starry West, Ithaca: Cornell University Press.

Rothko, Mark (2006) *Writings on Art*, New Haven: Yale University Press.

Rothko, Mark (2004) *The Artist's Reality. Philosophies of Art,* New Haven: Yale University Press.

Roy, Sanjoy (2008) 'Rosemary Butcher', *Guardian*, 6 November, http://www.theguardian.com/stage/2008/nov/06/dance (accessed 20 April 2015).

Said, Edward (1991) *The World, the Text and the Critic*, London: Verso.

Sontag, Susan (1966) *Against Interpretation*. New York: Farrar, Straus & Giroux.

Van Imschoot, Myriam (2005) 'Rests in Pieces: On Scores, Notation and the Trace in Dance', *Multitudes*, n° 21, Spring, p. 1–8.

Wilde, Oscar (1891) 'The Critic as Artist', in *Intentions and Other Writings,* New York: Doubleday.

CHAPTER 17
PERFORMATIVE CRITICISM AND CREATIVE CRITICAL WRITING
William McEvoy

Susan Sontag's 1964 essay 'Against Interpretation' called for new modes of engagement with art that bypassed the hermeneutic quest to decode meaning and that focused instead on surfaces, forms and appearances. Her critique challenged realist traditions that saw art as a representation of the external world, and proposed that critics try to capture art's sensuousness instead. Art criticism, she argued, needed to be descriptive rather than prescriptive. Interpretation was a betrayal, even a 'revenge of the intellect upon art' (Sontag 1978: 7). This essay looks at a number of recent examples of theatre criticism that take up Sontag's challenge to undo interpretation, substituting instead modes of writing that are creative, affective or in other ways questioning about their own form. It will look at both theatre theory and theatre criticism. The chapter will end by briefly exploring the journalistic theatre criticism of two of Britain's leading critics, Susannah Clapp, who writes for the *Observer*, and Lyn Gardner from *The Guardian*. Clapp's writing often suspends value judgements and instead tries to capture the singularity of performance through the use of figurative language and juxtaposed, vividly described details, while Gardner's reviews often register the psychical or physical impact of performance, creating a sense of an embodied, reactive spectator. I see their work as informed by feminist theories of writing that encouraged women to challenge prevailing forms and norms, and in dialogue with ideas coming from theatre theorists like Peggy Phelan about ephemerality, liveness and performative writing.

The reason this essay focuses both on theatre criticism, in the form of reviews and essays, and on theatre theory, is partly a result of Josette

Féral's insight that 'today it is easier to bridge the gap between journalistic and scholarly criticism' (Féral 2000: 311). Academic criticism nowadays often relies on and quotes from journalistic criticism and I view theatre theory in the same way that Terry Eagleton sees literary theory, 'a kind of 'metacriticism', a critical reflection on criticism' (Eagleton 1997: 172). Therefore, instead of compartmentalizing journalistic criticism, scholarly criticism and theatre theory, I explore them as part of a continuum in which the main difference is how much space you have to interrogate your critical assumptions and the wider cultural or artistic context of the work under discussion. In French, a common term for the critical analysis of theatre is 'théâtrologie', defined by Patrice Pavis as 'linking together different knowledges and reflecting on the epistemological conditions of theatre studies' (Pavis 2004: 381). But in a context in which liveness, ephemerality and the process of documentation and reconstruction have all become central to our understanding of theatre, the role of theatre criticism is increasingly important. This essay therefore focuses on both theatre theory and criticism as a way of suggesting that there are productive overlaps and dialogues between them. Often, when asking '[w]hat has happened? What survives after the event?' (Pearson and Shanks 2001: 57), theatre criticism is one of our key resources.

In both the theory and criticism under examination, the position of the writer in relation to the performance is crucial. Féral draws the distinction between the critic who is outside the work, analysing and evaluating, and one who is subjective, offering opinions:

> Must he/she be content with the analysis of the results, standing apart and above it all as an 'objective' onlooker, such as he/she claims to be? Or, taking the opposite stance, must he/she get involved and risk offering an opinion which is necessarily subjective?
>
> Féral 2000: 308

This difference maps on to Sontag's distinction between the hermeneutics and erotics of criticism: the former equates objectivity with mastery and truth, while the latter is associated with the subjective and a kind of merging with the art object that is more affective than logical, more romantic than classical, more unconscious than conscious. The objective position sees meaning as inherent in the text, waiting to be found, while the subjective one sees meaning as derived from the encounter between spectator and performance.

The move away from reliance on objectivity in theatre theory and criticism takes a number of forms, from performative writing (Peggy Phelan, David Williams) to self-reflexive theory (Daniel Mesguich, Howard Barker, Alain Badiou). Performative writing involves the staging of the critical self marked by the artwork; it is writing inflected by the multi-sensorial impact of performance, generated and performatively produced by theatre. Some of the writers under discussion, such as Mesguich, critique objectivity by rethinking the relationship between the verbal and the performed, asking what the limits of language are when dealing with theatre. In relation to Clapp and Gardner, who are writing criticism rather than theory, questions emerge regarding how the critical text channels the impact of the artwork into its own writing, with style becoming a kind of figuration of the performance, or a registering of its emotional impact. In both critics, there is an emphasis on the singularity and unrepeatability of performance.

Critiquing objectivity

In *Mourning Sex*, Peggy Phelan uses the term 'performative writing' to talk about a way of writing critically that is not direct, objective or conclusive, but informed and deformed by its own affective and subjective engagement with a work of art. Performative writing is generated by the work but is not necessarily directly about it. The texts produced 'enact the affective force of the performance event again' (Phelan 1997: 12), a phrase we will come back to in relation to Clapp and Gardner. In Phelan's words, it is 'writing [...] made vivid by the psychic process of distortion (repression, fantasy, and the general hubbub of the individual and collective unconscious), and made narrow by the muscular force of political repression in all its mutative violence' (Phelan 1997: 12). Phelan conceives of a type of writing that registers its own struggle towards verbalisation as well as being marked by the memory, impact and experience of performance, the '"scenes" that motivate it' (Phelan 1997: 12). Such writing for Phelan is triggered by and associated with performance, rather than being a reflection or summation of it [Féral likewise rejects the idea of 'critic as echo' as too passive to fulfil the critical function in a satisfactory way (Féral 2000: 309)].

As Mary Poovey suggests, performative writing can cite influences such as 'écriture féminine, Judith Butler's theory of performative gender, Freud's concepts of trauma and transference, or the development of performance studies as an academic discipline' (Poovey 2003: 123). To take the first of these, Hélène Cixous's classic text 'The Laugh of the Medusa' urges women to write in and through their body in a critical language which mixes discourses and transgresses conventions. The writing in Cixous's essay enacts its own rejection of norms of elegance and logical criticality: it is a text of excesses and rupture, of flow and fluidity, of the body and its verbal expression: 'laughs exude from our mouths; our blood flows and we extend ourselves without ever reaching an end; we never hold back our thoughts, our signs, our writing [...]' (Cixous 1976: 878). While Cixous's text is about the body's materiality finding form in language, Phelan's 'performative writing' is premised on absence, loss and the ephemeral, registering the insubstantiality of its object (performance). This critical writing, for Phelan, is the enactment of a difference from the performance which generates it, a kind of ripple or after-effect of the artwork that survives in the mind and the writing of the viewer.

In terms of the link with performativity in language and philosophy, Phelan suggests that 'performative writing' is in the first instance the making of a promise, in the Austinian sense (Phelan 1997: 16). It is the performative promise of its own critique of norms of logic and syntax, a marginal, queered text of otherness, outside a 'zone controlled by regulative syntax' (ibid). In a more general sense, this writing is performative in that it registers the effect and affective force as the artwork acts on and through the spectator. Such criticism is written to capture theatre's impact as it reverberates through language, a poetic re-enactment of performance in which emotion, associations, the private and the public converge, unpredictably, outside the regulatory structures of conventional critical writing.

A part of what performative writing does is to allow theatre to release associations and memories, producing writing not formed of argument and analysis, but of a chain of linked recollections and connotations. David Williams's essay on the use of fire in Peter Brook's productions, 'Except the Cinders – A Fire Trajectory', begins with a mosaic of associations with fire. His academic critical essay begins with a staging of the critic's own subjectivity, the private interplay of his own set of cultural references and intertexts:

[...T]he burning of the great library at Alexandria: the erasure of the archive. The nine day fire in Nero's Rome. The destruction of the Globe Theatre in 1613 during a performance of Henry VIII, its thatch ignited by the firing of a canon onstage; all those fires in theatres over the centuries. The Great Fire of London, in which over 13,000 houses were destroyed. The Hindu tradition of suttee. The burning of witches. The burning of Jeanne d'Arc. The burning of books. The fire-bombing of Cologne, Hamburg, Dresden. The Nazi crematoria. The burning of flags. [...] The fire I deliberately started in my family's back yard at the age of 6, then tried to stamp out, my shoe and sock on fire. Spitfire 'red-head' matches. At the age of 9, seeing a running man with his shirt ablaze, rolled and extinguished by passers-by; the smell of burning hair. Bunsen burners, magnesium, phosphorus, glass-blowing in school science classes. [...] Fire alarms, fire extinguishers, fireflies, fireworks, firearms. [...] Fire engines. Fire-fighters. Red-faced apologies. The self-immolation of a young Kurdish protester in the streets of London in 1999.

Williams 2000: 112–13

Williams's list moves between different orders of experience ranging from the world-historical, the traumatic, the mundane and the private, from an adult and a child's perspective and memory, showing how the critic is the vector of myriad different forms of knowledge, discourse and temporality. As writing, the text performs the singular and unique subjectivity of this particular critic while also recognizing how each spectator might have their own set of fire associations. Performance is conceptualized not as having objective meaning but as generating distinct processes of thinking, feeling and remembering for each spectator/critic.

This kind of asyntactical assembly of associations is reminiscent of what Mike Pearson and Michael Shanks call 'stratigraphy', writing formed of layers: '[a]nd within layers there may be the juxtaposition of different varieties of material, stylistic discontinuity and expressive diversity [...]. A collage then carried on simultaneously in different genres, styles and media [...] without value judgements on their relative worth' (Pearson and Shanks 2001: 25). Though they are talking about performance, this is also a useful term for thinking about Williams's critical list and its collage of connotations. The stratigraphic critic rejects the articulations of syntax for a 'paratactical', 'hypotactical' and 'katachresic' (Pearson and Shanks 2001: 25) critical language. Theatre criticism in this mould is neither objective (outside the work, measuring it) nor subjective (writing from the perspective of the self), but based on the premise that identity is a discursively structured set of associations. In this framework, the critic transcends the subjective/ objective binary, embodying a space through which events, associations, connotations and memories move, triggered by performance.

Performative writing therefore stages the impact of the work on the self. The theatre performance ripples through the critical text in a stratigraphic way, creating a poetics that aims to release the critic from the frameworks of either objective analysis or subjective impressions. Instead, it posits the spectator as an historical, discursively mediated subject whose writing captures that.

Theatricalizing theory

Performative writing can be seen as a rejection of the framing logic and structures of existing criticism. In its emphasis on the self as vehicle for the affects and effects of performance which are then transformed into writing, it rejects the desirability of a form of critical objectivity based on interpretation of meaning. In the following three examples of theatre theory, we encounter three different ways in which critical writing has become performative: staging language, staging the self, and staging the act of criticism itself.

Director Daniel Mesguich's book of theatre criticism and theory, *L'éternel éphémère*, is purposely fragmented and formally varied. It is both assertive and indecisive, dogmatic and full of ambivalences that threaten to undo certainty and logic. Rather than being divided into themed chapters, it is written almost like a script, conveying the idea of an author in dialogue with himself. The text dwells on the paradoxes of theatre texts (always 'to-be-performed', only completed by the ephemeral, vanishing, act of performance) and on the problematic attempts of verbal theory to articulate the choreographed, embodied, material art of performance. What Mesguich provides us with are a series of critical insights and moments rather than an overarching theoretical synthesis.

Furthermore, the essay is self-questioning, staging its own hesitation about beginning, and uses 'voices off', as if the critical page were a space, or place, for critical self-consciousness, almost confessional in tone: 'To talk, claiming to speak, however little, about the activity of theatre: such a claim is obviously false' (Mesguich 2006: 9; my translation). Fragmentation occurs not just at the visual level on the page, and in the disarticulation of critique, but at a discursive level, as the writing crosses over between the critical, the theoretical, the performative and the self-performative. The typography of the page also varies between italics and roman type to create a further level of textual variation.

The consequence of this is that the text is broken up and aphoristic rather than critically fluent. Its insights are meant to be seen as disruptive, incomplete, intuitive, fleeting and fragmentary, occupying the space between text and performance. They position performance as an art form that cannot be fully expressed or understood in language, that is located in the gaps between words. The aphorisms and visually varied paragraphs perform their own linguistic inadequacy to speak about theatre. Mesguich therefore can be said to create a critical text which registers the limits of language in dealing with performance.

If Mesguich borrows from the form of theatre texts themselves to create a generically hybrid critical text, with 'voices' from 'off' the page interrupting his critical fluency, Howard Barker takes this a step further by seeming to veer critically off course altogether into fiction, or into a text about love and desire which seems to forget it is about theatre at all. In *Death, the One and the Art of Theatre*, he combines aphoristic writing familiar from his earlier work *Arguments for the Theatre*, with longer sections of critical reflection on tragedy and death in which whole paragraphs deal with erotic desire. Crystalline theoretical observations are placed alongside digressions, sometimes overtly about love and its anxieties, '*The one* observed him through narrowed eyes. He had disappointed her and she did nothing to conceal this disappointment' (Barker 2005: 28), and at other times, offering insights that *might* be relevant to theatre, but equally might be part of this erotic sub-text. One example that balances indecisively between theatre and the erotic is his comment on photographs, which can feasibly be linked to theatre and visibility, but also to the desire to know the other's secrets: 'The old photograph. What is behind the tree? Something was behind the tree. To turn the photograph on its edge. To scratch away the surface of the tree' (Barker 2005: 13).

These digressions are not secondary or incidental to the exploration of theatre, since, as Barker constantly reminds us: 'All I describe is theatre even where theatre is not the subject' (Barker 2005: 2). The digression towards the fictional is explained by the recurrent reminder that the topic *is* theatre, so that these erotic, semi-theoretical statements become a new way of thinking about and talking about theatre, an oblique, even enigmatic one. They insist that the fictional, the erotic, desire and death are all part of how we respond to theatre, hence the new form of creative-critical writing to reflect this. Barker's text reconceptualizes theatre theory, not as having an analytical, meta-critical relationship to theatre texts or performances, but as a kind of disarticulation of the rational that allows desire and death to become mobile, disrupting the boundary between fiction and criticism, between erotic desire and the impact and status of theatre.

Generic hybridity is also central to Alain Badiou's recently translated *Rhapsody for the Theatre*. This text creates a bridge between theory and criticism, and between meta-textual analytical criticism and a more self-reflexive kind. It juxtaposes two modes of critical writing, one based on the assertion of philosophical positions about theatre and its relationship to the state and politics, the other as a series of dialogues between the writer, Badiou, and an empiricist version of himself.

Clearly invoking the historical use of the dialogue form from Plato onwards, the text juxtaposes philosophical rigour and theatrical dialogues to suggest that the two types of writing operate differently but in conjunction with one another. While the philosophical parts of the text offer theoretical statements, the empiricist acts more like a traditional theatre critic, demanding lists of specific productions, famous actresses or texts that qualify as the more serious type of theatre that Badiou is concerned with:

The Empiricist   It seemed to me that, in passing, you were proposing yet another list. Would you mind confirming this, so that I may take note of it on my empirical tablets?
Me   Damn! What list?
The Empiricist   That of the great authors of theatre, in the French language, and in the twentieth century. I heard: Claudel, Genet, Beckett.
Me   I consider excellent Vinaver, Vauthier, Kalisky, Koltès, and several others.
The Empiricist   Don't play tricks. Your minimal-list, as you say, the sure names, the contemporary classics that are already guaranteed?
Me   OK, those three.

Badiou 2013: 52

The theatrical, in the form of character-based dialogues, finds its way into the philosophical text as a comic mechanism, a critique of philosophical certainty, making Badiou's writing about theatre continuously self-critical about its conclusions and form. It therefore implies that theatre can only partially and inadequately be thought about through the meta-discourses of philosophy. Many of the interactions between the philosopher (Badiou) and Empiricist use humour, and comedy ends up being a mechanism for critiquing philosophy's theoretical ambitions.

Theatre criticism: Susannah Clapp and Lyn Gardner

We have looked at modes of theatre criticism which are performative, stratigraphic, self-critical, self-theatricalizing and generically hybrid. These are all creative deviations from the critical model based on objective meta-language that is often technical, abstract and disembodied. In turning to the theatre criticism of two leading British theatre critics, Susannah Clapp and Lyn Gardner, I want to suggest that their writing is concerned with capturing theatre's liveness, unrepeatability and singularity, staging the critic as an embodied presence, and deferring value judgements about quality in favour of communicating the performance's sensory impact.

Both Clapp and Gardner make regular use of a vocabulary of emotion and affect in their theatre criticism. They write about the mark theatre leaves on them, not merely cognitively, but bodily. Their writing often conveys the phenomenological experience of theatre, the situatedness of the spectator, their proximity to the work and the way such material and spatial experiences impact on them. Similarly, they register the 'affective force of the performance' (Phelan 1997: 12) on them as critics, and therefore move beyond value judgements and interpretation about the text (especially if it is a new play rather than a classic) and the mise-en-scène.

A notable quality of Clapp's writing is her creation of a highly distinctive style, a kind of verbal recreation of the power of the production she is reviewing. Theatre is translated into a richly figurative language so that style itself is a mode of theatre criticism, above and beyond the evaluative aesthetic judgements that might accompany it. Her writing is distinguished by its economy and concision. It is evocative, often reading like a series of discrete perceptions rather than attempts to quantify the theatre experience. In that sense, it could be called 'creative criticism', a term, as Poovey tells us, embraced by theorists in the 1970s to challenge the idea that 'critical language is denotative, transparent to its object, and simply points at what it faithfully describes' (Poovey 2000: 114).

The way in which Clapp translates spectatorship into a form of critico-poetic writing is evident in this review of David Mamet's *Speed-the-Plow* from 2008:

> What's not rickety is the testosterone-fuelled dialogue. It's both convincing and excluding: listening to it is like being trapped on some terrible, all-male squash court (poor old Laura Michelle Kelly just gets flat slabs of prose). It's hard to believe that Mamet has ever been more fully incarnated than here, where Spacey and Goldblum bark and snarl at each other's sentences as if they were tugging at opposite ends of the same piece of meat.
>
> Clapp 2008

The language is concrete and dynamic ('flat slabs'; 'like being trapped'), its metaphors visceral and vivid ('tugging at opposite ends of the same piece of meat'); it even resonates with the auditory experience of the performance ('bark and snarl'). The reader comes away with a strong sense of the writer searching for adequate figurative language, to find expressions to suit the impact of the work. The experience of theatre is not reframed via a critical meta-discourse but pulses in and through the innovative metaphors and similes.

In addition to a richly figurative critical language, Clapp is adept at capturing the singularity of performance in her theatre criticism. Her reviews often employ acts of critical noticing, observations that relate to the particular performance she has watched and that stem from her own individual experience. A more recent review of a West End revival of David Hare's *Skylight* provides a typical moment of observation incorporated into the texture of the writing: talking of Bill Nighy's performance, she observes how '[h]e scats around with jagged gestures and broken phrases. His bullying is the more effective because it is often oblique, and always stylish. Just look at the way he lopes over to the stove to take over his ex-lover's cooking' (Clapp 2014). Singular, unrepeatable moments like this reinforce the ephemeral nature of the theatre event, 'just look' or you'll miss it, whereas more conventional criticism tends to see one performance as exemplary of the whole production.

Such moments of singular noticing are consonant with theoretical ideas within the academy about liveness, unrepeatability and ephemerality. In Clapp's work, literary style provides a verbal analogue to the phenomenological and affective reception of the theatrical event, while acts of noticing convey the sense of an embodied, reactive spectator rather than a disembodied critical consciousness judging from an ahistorical and immaterial distance.

Lyn Gardner's theatre criticism likewise conveys the emotional force of performance and the way it reverberates through the critic. Her writing is often an expression of the passional and psychical impact of theatre, communicating a sense of the critic's placement in the theatrical space, her consciousness of intimacy or distance, of emotions being played and played out in performance. Gardner's reviews often articulate the impact of performance in terms of their disruption of the critic's state of mind. The emotional impact of performance is validated as a critical response in its own right, rather than being translated into rational, aesthetic or interpretive terms, as for example, in this review of the National Theatre of Scotland's production of Gregory Burke's *Black Watch*:

> John Tiffany's storming, heart-stopping production is all disorienting blood, guts and thunder, threaded through with the history and songs of the regiment and intercut with lyrical moments of physical movement, like some great dirty ballet of pulsating machismo and terrible tenderness.

Gardner 2006

Here, the writing registers the physical impact of the performance ('disorienting'; 'heartstopping'), the emotional tone of the acting ('pulsating machismo and terrible tenderness'), the way it vibrates through the body. Its metaphors and similes derive from the performance itself, its noisy sound effects and extraordinary range of choreography ('great dirty ballet [...] pulsating').

Like Clapp, her writing focuses extensively on the visual and the auditory, but it is much more frank about expressing a performance's emotional register, seeing the individual critic as metonymical of – not a substitute for – the audience as a whole. The move away from the objectivity of conventional criticism is not towards an impressionistic subjectivity, but invokes the importance of the subjective and the affective in the experience of theatre. Gardner's reviews seek to convey the impact of a performance on this one specific critic, and to ask the critical reader whether they wish to expose themselves to a similar emotional experience. For Gardner, passing value judgements or interpreting meaning seem less important than expressing the performance's emotional power and how it impacts on the critic's body.

In their construction of a writing style that searches for new figurations for the emotional and psychic vectors of performance, in their acts of noticing, and the way they record the passions and emotions generated by performance, Clapp and Gardner have paved the way for new modes of theatre criticism in the UK. Their writing of the body and emotions, of the visible, the audible, and the material presence of performance, are all a challenge to the disembodied objectivity of many of their (male) peers. They capture the singularity of the experience of performance, rather than speaking about one performance as if it applied to the production as a whole. Compare Michael Billington's *Guardian* review of *Skylight*, which prioritizes the play's text and meaning, rather than his experience of that one performance he saw, or Paul Taylor's *Independent* review of *Speed-the-Plow*, which conveys little sense of the reviewer listening to and watching a unique live performance.

This essay has looked at examples of theatre criticism that acknowledge the way performance impacts on critics, changing how they write. Powerful performances bleed into the critical texts that discuss them, triggering their metaphors, prompting the critics' memories, demanding a form of writing that incorporates the energy of its subject. This mode of performative criticism helps erode the difference between the theoretical and the journalistic, both of which use creative approaches to rethink their relationship to their subject. Whether juxtaposing theoretical and theatrical techniques, or generating poetic metaphors that capture the singularity or the bodily impact of performance, these texts often stage the challenges of writing about the material art of theatre, and they question the suitability of philosophical or reason-based analysis. Rather than seeking to understand theatre through critical interpretation, as if meaning were stable or fixed, they stage its impact on their writing and on the self, showing how it recreates critical language, or how it escapes the verbal in an endless difference.

Works cited

Badiou, Alain (2013) *Rhapsody for the Theatre*, London: Verso.

Barker, Howard (2005) *Death, The One, and the Art of Theatre*, London: Routledge.

Billington, Michael (2014) 'Skylight Review: Nighy and Mulligan in moving mixture of politics and love', *The Guardian*, 18 June.

Cixous, Hélène (1976) 'The Laugh of the Medusa', *Signs*, 1, 4, 875–893.

Clapp, Susannah (2008) 'Far More Than Mamet Deserves: Speed the Plow', *Observer*, 17 February.

Clapp, Susannah (2014) 'Skylight Review: Hare Revival is a Thatcherite Play for Today', *Observer*, 22 June.

Eagleton, Terry (1997) *Literary Theory. An Introduction*, Oxford: Blackwell.

Féral, Josette (2000) 'The Artwork Judges Them – The Theatre Critic in a Changing Landscape', *New Theatre Quarterly*, 16, 4, 307–14.

Gardner, Lyn (2006) 'Black Watch', *The Guardian*, 8 August.

Mesguich, Daniel (2006) *L'Éternel Éphémère*, Paris: Verdier.

Pavis, Patrice (2004) *Dictionnaire du Théâtre*, Paris: Armand Colin.

Pearson, Mike and Michael Shanks (2001) *Theatre/Archaeology*, London: Routledge.

Phelan, Peggy (1997) *Mourning Sex. Performing Public Memories*, London: Routledge.

Poovey, Mary (2000) 'Creative Criticism: Adaptation, Performative Writing, and the Problem of Objectivity', *Narrative*, 8, 2, 109–133.

Sontag, Susan (1978) 'Against Interpretation', *Against Interpretation, and Other Essays*, New York, Octagon.

Taylor, Paul (2008) 'Speed-the-Plow, Old Vic, London', *Independent*, 14 February.

Williams, David (2000) 'Except the Cinders – A Fire Trajectory', *Performance Research*, 5, 1, 112–119.

PART IV
SAMPLES OF CRITICAL PRACTICE

CHAPTER 18
HOW TO THINK LIKE A
THEATRE CRITIC
Alison Croggon

This piece was originally written for the Australian literary magazine Island *and was published in No. 137 in 2014.*

At first, you mustn't think. You arrive at the place assigned for performance. It may be a theatre, it may be a shed or an underground carpark. You wait for the ritual: the lowering of the lights, the hush in the auditorium, the slight unconscious holding of breath. Something is about to begin.

Even if it's a play that you know backwards because you've read it and seen it in countless interpretations, you have no idea what is about to happen. It will be different every time.

For days or weeks or months or years a group of people has been making whatever it is you are about to see. Theatre comes in many shapes, from many different processes, and is made for many different reasons. However it is done, it will end up in front of an audience. What makes theatre is the work of all those who created it – the performers, the writers, the directors, the designers, the back stage staff – meeting the unknown, which is the audience. The audience is you. They don't know what you think about it. You, ideally, don't know what you think of it either.

You watch and listen and feel. If you are a critic, it is your job to watch as hard as you can. You listen to the language, to the voices that articulate it, and you watch the bodies that move in front of you, weaving meaning out of a relationship and space. You listen to the soundscape that embraces the voices. There may be music, there may be ambient sound, there may be silence so profound you can hear the actors breathing and every step on the stage. You look at the shape of the stage, how the set and lighting create their own meanings, how the shapes open and determine the relationship of this performance to you, the audience. You open your body to the rhythms of the performance and the language and the colours and movement that weave their meanings before you. You create a relationship with the work that is occurring in front of you.

At the assigned time the performance ends. It may last for twenty minutes, or for twelve hours. You, the audience, will have experienced that performance in the time allotted. Even if you went back to the same theatre to see the same show, you will never have that experience again. It is now in the past tense, stored in your memory. If you watched hard enough, you will have noticed all sorts of details, which at the moment are mixed up in a generalized mash. In the immediate aftermath, you will have a reaction: you liked it, you hated it, you were indifferent, you were bored, you were so excited or so sad or so astonished that you couldn't speak at all.

None of that matters very much. You are not a critic yet.

You take your memory home and you begin to prod it. You begin to translate your experience into words. When you were in the theatre, you were living in the present tense. That is now over. Now you are a mortician, and language is your scalpel. Now you drag out the books. You may read the play again. You may research some aspect of performance history you don't know enough about. You may need to look up the history of English kings, or dog sledging, or what's going on in garment factories in Bangladesh in 2014. People make theatre about all sorts of things. You remember a quote by a critic writing in 1954. You remember a poem you love that seems apposite. You think about the shapes of everything you saw and you consider how they created the experience that is now living inside you. You let it all circle around your head.

Some experiences are easier to translate into words than others. The hardest are those that affect you most, the shows that possessed you so intensely while you were watching that their finishing is a kind of grief. You know that even if you had all the language in the world, what you write will never be equal to the experience of being there. If you were angered by the show, if you feel cheated or let down, you consider why. You write down sentences and you test them against what you remember. Is it true? Is it accurate? But always you are returning to the memory, which is the past tense of your present labour.

You will make mistakes. Everybody does. But you try to make as few mistakes as possible. You try to be true to what you experienced in the theatre.

What you write is conditioned by the context in which it will be published. You may have 400 words for a daily paper, or 5,000 for a theatre magazine that is asking you to remember works you saw years before.

It will be a response. You will bring to your response everything that you brought to the theatre: your attention, your knowledge, your experience, your sensibility, your life. You know that the less you bring, the less you'll have to respond with. You don't care about your opinion. Everyone has an opinion. You don't want to be the kind of critic who doesn't pay attention, whose responses are crafted out of their preconceptions or vanity or ignorance. You want to be a critic who thinks with all of their body, in the present and in the past.

You want to be invisible. You write.

CHAPTER 19
NOTA
Open Dialogues

This text was first published in Contemporary Theatre Review (online), February 2015 (http://www.contemporarytheatrereview.org/2015/ nota/). The selection of notes is published here for the first time, and spans all NOTA performances to date.

NOTA: NOT, NOTES, NOTER (NOTA), NOT/A, is a research framework produced by Open Dialogues (Rachel Lois Clapham and Mary Paterson) that presses on the time, place and quality of notes in relation to performance. Often unseen, notes are private materials produced in public space, which bridge the processes of critical viewing, writing and response. NOTA takes the form of performances, installations and a book published in ten chapters. As such, it draws (on) the performativity of note-taking, publicizing the content of notes, as well as the systems that create them, and the concept of 'work' in critical practice. To date, Open Dialogues has performed NOTA at SHOWTiME (London, 2012), Oh! Seminar (Florence, 2012), Critics and Cocktails (Copenhagen, 2014) and the Cross Cultural Live Art Platform (London, 2014). Chapter One of NOTA was launched at I'm With You: Index in February 2014, and is an 80 page book of risograph prints of notes produced at NOTA's first performance. The books were assembled during the launch – no two books are the same.

For each performance of NOTA, two (female) writers sit at a desk alongside a live event. We face the audience and write and stamp notes. Our position is both powerful and powerless – we could be sitting in judgement, or we could be discharging an administrative function; we are watching the audience, and we are subject to their gaze. This doubled status reflects the role of a writer: someone who is in a position of privileged communication, as well as part of a work-force charged with generating content for ever diminishing returns.

Neither on nor off stage, neither objective nor transparent, we are in process. Our process is with the performance, with the audience, and with the histories of writing, criticism and interpretation that circle them both. We perform the mediation – more or less explicit – to which these histories aspire.

The desk is significant: it is a location for administrative work, a staple item for a professional writer, and a choreographed table-top performance space that invades the distance between audience and stage. Labour, creativity and the aesthetic realm. As writers and as women we occupy all these modes at once.

During the performance, we mark each note with a customized, heavy-handled, rubber stamp dabbed in a pad of ink. Each stamp-mark shows the time and date, alongside the words 'NOTA' and 'RECEIVED.' 'Received' is a scar of the rubber stamp's humble origins in office stationery: in its un-customized form, this stamp lines the shelves of STAPLES next to calculators and index cards. 'Received' also suggests the movement of the note, from writer to reader perhaps; or through the theatre floor, rising up through our performing bodies, and out of the tips of our pens. The stamp, its action, seals this movement onto the page.

This administrative punch is the only form of editing the 'finished' notes receive. Instead, the editing of NOTA takes place in the foremath of the writing: the choreography of the installation, the choice of materials, the placement of the table.

The aftermath of the writing, the notes themselves, are displayed in the performance space after each event, without any editing – typos, inaccuracies, blunt questions and all. They NOTAte the performance, translate its experiences and become its remains. They exhibit the role of writing, as both form and action, in the production of meaning. Handmade, often unintelligible and critically unleashed from the subject that is their alleged focus, these notes appear to be exorbitant and unpublishable.

In NOTA, our notes make a particular invitation to the reader – as a form of conversation, they suggest there is space for other people to speak. And in fact, each element of NOTA – the public writing, the role of the writer/worker, the display of private documents, the delayed and deconstructed publication – is an attempt to open up the processes of writing to the possibility of dialogue and intervention.

NOTA's always already fallible notes are almost impossible to change after the fact, and any corrections simply draw attention to themselves as clumsy redactions. As a framework, NOTA performs these errors as innate, and the writing as bodily and simultaneous.

I'm waiting for you

Who decides the real?

Who desires the real?

How many decisions does the real thing demand?

Who cares about the real (anymore?)

Is this the real you?

What's the difference between these thoughts symbols souvenirs & their real life, real time replicas?

Reality is what stays when you've packed all the symbols away.

How does a symbol die?

What happens when you tire of the real?

Don't leave (me)

(Not really sure)

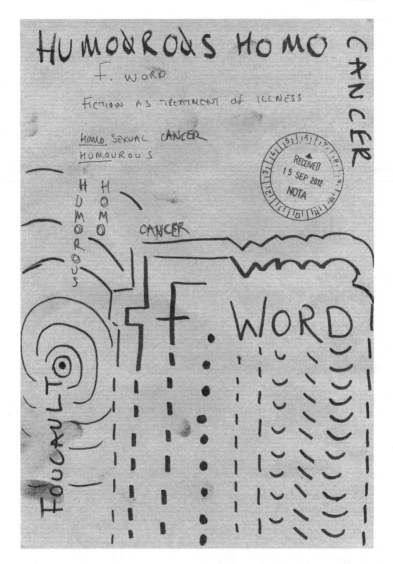

Theatre Criticism

CHAPTER 20
HUFF
Alice Saville

This review of the children's theatre show Huff *presented at the Traverse Theatre, Edinburgh by Catherine Wheels Theatre Company first appeared in* Exeunt *on 23 August 2014 (http://exeuntmagazine.com/reviews/huff/).*

Once upon a time there were three little pigs...

Well, not so little. Huff is billed as a children's show, but it's also an actorless art installation that adults — even grumpy critics — can enjoy too. Shona Reppe and Andy Manley have created a 25 minute promenade full of ingenious conceptual riffs, darkly shifting moods and moments of squealing terror, based on the tale of Three Little Pigs. This trio of intrepid audience members were told to shed their muddy shoes and wait their turn by a tiny white picket fence.

.1.

If you're scared during the show, you can raise your hand and someone will come and get you. But mostly you're left to adventure alone, and can peer inside, touch, or lift up anything you can As Long As You Put It Back. We begin by peering at a prodding-proof, glass-fronted cabinet full of pink china pigs. Some are sweet, some are twee and some are downright creepy.

As they slowly start to turn, the sound designer Danny Krass pipes a haunted music box medley of human voices and animal oinks. We never meet the pigs, but their ghosts are everywhere in this carefully greased, enchanted machine.

.2.

The prying proper starts in the kitchen. The unseen pigs have hay in their cupboards, tiles in their toaster and, most chillingly of all – bacon in their fridge.

The combination of pull-out interactivity and thought-provoking surprises makes it feel a tiny bit like a museum educational display – training kids in literary criticism and Meat is Murder. But there's a satisfying sense that cute – or silliness, or fun – doesn't need a reason here. We're instructed by a Charlie's Angels-style disembodied voice which tells us giggling porcine investigators to pull on the

.3.

toilet roll holder, or the y-fronts on the drier, to reveal hidden doors to the next room.

The spaces get smaller and more chaotic as the wolf's mighty puffs make their influence felt. The bathroom has a toilet on the ceiling, with a child-pleasing fake poo sticking out. We squeeze into a cubicle for a child-horrifying riff on the Psycho shower scene — red light soundtracked to Duran Duran's Hungry Like The Wolf.

.4.

After the horror, the show's most gorgeous moment is a still life of ravishing beauty. Where Dutch masters painted half-eaten meals or shrivelled, caterpillar eaten roses to demonstrate the futility of earthly vanity and the inexorability of time, Huff manages to suggest both these themes, and the immediate presence of a great big wolf with lungs the size of bouncy castles. A table spread with waxy fruit and Tunnock's tea cakes is tilted by an invisible gale, cutlery and wrappers hang in the air in chaotic disorder that, in Sergey Jakovsky's constantly ingenious lighting design, spells out "Help!" on the wall in hectic shadow.

.5.

Huff isn't a story told in soft watercolour washes. Instead, it plays with a whole paintbox of visual references. The dog-eared original fairytale has been collaged over and rebuilt in real straw, sticks and bricks, and decorated with shiny pop culture flourishes.

But it's also as sensitive as the smallest child to the power of a cleverly pointed spotlight and of subtle shifts in perspective that make a tiny plastic toy become a Big Bad Wolf, prowling across the wall in bleak shadow.

.6.

Huff's sense of reality and order being overturned recalls older, Grimmer fairy tales. But its emphasis on magical shifts of mood and atmosphere is foil-wrapped fresh — a triumph sealed by three discordant pigs, squealing along.

THE END

.7.

CHAPTER 21
TEH INTERNET IS A SERIOUS BUSINESS
Megan Vaughan

Megan Vaughan's review of the Royal Court production Teh Internet Is a Serious Business *was originally published on her blog* Synonyms for Churlish *on 23 September 2014 (http://synonymsforchurlish.tumblr. com/post/98220912603).*

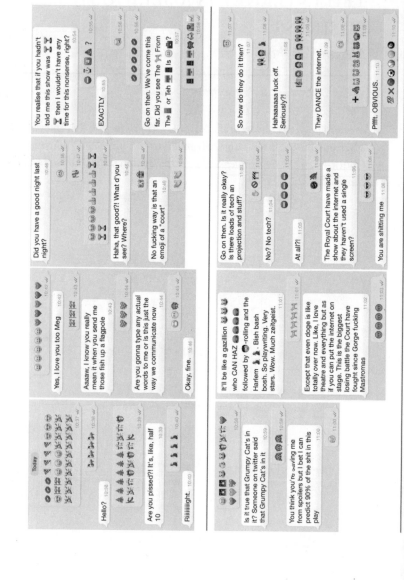

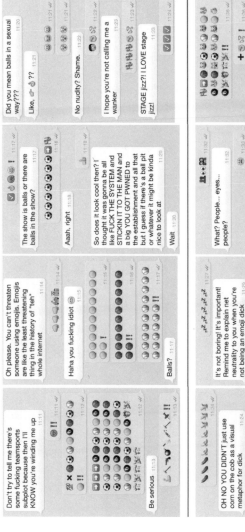

Don't try to tell me there's some fucking teamsports subplot because then I'll KNOW you're winding me up 11:11

Be serious 11:13

Oh please. You can't threaten someone using emojis. Emojis are like the least threatening thing in the history of "teh" whole internet 11:14

Haha you fucking idiot 11:15

Balls? 11:17

The show is balls or there are balls in the show? 11:17

Aaah, right 11:19

So does it look cool then? I thought it was gonna be all like FUCK THE SYSTEM and STICKIN IT TO THE MAN and a big YOU GOT PWNED to the establishment and all that but I guess if there's a ball pit or whatever it might be kinda nice to look at 11:20

Wait 11:20

Did you mean balls in a sexual way??? 11:20

Like, ?? 11:21

No nudity? Shame. 11:22

I hope you're not calling me a wanker 11:23

STAGE jizz?! I LOVE stage jizz 11:23

OH NO YOU DIDN'T just use corn on the cob as a visual metaphor for dick 11:24

A chicken leg?! Remind me NEVER to have sex with you. 11:25

Yeah yeah, whatevs. Be serious for a minute though. This is A SERIOUS BUSINESS after all. Does it say anything about censorship, intellectual property, the politics of the virtual realm? 11:27

It's not boring! It's important! Remind me to explain net neutrality to you when you're not being an emoji dick 11:29

You are a fucking child 11:30

THAT'S NOT AN INVITATION FOR YOU TO START BANGING ON ABOUT THE NETHER AGAIN 11:30

Yes, yes. We know. 11:31

What? People... eyes... people? 11:32

Oh! Anonymous read our emails then leak them for lulz 11:34

But I knew that already. Big whoop. 11:34

So I won't bother buying a ticket then? 11:35

Haha, gotcha. Cats, balls, stage jizz. What's not to love amirite 11:37

Thank you meg for that insightful cultural commentary 11:36

Stop it. 11:39

INDEX

Index

Berger, Jürgen 121
Berger, Maurice 5–6, 8
Berry, Wendell 288
Billington, Michael 15–16, 135, 146, 161, 170, 171, 172, 180, 303
Black Watch (Burke) 302–3
blogs *see* crowdsourcing; Feminist Spectator; insider role/'embedded' relationships; internet; online criticism/blogsphere
Bloom, Harold 273, 286
Boas, Fran 177
Bono, Francesco 101
Bourdieu, Pierre 61, 65
Brantley, Ben, fictional portrayal 155–6
Brennan, Mary 242
Briegleb, Till 121
Britain
    Critics' Circle 2, 10–11, 178–9, 237, 238, 241
    see also online criticism, England
British Theatre Guide (*BTG*) 136
Broadway and off-Broadway productions 40–1, 43, 44, 191
Brook, Peter
    The Empty Space 211–12
    'Except the Cinder – A Fire Trajectory' 295
Brustein, Robert 42, 43–4, 46–7, 49
Burke, Gregory: *Black Watch* 302–3
Butcher, Rosemary: *Episodes of Light* 278
Butt, Gavin 6, 7, 8, 99–100, 224
Bye, Daniel 212–13

Cage, John: *2 Pages, 122 Words on Music in Dance* 282–3, 284, 288
cannabalism metaphor 59–60
Cannella, Claudia 109–11
capitalism, 3, 16, 21, 27, 52, 112, 183, 205
Carey, John 7
Carroll, Noël 6–7
censorship
    Britain 10
    Russia 86
Chaudhuri, Una 1

chess game analogy 278–9
Chiaromonte, Nicola 102–3
children's theatre show (*Huff*) 317–24
'citizen critic' 174–5, 176
Citizen Kane (film) 162
Cixous, Hélène 294
Clapp, Susannah 291, 293, 300–2, 303
Cluetrain Manifesto 20
    '95 Theses' 236–7
code-switching 198
Collins, Eleanor 265
commercial and academic spheres, rift between 21–2
community
    of artists 276–7, 279–80, 281, 286
    and co-operation 20–1
    development and self-disclosure 16–17
comprehension and articulation, struggle for 245–8
conflicts of interest 109–10, 111
Conrad, Saxon 259–60
consensus and dissensus 230–2
conservatism 10
Constantine, Nathan 60
constellations of relationships 192–3, 205–6
contextualizing function 123, 129, 132
conversations
    audience *see The Porcelain Project*
    collaborative 261–4
    digital 23–6, 236–9
Cooper, Emmanuel 243
Cordelli, Franco 106–7
Costa, Maddy 203
Cowen, Tyler 23
craft of written criticism 169–70, 175, 180–1, 241–4
creative criticism 100–6, 301
'Critical Distance' (blog) 208
critical theory 6
The Critic (Sheed) 165–6
The Critic (Sheridan) 158
Critics' Circle 2, 10–11, 178–9, 237, 238, 241
Croatian artists 279, 281–2, 284–5
Croce, Arlene 5

Index

Index

Index